Cultural Complexes of Latin America

Cultural Complexes of Latin America: Voices of the South explores the theory and embodied reality that cultural complexes are powerful determinants in the attitudes, behavior, and emotional life of individuals and groups.

The contributing authors, all from several Latin American countries, present compelling historical, anthropological, sociological, mythological, psychological, and personal perspectives on a part of the world that is full of promise and despair. Latin America is a region marked with psychic "fault lines" that cause disturbances in its populations on issues of social class, ethnicity, race, religion, gender, and even geography. Many of these "fault lines" appear to have their origins in the "basic fault" that occurred with the conquest and colonization of the region, primarily by the Spanish and Portuguese.

This "basic fault" and its subsequent "fault lines" reside not only in various groups that compete for status, power, wealth, and meaning, but in the psyche of every Latin American individual who carries the emotional memories and scars of conflicts that have coursed through their mixed blood for generations.

Thomas Singer, MD, is a psychiatrist and Jungian psychoanalyst who trained at Yale Medical School, Dartmouth Medical School, and the C.G. Jung Institute of San Francisco. He is the author of many books and articles that include a series of books on cultural complexes that have focused on Australia, Latin America, Europe, the United States, and Far East Asian countries, in addition to another series of books exploring Ancient Greece, Modern Psyche. He serves on the board of Archive for Research into Archetypal Symbolism (ARAS) and has served as co-editor of ARAS Connections for many years.

Cultural Complexes of Latin America

Voices of the South
Senior Editor Thomas Singer

Edited by Pilar Amezaga,
Gustavo Barcellos,
Áxel Capriles M., Jacqueline Gerson,
and Denise G. Ramos

LONDON AND NEW YORK

Designed cover image: ©2023 Banco de México Diego Rivera Frida Kahlo Museums Trust, Mexico, D.F./Artists Rights Society (ARS), New York

First published 2024
by Routledge
4 Park Square, Milton Park, Abingdon, Oxon OX14 4RN

and by Routledge
605 Third Avenue, New York, NY 10158

Routledge is an imprint of the Taylor & Francis Group, an informa business

© 2024 selection and editorial matter, Thomas Singer; individual chapters, the contributors

The right of Thomas Singer to be identified as the author of the editorial material, and of the authors for their individual chapters, has been asserted in accordance with sections 77 and 78 of the Copyright, Designs and Patents Act 1988.

All rights reserved. No part of this book may be reprinted or reproduced or utilised in any form or by any electronic, mechanical, or other means, now known or hereafter invented, including photocopying and recording, or in any information storage or retrieval system, without permission in writing from the publishers.

Trademark notice: Product or corporate names may be trademarks or registered trademarks, and are used only for identification and explanation without intent to infringe.

British Library Cataloguing-in-Publication Data
A catalogue record for this book is available from the British Library

ISBN: 978-1-032-51039-2 (hbk)
ISBN: 978-1-032-51041-5 (pbk)
ISBN: 978-1-003-40082-0 (ebk)

DOI: 10.4324/9781003400820

Typeset in Times New Roman
by Apex CoVantage, LLC

Contents

Acknowledgments	vii
List of Contributors	viii

Latin America   1

   Introduction   3
   THOMAS SINGER

Brazil   13

1 **South and the Soul**   15
   GUSTAVO BARCELLOS

2 **Cordial Racism: Race as a Cultural Complex**   26
   WALTER BOECHAT

3 ***Non Ducor, Duco* I Am Not Led, I Lead**   39
   DENISE G. RAMOS

4 **São Paulo and the Cultural Complexes of the City: Seeing Through Graffiti**   58
   LILIANA LIVIANO WAHBA

5 **The Cultural Skin in Latin America**   85
   BRIAN FELDMAN

Chile — 99

6 At the Far End of the World: Exploring the Chilean
   Cultural Isolation Complex — 101
   CLAUDIA BEAS AND JAVIERA SÁNCHEZ

Colombia — 117

7 In the Shadow of the Virgin Mary — 119
   MARÍA CLAUDIA MUNÉVAR

Mexico — 131

8 The Right to Exist: Mexico's Spiritual Colonization — 133
   JACQUELINE GERSON

9 The Broken Bridge: Exploring the Mythic Core of Mexican
   Cultural Complexes — 146
   CLAUDE JUVIN AND ROCÍO RUIZ

Uruguay — 161

10 The Official Story of Uruguay: The Cultural Complexes
    Underlying What Was and Was Not Included — 163
    PILAR AMEZAGA AND PABLO GELSI

Venezuela — 179

11 The Gringo Complex — 181
    ÁXEL CAPRILES M.

12 Latin America: A Region Split by Its Cultural Complexes — 198
    EDUARDO CARVALLO

13 Venezuela: Cultural Complexes in Contemporary Context — 208
    MARGARITA MÉNDEZ

Index — *220*

Acknowledgments

Putting *Cultural Complexes of Latin America: Voices of the South* together was no easy task. It required the collaboration of editors and authors from several different countries who worked in three separate native tongues. The authors and editors were generous in sharing their ideas, their experiences, and their psyches, and this volume owes a great debt of gratitude to all of them. Northern Graphic Design and Publishing was unfailing kind and creative in the maps drawn for this book. The first edition of this book, *Listening to Latin America*, was published by Spring Journal Books and Nancy Cater, who deserves enormous credit for helping in every aspect of producing this book. From the outset, she supported the idea of the series on cultural complexes. She participated fully and equally in all phases of this book's creation – from the original meeting with the editors to discuss the idea of the book, to the choice of contributing authors, to the editing of the chapters and, not least of all, in the painstaking copy editing of the book. In every sense of the word, she was a partner in bringing the vision of what is now *Cultural Complexes of Latin America: Voices of the South* into reality.

Thomas Singer
Series Editor

Contributors

Pilar Amezaga is a Jungian analyst in Montevideo, Uruguay, where she serves as a supervisor and clinical psychologist. She is a founder of the Uruguayan Society of Analytical Psychology (SUPA). She teaches undergraduate and graduate courses in analytical psychology at the Catholic University of Uruguay. She is a member of the editorial board of the Journal of Analytical Psychology.

Gustavo Barcellos is a Jungian analyst in São Paulo, Brazil, a member of the Associação Junguiana do Brasil (AJB) and the International Association for Analytical Psychology (IAAP), and editor of *Cadernos Junguianos*, AJB's journal. The author of many books and articles in Brazil and abroad, he also writes and teaches in the field of archetypal psychology. He maintains a private practice in São Paulo, Brazil.

Claudia Beas, MSc, is a clinical psychologist who is training in the Jungian tradition in Santiago, Chile. For the past ten years, she has led university workshops on dreams and has taught in the master's program in analytic psychology at Adolfo Ibañez University. She works as a psychotherapist for adolescents and adults for a municipal mental health center and is in private practice.

Walter Boechat, MD, PhD, is a diplomate of the C.G. Jung Institute Zürich (1979). He is a founding member of the Jungian Association of Brazil (AJB) and a member of the executive committee of the International Association for Analytical Psychology (IAAP) (2007–2010 and 2010–2013). He is working on the Brazilian edition of The Red Book by C.G. Jung and maintains his clinical practice in Rio de Janeiro.

Áxel Capriles M. is a Venezuelan analyst who graduated from the C.G. Jung Institut-Zürich. With a doctorate in economics, he is a professor of psychological economics at the Universidad Católica Andrés Bello, Caracas. He teaches in the training program of the Venezuelan Society of Jungian Analysts and is the director of the C.G. Jung Foundation of Caracas. The author of four books, he has an editorial weekly column in the newspaper El Universal.

Eduardo Carvallo is a psychiatrist and Jungian analyst originally from Caracas, Venezuela. He participates in the training of analysts and has written numerous articles on clinical issues as well as on cultural and archetypal topics. He ran a Jungian-oriented day hospital in Caracas until the political situation in Venezuela caused him to move to Bogota, Colombia, where he now teaches and maintains a private practice.

Brian Feldman is a clinical psychologist, a Jungian analyst, and an infant observation seminar leader (Esther Bick method). He is a member and on the teaching faculties of the Jung Institute of San Francisco and the Interregional Society of Jungian Analysts. He is currently a visiting professor at the State Academic University in Moscow. Brian studied anthropology in Mexico at the Universidad Nacional Autónoma de México (UNAM), was a visiting scholar in the Departments of Psychiatry and Pediatric at the University of Campinas, São Paulo, and has been on the teaching faculty of the Jung Center of Mexico City.

Jacqueline Gerson is a Jungian analyst with a private practice in Mexico City, where she works as an analyst, teacher, and supervisor. With a lifelong passion for dance and movement, she first approached dreams as spontaneous choreographies created by the psyche. She lectures and writes on topics related to analytical psychology. Her special joys are movement, writing, and the newly discovered pleasure of grandmothering.

Claude Juvin is a Jungian analyst. She lived in Mexico for 45 years and recently returned to Tours, France, where she was born. She is a member of the C.G. Jung Institute of Chicago (CSJA).

Margarita Méndez is a licensed social psychologist from the Universidad Central de Venezuela and has been a Jungian analyst since 1998. She is the director of studies of the Sociedad Venezolana de Analistas Junguianos (SVAJ) in Caracas. She is interested in incorporating the psychic body in Jungian analysis, using active imagination in body movement.

María Claudia Munévar is a Colombian clinical psychologist, currently training in the Jungian tradition. She has a master's degree in ethics and human rights. She maintains a private practice and provides psychological support to social projects in vulnerable communities.

Denise G. Ramos, PhD, is a Jungian analyst and professor at Universidade Católica de São Paulo, where she is the chair of the Center of Jungian Studies in the graduate program in clinical psychology. She is a member of the International Society of Sandplay Therapy and the Academy of Psychology of São Paulo. She has served as the editor-in-chief of Junguiana – a Jungian journal edited in three languages. She is the author of several articles and books, and lectures in Europe and the USA on psychosomatics.

Rocío Ruiz is a Mexican Jungian analyst and has lived in Mexico City for most of her life. She is a member of the C.G. Jung Institute of Chicago (CSJA). She is a clinical psychologist and holds a master's degree in couples psychotherapy. She has worked with shamans interested in analytical psychology and also serves as a teacher and supervisor. She now lives in Cancún, Mexico, where she has her clinical practice, and travels periodically to Mexico City to work with patients.

Javiera Sánchez, MSc, is a clinical psychologist who participates in the Jungian Router training program and maintains a private practice in Santiago, Chile. She works as a psychotherapist in a clinic and conducts a private analytic practice with adolescents and adults. She has also taught at Pontificia Universidad Católica de Chile.

Liliana Liviano Wahba, PhD, is a psychologist and Jungian analyst. She is a former president of the Brazilian Society for Analytical Psychology. She is a professor at the University of São Paulo and former Honorary Secretary of the Ethics Committee of the International Association for Analytical Psychology (IAAP). She also serves as director of psychology of the Association Ser em Cena (Theater for Aphasics).

Latin America

DOI: 10.4324/9781003400820-1

Introduction

Thomas Singer

The Cultural Complex Series

This is the second volume in a series of books on cultural complexes in various parts of the world. The main goal of this series is to explore that part of the individual and group psyche which swims in the history, memory, affect, images, thought patterns, and behavior of past generations of peoples in a particular region. How is psyche shaped by landscape, language, and the various groups that have intermingled with one another over centuries in a specific locale? A secondary goal of this series is to test the cultural complex hypothesis and see if it offers a useful approach and perspective when addressing these interwoven topics of psyche, place, and history. By the nature of the inquiry, our methodology is qualitative, not quantitative, and we circle around these themes through myths, stories, history, anecdote, images, and psychological reflection.

Another volume in the series, *Cultural Complexes of Australia: Placing Psyche*, focuses on Australia, while this volume focuses on Latin America. Australia and Latin America are two extremely different continents with vastly different histories, landscapes, populations, and cultural complexes – although they perhaps are united in historical and imaginal geography by both being in the Southern Hemisphere. With regard to cultural complexes, the major similarity between these two regions is that both were inhabited by indigenous populations who had lived there long before the arrival/invasion and conquests of these "new lands" by colonizers. The impact of the colonization process on indigenous and nonindigenous populations of both continents has been a major factor in the formation of the cultural complexes in each area. This observation brings to mind what Jung wrote about conquerors and the conquered in his 1927 essay, "Mind and Earth." What Jung wrote with regard to North America and the "usurpers of foreign soil" clearly holds true in our studies of cultural complexes in Australia and Latin America:

> Thus the American presents a strange picture: a European with Negro behavior and an Indian soul. He shares the fate of all usurpers of foreign soil. Certain Australian primitives assert that one cannot conquer foreign soil, because in it there dwell strange ancestor-spirits who reincarnate themselves in the new-born. There is great psychological truth in this. The foreign land assimilates its conqueror.[1]

However, there are major differences between the experiences of the indigenous peoples of these two continents. For the most part, the Aborigines of Australia remained separate from the colonizers, and although their way of life was decimated, they remain a well-defined minority today. In Latin America, while some of its indigenous people have retained a separate identity, it has experienced a far greater mixing of the "blood" of the different groups of its people: the indigenous Indian populations, the Europeans (primarily Spanish and Portuguese), and the Blacks, who originally arrived as slaves. The extensive intermingling and intermarriage that has taken place among these groups has resulted in the development of different dynamics between the indigenous and nonindigenous populations in Latin American than occurred in Australia. Yet the impact of colonization on both continents continues to express itself in long-standing tensions, conflicts, and cultural complexes between segments of the population, including the indigenous and nonindigenous.

What Is a Cultural Complex?

If one studies Jung's 1926 diagram of the human psyche, The Geology of Personality, shown in Figure 1, it is clear that Jung thought of the individual human being as a tiny dot that rides just above the surface of the oceanic depths of the evolutionary development of the human psyche.[2] This diagram shows us that Jung believed

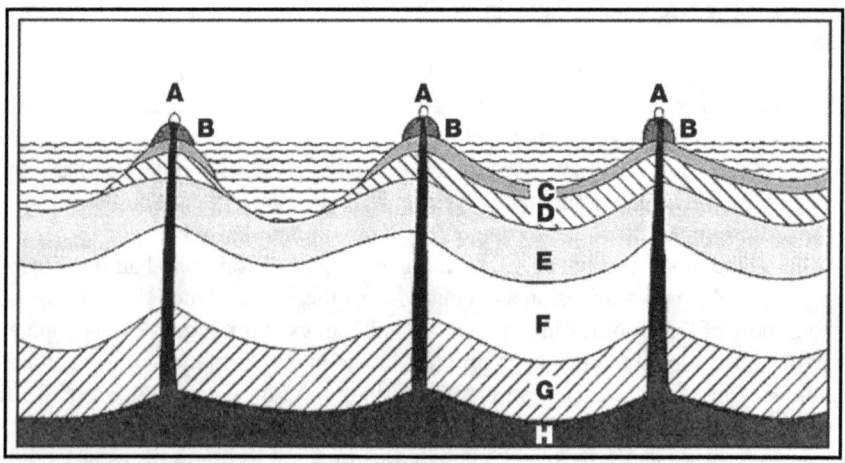

A=Individuals   E=Large group (European man for example)
B=Families   F=Primate ancestors
C=Clans   G=Animal ancestors in general
D=Nations   H="Central fire"

Figure 1 Jung's diagram of the human psyche.

that inside each human being the psyche connects the individual to the history of life's evolution, from human to primate to the very origins of life itself in what Jung termed "the central fire" at the bottom of the diagram. And in terms of this book's topic, as described in Gustavo Barcellos' first chapter, "South and the Soul," Jung, like Freud, imagined in his diagram – almost unconsciously – that this downward, reverse evolutionary movement of the psyche was towards the "South." In that regard, the so-called "personal unconscious" was a relatively small entity that sat on top of its much deeper, more "southern" origins in the cultural and collective unconscious.

In recent years Andrew Samuels and Michael Vannoy Adams, among others, have opened up the largely neglected area in the development of analytical psychology that is indicated in the regions between C and E in Jung's diagram.[3] In this realm, one sees the individual as part of a greater whole of clan, nation, and "large group" – for instance, using Jung's example, "European man." Our current inquiry into cultural complexes takes root in the fact that the individual psyche is embedded in this greater whole of the human community.

I include Jung's early diagram of the psyche in this introduction to underline the fact that Jung was not only interested in the individual and his relation to the collective unconscious but was also interested in the individual and his relation to the psyche of his surroundings and origins. In other words, Jungian psychology is not just about the inner life of individuals and their individuation or their relationship to the collective unconscious, to the world of archetypes. The Jungian tradition also has a long history of exploring the vast region of psychological experience that exists in the realms between the individual and the collective unconscious. This part of our psychological experience is often referred to as "the collective psyche" and is sometimes viewed among Jungians as a shadowy nuisance to the "real" work of individuation and the individual's relationship to the collective unconscious.

The term "collective psyche" itself may be confusing to some readers who might wonder what the difference is between the "collective psyche" and the "collective unconscious." In my use of the term "collective psyche," I am not referring to the "collective unconscious" but instead to the level of psychological experience that occurs in groups – whether it be the family, the local community, the tribe, the region, or the nation. This, in general, is the area in Jung's diagram designated by B, C, D, and E. It is the realm of our "collective" or social or cultural life. In short, it is often referred to as "the collective" or "the collective psyche."

The confusion in speaking of the "collective psyche" may be further compounded by the fact that the word "psyche" itself has come to mean many different things to many different people. I am using "psyche" to refer to a fine thread of mental, somatic, and even soul experience – both inside the individual and in the life of the group – that is partly conscious and partly unconscious. This "psyche" may be more obvious to an intuitive person who can sense this thread and "know" it without having to think about it. The fact is that "collective," "psyche," and "soul" are all somewhat elusive terms, and one has to develop a "feel" for them by following the "thread" as it expresses itself in the life of groups. In summary, as I use it, "the collective psyche" refers to the psyche of the collective or social order, and it has both conscious and unconscious aspects, which dwell in both the individual and in groups.

Whether we refer to it as the collective psyche, the cultural psyche, or the social psyche, the Jungian tradition largely turned away from Jung's earlier interest in it in the first decades of the twentieth century. This turning away was in part a result of Jung's own recoiling from or perhaps just leaving behind his earlier studies on national character and other aspects of the collective psyche, which got him into such trouble and led to allegations that he was pro-Nazi and anti-semitic. Indeed, from his early fears of becoming psychotic based on a series of horrifying visions, he experienced just prior to the outbreak of World War 1, Jung had deep suspicions of the collective, and the tradition that grew up around him mostly saw the collective as a shadowy realm out of which individuals needed to differentiate themselves. In its apparent withdrawal of interest in the more social and collective aspects of life, the Jungian tradition came to be seen as primarily focused on the inner life of the individual and his relationship with the collective unconscious as well as upon more esoteric traditions, such as alchemy and mysticism.

But in our returning to Jung's early fascination with the collective and its influence on the human psyche, so apparent in his 1926 diagram, we can build on Jung's earliest work on complexes and begin to discover anew their role not just in the individual psyche but also in the cultural or collective psyche. We define a cultural complex as an emotionally charged aggregate of historical memories, emotions, ideas, images, and behaviors that tend to cluster around an archetypal core that lives in the psyche of a group and is shared by individuals within that identified collective. It is a good bet that a cultural complex is at work in the psyche of an individual or a group when one encounters the following characteristics, which can feel much like one has stepped on a landmine or as though the level of surrounding cultural confusion is like being in a thick fog:

1 A cultural complex expresses itself in powerful moods and repetitive behaviors – both in a group as a whole and in its individual members. Highly charged emotional or affective reactivity is the calling card of a cultural complex. This is true for the most part, unless the cultural complex is so ego-syntonic with the identity of the group that it becomes seamlessly part of the individual's personality without causing any disturbance.
2 A cultural complex resists our most heroic efforts at consciousness and remains, for the most part, unconscious.
3 A cultural complex accumulates experiences that validate its point of view and creates a storehouse of self-affirming, ancestral memories.
4 Cultural complexes function in an involuntary, autonomous fashion and tend to affirm a simplistic point of view that replaces more everyday ambiguity and uncertainty with fixed, often self-righteous attitudes to the world.

5 Cultural complexes have archetypal cores; that is, they express typically human attitudes and are rooted in primordial ideas about what is meaningful, making them very hard to resist, reflect upon, and discriminate.
6 Cultural complexes often, but not invariably, originate in traumatic events that have befallen groups of people, sometimes centuries, even millennia, ago.

These markers are relatively easy to spot. Indeed, it is quite likely that in the not-too-distant future, what we are calling "cultural complexes" will be activated by trigger words (just like what happened in Jung's early word association tests) under experimental conditions in the neuroscientists' laboratories, showing the links in the brain between centers of affect, image, historical memory, cognition/ideation, and behavior. These experiments may demonstrate anatomically and neurologically what we already know to be true, namely, that cultural complexes are real, powerful, and often determinative of how both individuals and groups think about and respond to one another.

Why a Theory of Cultural Complexes?

I introduced the subject of "What is a cultural complex?" by showing Jung's 1926 diagram of the psyche to indicate that he clearly envisioned a significant realm of psychic activity that corresponds to the realm that we are calling "collective," "cultural," or "social." This is another way of saying that a study of culture and its conflicts is a legitimate realm for Jungians to address in terms of considering the role of psyche in these dynamics. This is important because some may question why we even need a concept of "cultural complex" when such topics have been studied and analyzed effectively by other disciplines. What are analytical psychologists – Jungians – doing mucking around in matters that are best researched by historians, anthropologists, sociologists, and even economists? This criticism of the cultural complex hypothesis might lead us to believe that, as psychotherapists, we would be well advised to mind our own business and stay in our consulting rooms where we belong, treating individuals and their development about whom we know much more than we do about these other spheres of human activity. Those favoring this argument may go on to point out that the notion of a "cultural complex" itself is conjecture at best and should be questioned as an unproven concept of little value that is itself a historical hangover from Jung's early word-association tests that have long outlived their not very useful life. In a way, the answer(s) to those who might say we are outside our area of expertise, using a long antiquated, primitive, and simplistic concept from another century, is rather simple. I would argue in answering the question of "why do we need a theory of cultural complexes" that it focuses on the human psyche, something that is rarely, if ever, held in the forefront by other disciplines, such as sociology, anthropology, and history. The theory of cultural complexes most directly tries to answer the question, "How do those spheres of human experience described by historians, sociologists, and anthropologists actually 'live' in us as individuals and as members of groups, tribes, and nations?" They live in our inner history, in our inner anthropology, in our inner sociology.

The inner, more subjective representations of history, anthropology, and sociology in each one of us is the arena of psyche and its cultural complexes. And how these realities live inside each of us and the groups we belong to is often quite different from what the professors of these "outer" social studies might have to say about them. Each of these disciplines has its own central focus, in which the role of psyche or even soul is rarely considered, much less placed in the center of attention. The fact is that every individual and group swims in a multileveled collective psyche that moves from deeply unconscious to conscious and back again over many generations. This is the realm of analytical psychology and the special arena of the theory of cultural complexes. Another way of saying this is that cultural complexes are among the basic building blocks of the human being's inner world of sociology, anthropology, and history and that analytical psychology, through the theory of cultural complexes, places psyche at the center of its interest. The short answer to why analytical psychology should study these phenomena is because these are alive and potent in the psyche of individuals and groups.

Latin American Cultural Complexes

To mix geological and psychoanalytic theories rather shamelessly in a metaphoric language just as Jung did in his 1926 diagram, the psychic "fault lines" of Latin America run deep and many seem to originate in a "basic fault." The fault lines of Latin American society, like their geological namesakes, occur throughout the region and cause periodic upheavals in the same way that shifting tectonic plates cause earthquakes, volcanoes, and the creation of vast mountain ranges. This book is filled with stories and myths of faults lines that express themselves in frequently recurring Latin American cultural complexes related to race, ethnicity, religion, socioeconomic status, and gender. Each of these arenas is fertile ground for intense "tectonic shifts" around issues of inferiority/superiority, victim/perpetrator, belonging/excluded dynamics. Here is how Jung put it:

> Alienation from the unconscious and from its historical conditions spells rootlessness. That is the danger that lies in wait for the conqueror of foreign lands, and for every individual who, through one-sided allegiance to any kind of -ism, loses touch with the dark, maternal, earthy ground of being.[4]

Even more powerful than these multiple fault lines is the fact that so many of these cultural complexes, as described and experienced by this book's authors, seem to originate in a "basic fault" of Latin American culture. In this regard, it seems apt to extend Michael Balint's psychoanalytic notion of a "basic fault" to a much larger cultural context than the application to the individual that Balint originally intended. The cultural application of the basic fault idea is that a primary injury occurred to the Latin American psyche during the time of the Conquest and into which it often regresses in times of transition, stress, and crisis. So many of the contemporary Latin American cultural complexes can be traced back to a basic fault that fractured the psyche of the region as a result of the Conquest.

John Beebe has spoken to the fundamental fracturing of the psyche in the following psychological formulation:

> The collective unconscious often sends up archetypal compensations which are bewildering, unless one realizes that like volcanic eruptions that occur to relieve pressures that have built up between the tectonic plates of the earth, the archetypes have emerged to right imbalances produced in collective consciousness by the cultural complexes. These forceful, sometimes violent compensations are all but inevitable because cultural complexes so to speak "pressure" collective consciousness into accepting what are in fact distortions of consciousness. When these are accepted, sometimes for long centuries, as if they were objective, indisputable perceptions and judgments, when they are in fact little more than prejudices and presuppositions, the Self has little choice but to assert its more comprehensive relation to reality in a way that will dislodge them.[5]

Just about every chapter in this book makes reference to painful, often violent eruptions in time and culture caused by the Conquest and colonization that echo in contemporary Latin American culture with a recurring horror that continues to violate the spirit of the place and its inhabitants. Jung was not writing specifically about Latin America when he penned these ideas, but they clearly connect with its land, history, and psyche.

> The very fact that we still have our ancestral spirits, and that for us everything is steeped in history, keeps us in contact with our unconscious, but we are so caught in this contact and held so fast in the historical vice that the greatest catastrophes are needed in order to wrench us loose to and change our political behaviour from what it was five hundred years ago.[6]

The ancestral spirits of every country in Latin America continue to roil with the impact of the Conquest on the psychic tectonic plates of its populations – primarily the European, indigenous, and black populations. This book bears witness to the distress and violence that erupts periodically from this basic fault in the Latin American psyche.

In order to orient the reader to the basic contents of the book, I offer a brief synopsis of its chapters, which seem to invariably touch on cultural complex themes of inferiority/superiority, conqueror/conquered, perpetrator/victim, inclusion/exclusion – whether the topic is race, gender, religion, ethnicity, or geography.

1   The book begins with a study of the word "South" itself. Gustavo Barcellos, a Brazilian, reveals that "South" has become a trigger word in geography and psychology denoting unconsciousness, primitivity, the underworld, and the very notions of depth

and soul. Barcellos writes, "We in the 'South' become the true carriers of body, lust, instinct, spontaneity, nature, joy, song, nudity. Again, a huge cultural complex."[7]

2. Walther Boechat's chapter on "cordial racism" in Brazil looks at the cultural complex of race as it has played itself out in the mixture of Native Indians, the Portuguese from Europe, and the blacks from Africa. "I suggest that the image of the sadistic master and the suffering slave may be considered as a cultural complex that has manifested itself in the very stratified system of Brazilian society."[8] Furthermore he notes that "Brazilian racial prejudice appears in disguise and goes hand in hand with social class prejudice."[9]

3. Denise G. Ramos studies the fascinating history of the city of São Paulo in terms of a cultural complex related to the dynamics of superiority/inferiority as they play out in Brazil. As an economic and cultural powerhouse, the city of São Paulo holds the memories, affects, self-definition, and imagery of a place that inspires in the psyches of its citizens and those of its regional rivals intense feelings that alternate between pride and scorn.

4. Liliana Liviano Wahba examines the graffiti of São Paulo, Brazil, to understand the psyche of its people in the grips of postmodernity or hypermodernity in which "fragmentation, dispersion, and uncertainty" are the norm. Her analysis of a large variety of images reveals a collective psyche that seems overwhelmed, numbed, and tortured by the pace and dehumanization of the urban environment.

5. Brian Feldman, a North American, explores the notion of the "cultural skin" in Brazil as a container for the individual and collective psyche of its people. His study is based upon anthropological fieldwork he has conducted in an Amazonian elementary school, infant observation of a baby of Mayan origin, and a keen sensitivity to the contemporary Brazilian soul as it lives in music and culture. He postulates that "The cultural skin mediates experience between the subjective and symbolic realm of images, and the intersubjective dialogues which take place in the social spaces between self and other."[10]

6. In writing about Chile, Claudia Beas and Javiera Sanchez tease out what they call the "Cultural Isolation Complex." Geography, history, and family dynamics all contribute to a series of opposites in the Chilean psyche that tip to their more negative poles with regard to isolated/bonded, mistrust/trust, submission/domination, and superiority/inferiority.

7. María Claudia Munévar of Colombia tells a chilling tale of witnessing the murder of a 16-year-old boy as he was entering his schoolyard. It leads her on a long odyssey of trying to understand how children who are the victims of exclusion, disenfranchisement, and poverty are recruited and trained to become assassins.

8. Jacqueline Gerson explores how the gap between what is promised and what is delivered in daily exchanges in Mexico opens up a window for understanding a Mexican cultural complex that reveals a "basic fault" embedded in its collective psyche. She writes,

> The conqueror-conquest poles are present in the Mexican psyche, and it is the identification with one of these polarities that creates the Mexican cultural complex that gives the other no right to exist. One side of the equation

loudly demands work, completion, and concretization of results in a chronological measure of time; and the other, silently, expects consideration of its mythological, ritualistic, and contemplative way of living life's cycles.[11]

9 Claude Juvin and Rocío Ruiz's "The Broken Bridge" take the reader on a mythic journey in search of explanations for the disintegration of contemporary Mexican society:

> Following our path through Mexican mythical images, we propose that the myths of creation form the psychic substratum of our culture and account for some of its specific dynamics. The archetypal energies of the mythic substratum express themselves in the contemporary, chaotic cultural complexes devouring Mexico today.[12]

10 Pilar Amezaga and Pablo Gelsi examine the "Official Story" of modern Uruguay and argue that what has been left out of this narrative has become the very building blocks of the country's most powerful cultural complexes. They write,

> The Official Story denied the country's origins in "nothingness." It denied the country's smallness, its natives, its gauchos, its blacks. It denied the diversity of its European immigrants. It denied the desire to be part of what is today Argentina. It denied the heroism of the immigrant, the importance of individual effort, its colonial origins, and it denied the precariousness, frailty, and failure of its ultimate hero.[13]

11 Áxel Capriles M. of Venezuela takes the reader on a memorable journey through the historical origins and many uses of the word *gringo* that is at the heart of a major cultural complex that exists between North and South America. Dr. Capriles writes,

> The Gringo Complex is the bearer of many racial and sociohistorical conflicts that hinder cultural cohesion and appear in personalized form as prejudices and aversion to foreigners with contrasting values. It is a symbol of unresolved collective contradictions that demand consciousness. We condemn the *gringo's* cold pragmatism and the inhumanity of American Capitalism but we are furious consumers of all type of American goods and services. The Gringo Complex contains a cluster of representations that confront us with the archetypal themes of failure and success, of alienation and identity, of informality and order, of the sense of self and the construction of the Other.[14]

12 Eduardo Carvallo, a Venezuelan, examines primary differences between the European and indigenous psyches as a way of exposing the "basic fault" that developed Latin America as a consequence of the Conquest:

> The archetypal structure of the Spanish colonization of the New World . . . was a rigid and authoritarian warrior pattern within a strict monotheism that

contrasted sharply with the archetypal framework among the indigenous peoples which included polytheism, a balance between male and female forces, and a close relationship of mutuality with the natural environment.[15]

13 Margarita Mendez traces the emotions of envy and resentment that originate in the experience of class and social exclusion in Venezuela:

> In Venezuelan history the experience of exclusion results in the expression of resentment, both individually and collectively. This combination of exclusion and resentment erupts from the unconscious seeking vengeance and retaliation.[16]

As is apparent from this brief synopsis of the book's chapters, our explorations of cultural complexes in Latin America paint a picture filled with pain, suffering, conflict, turmoil – a region full of fault lines built, at least in part, on a basic fault, the injury to the collective psyche that resulted from the Conquest. After venturing down such a dark tunnel, we all yearn for the waters of renewal and transformation that the book's cover image by Diego Rivera evokes with such earthy flow in his "The Hands of Nature Offering Water."[17]

Notes

1 C.G. Jung, "Mind and Earth," in *Collected Works*, vol. 10 (Princeton, NJ: Princeton University Press, 1927), § 103.
2 C.G. Jung, "Analytical Psychology," in *Notes of the Seminar Given in 1925*, ed. W. McGuire (Princeton, NJ: Princeton University Press, 1989), pp. 41–42.
3 Andrew Samuels, *The Political Psyche* (London and New York: Routledge, 1993); Michael Vannoy Adams, *The Multicultural Imagination: "Race," Color and the Unconscious* (London and New York: Routledge, 1996).
4 Jung, CW 10, § 103.
5 Personal communication with the author.
6 Jung, CW 10, § 103.
7 This volume, p. 24.
8 Ibid., p. 36.
9 Ibid., p. 38.
10 Ibid., p. 109.
11 Ibid., p. 183.
12 Ibid., p. 204.
13 Ibid., p. 229.
14 Ibid., p. 255.
15 Ibid., p. 265.
16 Ibid., p. 281.
17 Diego Rivera, *Water. The Source of Life. The Beneficent Hands of Nature Bestow the Gift of Water* (Mexico City, DF, Mexico: Carcmo del Rio Lerma, 1886–1957).

Brazil

Chapter 1

South and the Soul

Gustavo Barcellos

Départ dans l'affection et le bruit neufs.
(*Departure in new affection and new noise.*)

— Arthur Rimbaud, *Illuminations*

I would like to concentrate in this chapter upon the idea of "south" and what it means for soul, in an attempt at reimagining Jungian archetypal psychology's celebrated *southward direction*. In South America, of course, we are inclined to see "south" as a great metaphor for depth psychology in general. We cannot escape the feeling of "south" into which we are born. So we need to reflect upon it, that is, create ever new images. It is a huge cultural complex; in a sense, it is the complex of inferiority, of that which is felt or feels itself as inferior, the underside, even underworld, and we are those *inferiores*. But it is also that "intimate south" of Jorge Luis Borges, who felt it as a tragic or melancholic destiny, the south of his "Poema Conjectural" ("Conjectural Poem") (*"al fin me encuentro/con mi destino sudamericano"*),[1] as in the atmosphere of his famous short story "The South," in his collection *Ficciones*. We need to see through this metaphor, and for this I feel my words must turn inevitably to geography – by this I mean *imaginal geography*, or a geography of images – if we are to listen to new *anima* noises. I believe the Brazilian experience can help depth psychology rethink one of its most fundamental metaphors.

But to attempt an archetypal revision of the idea of "south" in our psychology, and to give it a deeper significance in our lives, we should not at all go by the way of simple reversion, merely putting north-south upside down, trying for a moment to disturb optics and soul, seeing south as "superior." That would be "psychopathic geography": south in the place of north so that nothing is really changed in our perspective. Nor would I wish to fall here, once again, into "those tiresome dilemmas of North and South"[2] – historical geography. No, to be sure, I want to avoid the rhetoric of oppression altogether so archetypal for the relations between North and South, and so paradigmatic to our continent, the Americas, as James Hillman brilliantly expanded upon the one occasion he spoke of South America, in the article "Culture and the Animal Soul," published in *Spring Journal*, in 1998 – which article, along with another, "Notes on White Supremacy," from 1986, are the main references for my notes here; for that too, would be to continue looking at these issues from the northern perspective, and so to remain in a "*money*theism" of the North.[3] I would like to attempt a step forward.

The mythologem "New," for instance – New World, new land – as well as the mythologem "Antarctic" (from the Latin *antarcticu*, not-Arctic, anti-Arctic, anti-north, opposed to the Arctic pole of our planetary *rotundum*), although we may be still trapped in them, are no longer sufficient, no longer speak to the soul – or did they ever? "Newness" is the *prison* of the Americas.[4] And "Antarctic" is, of course, the rhetoric of negation. So maybe the mythologem "South" can be more affirmative and would thus have more to show about soul in general, about us Latin Americans in particular, and more to say to the theoretical imagination of psychology itself. Revelation, not contrast or conflict – sociological and/or anthropological. Again, not historical geography, but *imaginal geography*.

Archetypal psychology has brought back this metaphor – in particular, "south" – to make a major theoretical move. This move has to do with the turning of the West-East axis into a North-South axis, which for Jungian psychology meant that we no longer had to go East to go deep. This "south" was meant to be essentially the Mediterranean culture – from Greek myths and religion to Renaissance civilization, philosophy, and modes of living: imaginal sources that brought sensual as well as tragic perspectives to psychology and to psychotherapy.

We all know the significance and the power of the south metaphor: it is truly archetypal. Since Freud and the early days of psychoanalysis, it was *the* place to go when imagining a direction towards the unconscious, towards soul: the vertical direction. To find soul we go downwards: personal memories, childhood, ancient myths, complexes, archetypal reality – all this is imagined to be stored deep down inside, the "south" of ourselves. True character is also imagined to be down inside our acts. And we must not forget this "south" stands as well for the lower part of the body.

Since the psycho-topographical descriptions of Freudian days – and Freud was the first in our tradition to bring a truly topographical, or geographical, imagination to psychology – the downward direction is, simultaneously with the inward direction, *the* way to follow in the imagination of psychology (regardless of the school) when psychic reality is to be found, understood, attended: we go "down," we go "south," either in the individual, or the culture. Many may know that in his *Archetypal Psychology: A Brief Account*, James Hillman imagined this direction even further in his geographical *poiesis* and said that it, archetypal psychology, "starts in the South."[5] He also wrote, "venturing South is a journey for explorers."[6] Old or young, yes, Mr. Eliot, we should turn into explorers: *International Geographic*.

In Brazil we are well aware of all this, for we too start in the South. My main point here is that now, beyond Mediterranean culture, this archetypal "south" can be reimagined. Brazilian South American syncretic polytheistic culture shines and, in itself, continues to offer a challenge for psychology regarding "south" as a cultural, ethnic, and imaginal location, a region of the soul, beyond what it has already acknowledged as "south." I am trying to suggest that beyond what Hillman showed us of value for psychology in Mediterranean classical culture, cultures below the equator (such as Brazilian culture) can help archetypal psychology continue to imagine even more radically its fundamental metaphorical direction in thought and research.

Here we remember that what we formulate as psychology "emerged from the Protestantism of northern and western Europe and its extension westward into North America."[7] *Northern* Europe, *North* America. *Northern* Psychology. We all know how *north* we are when we speak psychology, and how much to avoid "north" was indeed necessary to move psychology *soul-wards*.

Maybe that is the reason why I want to talk about south – first because I live, work, and come from what in psychology's main perspective is called the "South." But also, and most importantly, because perhaps re-imagining south is a way of re-imagining soul. For me, that would essentially mean to continue imagining soul, while continuing imagining world; for soul, as we all well know, is what is continually imagining in us. Psychology cannot stop short at its first south – Mediterranean, Greek, ancient. It seems essential that the soul continues to be imagined so that we can find more and more images, more reflections, in theory and in practice (as well as in the world) to recognize its presence and its works in our lives. So I want to suggest that maybe *south* and *soul* have yet more in common that has already dreamed our psychology. I want to call attention to the Brazilian way of imagining soul, affection, culture, and psychology and how it can respond to the challenge of an archetypal perspective that lies beyond the cultural complex "south."

I believe this discussion is "central" to our depth psychology. And I want us to recall that archetypal psychology states that what divides North and South in our tradition – transalpine and cisalpine mentalities or psychological landscapes, Reformation and Renaissance – are, in one image, *mountains* – a powerful metaphor. The Alps, as Hillman stressed many times, with all those *albedo* tops. So we all are still, metaphorically, in Europe – even when we speak psychology in places like Brazil. We continue to divide our souls into what Hillman called the Hebraic monotheistic consciousness and Hellenic polytheistic consciousness. Hebraic, Hellenic: it seems there is no way out of that division – even when we speak archetypal psychology. We are, psychologically speaking, either monotheistic or polytheistic, with the Gods or without the Gods.

When I want to speak here about a *south souther than south*, in what is now an alchemical mode of speaking, it is to point, *first*, towards a division that makes itself felt by the presence of nothing less than an *ocean* – one would say, an Atlantic gap. Here we are, I believe, with the central images for this reflection – for I am trying all along to think in images, the pagan mode. What then divides northern Europe (even its Iberian or Mediterranean consciousness) and tropical South-American Brazil is an ocean, that is, an enormous amount of salt water, which indicates, of course, an Atlantic (that is, Titanic) distance, and certainly more profound projections – a deeper unknowing. "Mountains" and "ocean" speak for the imaginal difference in the division. When we speak of *mountains*, even in psychology, we are still, somehow or somewhere, inevitably involved in the rhetoric of the spirit; what we have to trespass is, nonetheless, The Spirit, as if psychology had to "jump" the spirit – that is, lose all abstract conceptualizations and borrowed language – to meet the very soul it searches. Whereas when we speak of an *"ocean,"* maybe Soul is immediately closer, that is, its presence not mediated, already given by the image, already given in the imagination. Perhaps water in this case has more to do with soul than air, for souls take pleasure in moisture, that is, the soul is aroused by water (in a Venusian sense), even if we go on recalling Heraclitus saying that the *dry* soul is the wisest (Frag. 118).[8]

But *secondly*, I want to talk about Brazil as a place where the division "monotheistic/ polytheistic" is, in fact and in psyche, no longer operative in a positive sense. It is my impression that maybe it has never been really operative, since the beginning. The Afro-Brazilian polytheism (along with all its different ramifications) is very much alive *inside* the monotheism of the Christian official culture in Brazil, even though more conscious in some parts of the country than in others. Some speak here of paradox, others of tolerance or syncretism. Some attack this very syncretism, trying to purify influences; others celebrate it. The psychological reality in Brazil indicates, anyway, this peculiar synthetic state of soul. This is a way of *south*.

Brazil is the largest Catholic country in the world, but it is as well a place where a polytheistic religion – the Afro-Brazilian religion of the Orixás – is alive and largely practiced every day with such a power that, unlike other places, it also dwells strongly in urban areas, in the cities – psychotherapy's enthroned territory since the beginning. Of course, it is not always practiced literally in rituals by everyone, but certainly, and most importantly, in deeper levels, in the mind, in psyche, in thinking and feeling processes.

One way to understand it is as a clear result of the melting of the three absolutely different races that originally combined to form Brazilian people: the American Indian, the Portuguese, and the African slave. Alchemy again, *coniunctio* as *solutio*. Miscegenation. And it is clear to me that *miscegenation* is the main contribution to psychology from Brazil. It represents a totally different style of consciousness, more inclusive and receptive, less abstract and conceptual. And it is for psychology a chance to overcome what Hillman refers to as "white supremacy": ego psychology, empiricism, subjectivism, spiritualism. It represents a true descent into the "south."

But then we have to go back here to the metaphor "south" and enter the cultural complex that has as its basis this archetypal fantasy.

"South" has always been emblematic for psychology, especially for depth psychology. James Hillman himself admitted that "going South means leaving our psychological territory at the risk of archetypal disorientation."[9] We know Freud and Jung pathologized when they attempted going towards their own "souths" – Greece, for Freud, and Italy, for Jung. In fact, Jung, in old age, fainted at the railroad station when he was finally buying tickets to go to Rome for the first time. The trip never took place. In his autobiography, when writing about Italy, he mentions unexpected things becoming conscious, "unforeseen vistas opened," and questions posed "which were beyond my powers to handle."[10] Paradoxically, "south" is the psychological route and destination *par excellence* and, at the same time, seems to inevitably bring with it some pathologizing.

And not only for psychology. We may recall just a few examples: Arthur Rimbaud, who renounced poetry forever, went to Africa and was never Rimbaud anymore, returning to Europe ill, to die young back in Marseilles;[11] Henri Cartier-Bresson, whose voyage in Africa was characterized as an *échec*, a failure, but gave him the "eyes" he needed for profound photography;[12] Claude Lévy-Strauss traveling his *tristes tropiques*;[13] Pierre Verger, the superb French photographer and writer that lived in Africa and in Brazil who had to assume another *persona*, another faith, another name (Fatumbi) to find himself, and became an initiate into the Yoruba Candomblé of Bahia;[14] André Gide in the Congo, who had to turn into an "immoralist," had to lose his European ethics – all explorers of the south, *blue* voyagers, melancholic voyagers, like so many others (Jung himself in Africa) that, crossing the Equatorial line, have had strong experiences of transformation.[15] And of course, the most paradigmatic of all examples, that of Kurtz, a main character in Joseph Conrad's *Heart of Darkness*. Conrad himself had in the Congo an exasperating and humiliating experience, "an extreme personal crisis which shocked him into a greater moral and emotional maturity."[16] More than "geographical panic," this is the *horror* of "south."

"Athens" and "Rome," as imaginal places,[17] were for those men, Freud and Jung, those pioneers in depth psychology, the core of a complex (as was so diagnosed by Hillman)[18] that can only be understood in terms of its depths and/or the archetypal fear of depth. Archetypal psychology, I think, stands in a somewhat special position here, since it has already ventured in moving psychology southwards, it has already "entered" the metaphor, so to speak, thus altering vision and depth in psychology.

However, I am suggesting that "Rio de Janeiro," or the Afro-Brazilian deeply colonial landscape of the city of "Salvador," in Bahia, for instance (to mention two former capitals of Brazil), "São Paulo," or the architectural collective dream of "Brasilia" are, as well, imaginal places that can lead depth psychology even further towards the south of its depths, or the depths of its south. This is not merely a play with words but a play with images: geography as *mythopoiesis*. These places would lead psychology to a "south" where, it is my impression, a psychological *solutio* is being engendered in the world soul.

Nevertheless, when we equate "south" with the repressed, we should expect its return. And when it does so, as it will surely do, it "comes from the other side of any mountain, across any border, as Italian, Arab, Mexican, Jew, Caribbean," as Hillman observed.[19] Note he does not mention South America. Yes, across *any* border: but what about the "Equatorial border"? Am I being too literal here? Well, this is not, in my view, a simple detail. It is significant that a south really south of the border is not imagined. It is as if an unconsciousness still pervades archetypal psychology's southward *solutio*. But the *opus* goes on "operating" in the world soul. The failure to see a south on the other side of the ocean (not the other side of the mountain) reveals a *projected* emotion that fails the radicalism of this psychology's *project*. Is this, at a deeper level, the same old fear of "archetypal disorientation"? Perhaps this emotion, this neglect, could be well described by those famous lines by T.S. Eliot, in the Tarot scene from *The Waste Land*, when Madame Sosostris says to the protagonist: "Fear death by water."[20]

This water, *mare nostrum*, again, is both *salty* and *titanic* (Atlantic, we now call it) – thus pertaining to Atlas, but also to the alchemical imagination of salt, so it should necessarily bring a *solutio* as an archetypal move. And it is as well, as an ocean – like any ocean – let us not forget, wherefrom Aphrodite, goddess of beauty and pleasure, is born. I can imagine this water as a great factor, the great foaming untamed image dividing for us "North" and "South," two completely different styles of consciousness. Now, an Atlantic disproportionate projection of beauty and pleasure and freedom takes its course, so that we in the "South" become the true carriers of body, lust, instinct, spontaneity, nature, joy, song, nudity. Again, a huge cultural complex.

In South America, "south" stands clearly for everything that is located below, repressed above, all that has always been seen from the North as *inferior* (as the "imaginal geography" of Figure 1.1 shows), intriguingly inviting on its way across the sea a radical *reversion* to dark projections. This darkness has historically ranged from the Christian Hell of the missionaries, to the mythological Hades of the

Figure 1.1 South as the Underworld: From Andrea de Jorio, Viaggio di Enea all' inferno, ed agli elisii secondo Virgilio (3rd ed.; Naples: Fibreno, 1831)
http://ancienthistory.about.com/od/maps/ss/mapsindex_6.htm

psyche: inferior, unknown regions, a true *under*world; land of the *inferiores*; land, not of the brave, but of the serpent and the dragon.

We all know those dark projections that landed below the equator (the equator, that abstract line of the spirit that does not really *equate* anything): tropical-south as irrational, sexually free, Dionysian, pagan, perverse, archetypally mother-bound due to an extravagant and extraordinary appeal of nature and climate, instinctive, irresponsible, lazy, cannibalistic. Are these projections still in operation? What was at first perceived by the *conquistadores* as heavenly, a paradisiacal projection, soon turned into a hellish project to steal, to usurp, and to abuse land and people in the Tropics – gold rush, wood traffic, slavery, soul mutilation. But this is history or, at best, psychology. And here we want geography, psychic geography.

My question would then be, at the verge of a new psychological era, will psychology have the courage ("courage" here because I mentioned "fear") to go "souther," further south, to continue imagining its fundamental imaginal direction and so leave for a moment its focus on Greek gods and goddesses, its polarization of soul into a mono *or* poly experience of itself, its Mediterranean landscape and modes of thinking, and see that world and soul, and the world-soul, do not end in a soft sea, an "in-between-lands" sea, but go further south across a titanic, rough, and open ocean (once called "tenebrous," *tenebrositas*), towards a new, salty *solutio* that lies perhaps waiting in a new ("new," of course, only from the European historical perspective) world? Can we now finally avoid pathologizing when we go south, avoid the archetypal fear and the archetypal neglect of it? Would we dare to see what kind of *solutio* is being possibly imagined in the South? Can our psychology finally conclude its *circumambulatio* of the soul?

Our play with imaginal geography seeks to bring "south" as soul-making once again – a move towards Brazilian imagining, imagined as a move of soul-making, more soul-making, new soul-making.

I would like now to make some concluding observations about this move, adding a few words on what is otherwise certainly a vast theme. One fundamental aspect of the reality of the salty solution that I mentioned will always be, for me, *baroque*. I want to suggest that one true image that South American and Brazilian soul (or the soul in South America and Brazil, the soul in the South) can open to psychology is to be first found in Colonial baroque, or has its origins in Colonial baroque. So I need to say two or three things about this Brazilian baroque, first because the North has not been impacted by the baroque as the South has been, but also to end on a truly imaginative note.

The baroque in Brazil, as in all South America, is not simply a transitory artistic movement, imported from Europe and so attached to this origin and its canons. What the art historians insist is that, rather, tropical baroque has to be understood on its own terms, as the first full legitimate manifestation of art and culture to flourish outside Europe in the Colonies, one that has little more to do directly with Europe, and is no longer a marginal artistic expression but something in itself. In fact, it is the first original cultural manifestation in the South, and being so, I believe

22 Gustavo Barcellos

it strongly reflects the very soul that was being formed in this "new" land. So the baroque is part of the foundation of the Brazilian soul. This "new soul" – or new step in the world soul-making – this mixture that was being engendered in Brazil through the encounter and mixing of three races, begins to speak right here, right with the baroque. Brazilian baroque incorporates thus, apart from European

Figure 1.2 Baroque image in Brazil: Our Lady surrounded by musician angels, in Ouro Preto, painted by Mauel da Costa Ataide. http://en.wikipedia.org/wiki/Manuel_da_Costa_Ataíde

(Portuguese, Spanish, and Roman) elements, those from Indian and Black influences. The baroque merges itself with many aspects of our deepest soul (see Figure 1.2).

Opposed to the rationalist aspect of the Renaissance culture, the magical universe of the tropical baroque is rooted in the imagination – sensorial extremes of imagination. It is an art that can only be perceived in its full impact by the soul, *not* by the mind. The baroque, specially in Brazil, is the ongoing subversion of the Council of Trent, the affirmation of fantasy as the deepest truth. It is a *contredance*, freedom to imagine, and it is the moment when we speak, not of a Renaissance, but of a *naissance*, a birth, for the baroque made possible independence (and not only for Brazil).

Baroque: images constantly moving, the play of light and darkness continually disturbing spatial and temporal orientation, orienting the soul to dance and to celebrate the senses, enlightening the soul – but also seducing, disturbing it: the baroque is the most dangerous movement of the soul. In Brazil, it reveals a true soul atmosphere: extremes of colors, shades, darknesses, textures, candles, smoke, perfume, costume, emotion, ritual, recitation, theater, music, fantasy, pain, joy, feeling, exaltation, street celebrations, carnival, body – all an attempt to represent and respond to the impact on the soul of an all-exuberant, colorful, wild, dangerous, and luminous nature. The early mixture of cultures, of skins, of libidos that took place in Brazil, and all those "eyes" (white, black, and native), all well immersed in the torments, marvels, and secrets of the tropical forest, are the *prima materia* of this baroque.

This baroque still defines, to this day, much of our soul; our urban soul, and our idea and experience of "south," is born under the sign of the baroque. So there is a latent "baroquism," so to speak, that continues to inform and characterize, deep down, much of the way Brazilians feel and live soul, south, and affection: the extremes of faith, the inclination to contradiction and ambivalence, the attraction for emotional vertigo, dance, and festive ecstasy, the exaltation of the senses, the mystical impulse, aesthetic pleasure, tragedy, confusion, illusions of grandeur, the erotics of power *and* the power of erotics, the magic of words, excessive use of adjectives, and most of all, an image-sense, a sensibility for the image – this is all in the baroque. *Anima* phenomenology? Maybe. If so, then we have a rich soil for a psychology based on image to flourish, an imaginal psychology. We can say that the cult of the image in Brazil is as old as its history, since the first ship to arrive at the Brazilian coast, five hundred years ago, was carrying inside it not only men, projects, projections, problems, but also a powerful marble image of the Christian Great Mother, the *anima* principle, in this case, Our Lady of Hope! And of course, both the Indian and the African heritage are full of images.

But it is my impression – and here we come to my final conclusion – that this "baroquism" is exactly, as well, where in Brazil monotheism and polytheism began mysteriously to merge or disappear as psychologically conscious, excluding clear and experienced categories. It seems to me the baroque is the moment in Brazil, on a deeper soul/south level, where the very division "monotheistic/polytheistic" first ceases to be relevant – for Brazilian baroque, may I suggest, is a *pagan* baroque, as was once pointed out to me by a patient during an analytical session. The enormous variety and number of Catholic saints that are observed in Brazil, covering a vast field of human and spiritual experience (from love and marriage to diseases and death), honored like gods in themselves, attest to the strong influence on consciousness of a polytheistic soul active right underneath the Christian monotheistic layer, not to mention the syncretic amalgam of those saints with the African Yoruba divinities. (This syncretism, as is well-known, was the historical way found by the African slaves to maintain alive their religious beliefs and rituals in the new environment.)

So yes, we go to church on Sundays but beat our drums on Monday nights. It is not unusual to see shrines in Brazil where the statuette of Christ shares the altar with, for instance, the siren-shaped figure of Yemanjá, the African Yoruba Goddess of the sea, a Great Mother from the salty waters – or Saint George with the sword killing the dragon. *Macumba.* I believe then that this polytheism, acted literally (although still full of poetics) in this contemporary form, lived as a true religion for some Brazilians, also spreads itself inwardly in the soul, making every Brazilian feel, think, and relate polycentrically within a somehow fantastic, unitary, collective atmosphere.

I would like to suggest that this is the *prima materia* of the "south" I have been speaking of. Again, "south" as *an imaginal attribute in the world soul*. The cultural synthesis that Brazil and its image of "south" represent in the world soul is also a psychological synthesis, I dare say, a synthesis in soul. I can see here a south image that is for me a soul image. It is the true image this "south" I have been playing with can bring to psychology and culture today.

Notes

1 Jorge Luis Borges, *Selected Poems*, ed. Alexander Coleman (New York: Penguin Books, 1999), p. 159: "I who dreamed of being another man,/well-read, a man of judgment and opinion,/will lie in a swamp under an open sky;/but a secret and inexplicable joy/ makes my heart leap. At last I come face to face/with my destiny as a South American." Translation by Alastair Reid. [*"Yo que anhelé ser otro, ser un hombre/de sentencias, de libros, de dictámenes,/a cielo abierto yaceré entre ciénagas;/pero me endiosa el pecho inexplicable/un júbilo secreto. Al fin me encuentro/com mi destino sudamericano."*]
2 James Hillman, "Culture and the Animal Soul," in *Spring 62* (Woodstock, CT: Spring Publications, 1998), p. 11.
3 Ibid., pp. 10–37; James Hillman, "Notes on White Supremacy," in *Spring 1986* (Dallas, TX: Spring Publications, 1986), pp. 29–58.
4 Hillman, "Culture and the Animal Soul," p. 19.
5 James Hillman, *Archetypal Psychology: A Brief Account* (Dallas, TX: Spring Publications, 1985), p. 30.
6 James Hillman, *Re-Visioning Psychology* (New York: Harper Colophon Books, 1975), p. 223. See, "Old Men Ought to Be Explorers . . ." *Four Quartets*, "East Coker," in T.S. Eliot, *The Complete Poems and Plays of T.S. Eliot* (London: Faber & Faber, 1969).
7 Hillman, *Re-Visioning Psychology*, p. 219.

8 Alexandre Costa, *Heráclito: fragmentos contextualizados, tradução, apresentação e comentários de A. Costa* (Rio de Janeiro: Difel, 2002).
9 Hillman, *Re-Visioning Psychology*, p. 223.
10 C.G. Jung, *Memories, Dreams, Reflections*, ed. Aniela Jaffé, trans. Richard and Clara Winston (New York: Vintage Books, Random House, 1965), p. 288.
11 http://en.wikipedia.org/wiki/Rimbaud.
12 http://en.wikipedia.org/wiki/Henri_Cartier-Bresson.
13 http://en.wikipedia.org/wiki/Claude_Levi-Strauss.
14 http://en.wikipedia.org/wiki/Pierre_Verger.
15 http://en.wikipedia.org/wiki/André_Gide.
16 Paul O'Prey, "Introduction" to Joseph Conrad's *Heart of Darkness* (New York: Penguin Books, 1983), p. 12.
17 "I mean rather the specific geographical and historical psychic complexity that is implied in the image 'Italy' and which Jung sensed in the meanings and emotions released by 'Rome.'" "By considering 'Italy' and 'Rome' as genuine psychic geography and history, they become areas of the cultural imagination, genuine expressions of regions of the soul" James Hillman, "Plotino, Ficino and Vico as Precursors of Archetypal Psychology," in *Loose Ends: Primary Papers in Archetypal Psychology* (Dallas, TX: Spring Publications, 1983), p. 160 and p. 169, note 68.
18 Ibid., p. 160.
19 Hillman, *Re-Visioning Psychology*, p. 224.
20 *The Waste Land*, Section I, 55, "The Burial of the Dead," in T.S. Eliot, *Complete Poems*, p. 62.

Chapter 2

Cordial Racism
Race as a Cultural Complex

Walter Boechat

Author's Note: This paper was presented at a plenary session of the XIXth International Congress of the IAAP in Cape Town, South Africa, in September 2007. It was published in the proceedings of the Congress, *Cape Town 2007: Journeys, Encounters: Clinical, Communal, Cultural*, Pramila Bennett, ed. (Einsiedeln, Switzerland: Daimon, 1999). This conference paper also included comments and interpretation of a clinical case with race implications by Paula Boechat. It appears here with various modifications and expansions.

Introduction

When the Brazilian Jungian group was starting to form its first society, the International Association for Analytical Psychology (IAAP), back in 1978, we received a visit from Adolf Guggenbühl-Craig of Zürich. Although almost 30 years have passed, I can well remember the days he spent with us in Rio de Janeiro. Driving with him along the seaside, he told me:

> Brazil is well known for its *racial democracy*. Its crowded beaches where everybody can go, no private places in which people have to pay to enter as we sometimes have to do in places that are called "public" in Zürich. You can see, as we now see, White, Mestizos, and Blacks all together on Brazilian beaches. But if you go to good restaurants, you notice a whitening of the atmosphere at the more expensive places. But at the less expensive establishments, like small bars on the corners, it is the other way around: there is a darkening of the place, you see more Blacks.

With his sharp social eye, Guggenbühl-Craig had an intuitive understanding of a crucial problem in Brazilian cultural identity – that is, the close connection between our social prejudice and a very subtle "racial" prejudice not always admitted in different groups, amongst scholars and laypeople.[1]

In this chapter we will describe the unique style of multiple "races" that constitutes the social structure of Brazil. The peculiar way in which multiple people of

DOI: 10.4324/9781003400820-5

different origins have composed Brazil's social structure since colonial times led the famous sociologist Gilberto Freyre to state that a "racial democracy" exists in Brazil.[2] This assertion has been challenged for a long time by many anthropologists and scholars who began to demonstrate that racial democracy does not, in fact, exist in Brazil; rather, there is strong evidence of a peculiar kind of racial prejudice.

The problems of class, wealth distribution, and skin color are closely intertwined, a topic of endless debate among Brazilian anthropologists and sociologists. We will discuss these issues and their historical, sociological, and symbolical implications. In my approach to Brazilian culture, some psychological models for understanding larger groups are very important. Among them, the concept of the cultural complex is central. As defined by Thomas Singer and Sam Kimbles:

> Cultural complexes are based on repetitive, historical group experiences which have taken root in the group's cultural unconscious. At any ripe time, the slumbering cultural complexes can be activated in the cultural unconscious and take hold of the group's collective psyche and of the individual group members' individual/collective psyche. The inner sociology of cultural complexes can seize the imagination, the behavior and the emotions of the collective psyche and unleash tremendously irrational forces in name of their "logic."[3]

We consider this approach to be very significant for several reasons. First, it revitalizes Jung's complex theory, which has at times been neglected in favor of a more purely archetypal approach. Also, it provides an important theoretical tool for working with larger groups and societies. We now observe significant changes all over the world in the coming together of groups, societies, and nations that were previously more isolated. Faster communication, including the Internet, and better transportation have created dynamic and unparalleled interactions among groups leading to new values, symbols, and social changes.

Other psychological tools helpful in understanding groups and societies from the point of view of analytical psychology have been developed by Andrew Samuels with his in-depth studies of the psychodynamics of politics,[4] by Joseph Henderson with the concept of the *cultural unconscious*,[5] and by Michael Vannoy Adams, who studied the problem of multiracial groups and developed the idea of *stereotypes and stereotypical images* in the collective psyche of societies.[6]

Considering the growing importance of psychological studies of groups and communities, we believe that a psychological perspective on the cultural identity of Latin America is of major significance. We must always remember that Jung emphasized that psychology is a peculiar science since the psychologist is both the observer and object of its work. He also said that a psychological theory is always a personal confession. So I believe it is important for us Latin Americans to have a specific perspective in analytical psychology that takes into account the points of view of our continent. I believe the concept of cultural complex is central to this endeavor.

We consider that the color prejudice that took shape throughout Brazilian history represents one of the most important cultural complexes in Brazil. But to understand Brazilian society, we must first take a look at Brazilian history. To grasp the particular kind of racism constellated in Brazilian society, we will approach it as a cultural complex in the context of the general behavior and attitudes in this country.

The Role of Crossbreeding in the Evolution of Brazilian Identity

The history of Brazil has been one of journeys and encounters among different peoples and races since its discovery in 1500 by the Iberian Portuguese. There has always been an intermixture of populations of various origins throughout the history of the country. This is explained in various ways. The Portuguese ships that arrived on the coasts of Bahia, Brazil, in 1500 were not manned by stable Puritan families, like those on the Mayflower who arrived in North America to populate the Brave New World. Very few women and families were among the first Portuguese who arrived on Brazilian coasts. Rather, solitary men who had no professional opportunities in Portugal or elsewhere in Europe, many of whom had been in prison, were the first arrivals. Many were called *degredados* (outcasts).[7] From the beginning of colonial times, these solitary men found Indian women and had children with them. So the intermixture of the Portuguese with Indians started at the beginning of colonialization in Brazil. The first mother of all Brazilians is an Indian, *a great Indian mother*.[8]

The expansion of Portuguese domains into inland Brazil to build the identity of a new nation was the product of this breeding between the White Portuguese and the Native Indians. Their offspring, the mestizos, paved the way for some degree of integration between the Portuguese and the Indians. This does not mean that the two races' coexistence was always peaceful, for as soon as the Portuguese needed more hands for labor, they tried to enslave the Indians – an attempt that proved very difficult. Many Indians fled to the interior of the Amazon forest and other hidden parts of inland Brazil. Others died amidst the cruel, hard work imposed upon them by their Portuguese masters, or by diseases brought by the Whites in their initial contacts with them.

These early colonial times also marked the onset of human trafficking from various countries of Africa, where men were captured and shipped for slave work at sugar cane plantations and gold mines in central Brazil. The systematic import of slaves from Africa began at the end of the sixteenth century and did not stop until 1895! In fact, slavery was abolished by decree in 1888, making Brazil the last country in the civilized Western world to do so. When slavery was finally abolished, the Africans were so unprepared to live as free men that many returned to labor at the large farms where they had previously worked as slaves.

While many Indians died in slavery or fled to the Amazon forest and other regions of inland Brazil to escape it, the Blacks were better at slave work and thus continuously lived side by side with the Whites, a situation that has always been a focus of interest for Brazilian ethnologists and sociologists. Sociologist Gilberto

Freyre wrote the most important research about the coexistence of races in Brazil. His book *Casa Grande e Senzala* (*The Masters and the Slaves*)[9] describes how the cohabitation of masters and slaves contributed to the formation of the patriarchal colonial family in rural Brazil during the colonization period. This book became his masterpiece and was translated into many languages.

The history of slavery in Brazil is painful and full of suffering. The Blacks were captured by chance from among the hundreds of tribal societies in Africa, which spoke completely different dialects and had different social traditions. There was no uniformity in language or culture among them, and the slave trafficker wanted it that way to avoid the creation of solidarity among the slaves while being transported from Africa to Brazil.

The slaves of that era, almost totally cut off from their traditions and cultural roots, were forced to live in a completely alien landscape and milieu. To communicate and survive, they had to learn the Portuguese language of their masters. To survive the inhumane transportation conditions onboard the ships where many died, and of slavery itself when they arrived in Brazil, the Africans had to cling to their deepest inner values, their religious beliefs and magical practices, many of which are still widespread in the Afro-Brazilian religion called *Candomblé*.[10] *Candomblé*, with African gods, and *Umbanda*, a syncretic religion that includes African and Christian gods, functioned as safeguards to protect Black identity in the new world. A great variety of condiments for foods and all sorts of musical rhythms also served as references for identity in the Black culture. Since then, Black music has had a phenomenal development in the tunes and rhythms of popular music in Brazil. Some of these elements were purely African, and some were mingled with Portuguese or other influences. Samba, chorinho, bossa nova – all have Black influence.

Darcy Ribeiro describes the impact of slavery on the psyche and *cultural unconscious* of modern Brazilians in the following way:

> No people that went through this [the slavery period] as a daily routine through the centuries could come out without being indelibly imprinted. All of us, Brazilians, are of the same flesh of those tortured Blacks and Indians. All of us Brazilians are, in an equal way, the possessed hand that tortured them. The tenderest sweetness and the most atrocious cruelty conjugated themselves here to make us the suffering and sorrowful people that we are, and also the insensible and brutal people that we also are. Descendants of slaves and slave masters, we will always be servers of the malignancy distillated and installed in us. . . . The most terrible legacy of our heritage is to carry the scar of the torturer imprinted in our souls, ready to explode in classicist and racist brutality.[11]

This is a precise description of a cultural complex constellated in the Brazilian psyche after almost three centuries of uninterrupted slavery. I suggest that the image of the sadistic master and the suffering slave may be considered as a cultural complex that has manifested itself in the very stratified system of Brazilian society. Here we come face-to-face with the deeply intertwined relationship between *cultural complex* and *cultural trauma*. Luigi Zoja touches upon this theme in his sensitive essay on the arrival of the Spanish navigator Cortez amidst the Aztecs in Mexico.[12] He compares cultural trauma to personal trauma, drawing on the ideas of Donald Kalsched, who reminds us that in severe trauma, the ego's defenses are unable to cope with the dangers that threaten the whole psychic system. As a result, archetypal defenses arise to protect the self.[13]

The cultural complex constellated in Brazil by slavery for more than three centuries has also caused trauma and archetypal defenses in the cultural unconscious. Luigi Zoja suspects that the whole Mexican culture was traumatized and that this trauma had an indelible effect, even on future generations.[14] In a similar way, the Brazilian culture was also traumatized. No doubt the prolonged sadomasochistic relationship between the slave and his master is a *stereotypical image*[15] that continues to exist in the cultural unconscious, affecting the psyche of all Brazilians. The cultural complex continues to influence society in various ways. One is through the sadistic class system, with its low salaries and lack of opportunities.

In fact, a central problem in Brazilian society is the concentration of wealth among a small portion of the population. The lack of income distribution has become one of the most serious problems in the history of Brazilian society. And there is a strong prejudice against the lowest classes. This goes hand in hand with an ethnic prejudice, since Blacks and mestizos predominate in the lowest classes and have tremendous difficulties achieving better living standards.

Social Colors and Social Classes

However, mulattos and mestizos have often participated in Brazilian culture with significant success. For instance, the Mulatto Machado de Assis, son of a laundress mother who was an immigrant from the Azores archipelagos and a Brazilian mulatto father, is considered one of the best writers in Brazil's history.[16] Recently the Anglo-Indian writer Salman Rushdie said he "considered Machado de Assis the anticipator of Jorge Luis Borges and Gabriel Garcia Marquez" and regarded him as being among the best of Latin American authors.[17] One of the greatest Brazilian artists, Antonio Francisco Lisboa, a sculptor from the baroque period, was affectionately known as *Aleijadinho* ["the little crippled"], and he was also a mulatto. These are only two examples of many individuals who have achieved an exceptionally positive integration into the creation of Brazilian culture.

Yet the role of mestizos and mulattos in Brazil's civilizing process is generally disregarded. As a rule, they are seen as by-products of little importance in the history of Brazil, but their influence and importance in the creation of Brazil's ethnic identity should not be dismissed. Their peculiar status is essential to understanding the unique kind of racial prejudice in Brazil, which is quite different from Anglo-Saxon racism. Anglo-Saxon racism has a more defined character, based on the separation of races and places. The word *apartheid* means separation. In the USA, for instance, Martin Luther King confronted the fact of segregation where there were separate buses for Whites and Blacks. But in Brazil, strong racial prejudice is hidden, and that is why many hold Brazil out to be a *racial democracy*, which is not completely true. Brazilian racial prejudice *appears in disguise and goes hand in hand with social class prejudice.*

The prevalent crossbreeding in Brazilian history is a major factor in its social makeup. According to the Brazilian historian Laurentino Gomes, 90 percent of Brazil's population in 1882 – the year of independence – was made up of Black slaves, recently liberated slaves, and mestizos. Only a minority of Whites, a true elite, had a proper education and were literate.[18] The relationship between social class structure and skin color may be observed already at the very beginning of Brazil as an independent country.

These two different problems – race and social class – became intermingled at Brazil's origin as a nation. First, there were immense social class differences with only a minority of the population having access to information and power, while the large majority of recently liberated slaves, Mestizos, and poor people had none. Second, there were racial differences, with only the White elite having access to money, education, and power. We must emphasize that this mixture of social class and color differences is fundamental to Brazil's social structure and identity as a country. These social class differences, despite all the cultural changes that have taken place in the 190 years of Brazil's history as an independent society, remain a major issue.

The Peculiar Racism in Brazil: The Ethnic Persona and *Cordial Racism*

In a multicultural society such as Brazil, it is important to consider what I call the *racial persona*. Here is how Jung described the persona:

> The persona is a complicated system of relations between individual consciousness and society, fittingly enough a kind of mask, designed on the one hand to make a definite impression upon others, and, on the other, to conceal the true nature of the individual.[19]

The *racial persona* is a derivative of the concept of persona: it encompasses the totality of racial traits that define the external appearance of the individual, that is, skin color, hair texture, and other racial features.

The strong crossbreeding in Brazilian history favors a *racial prejudice that continues to exist in disguise, hand in hand with social prejudice*. This consequently causes racism to be a central element in Brazil's collective shadow.

The daily paper *Folha de S. Paulo* conducted very careful and specific research on the prevalence of racial prejudice in Brazil. This research demonstrated the extent of racial prejudice among the general population. The research included all "races" – Whites, Blacks, Indians, mulattos, and mestizos – of all educational strata and income levels: richer classes, middle class, the poor, and the destitute. This research was published in a small book titled *Cordial Racism*.[20] I find the term *cordial racism* very useful and descriptive in understanding the peculiar nature of racial prejudice in Brazil.[21]

This curious name given to Brazilian racism is based on the notions of *Brazilian cordiality* introduced by the historian Sergio Buarque de Holanda, who developed this idea in his 1936 book, *Raízes do Brasil*. This is one of the most famous works in Brazilian social history and is required reading for Brazilianists, anthropologists, and sociologists specializing in Latin American culture. According to Holanda, Brazil's contribution to civilization will be "cordiality." He writes,

> We will give out to the world *the cordial man*. The affability in dealing with other people, hospitality, generosity, virtues so praised by foreigners who visit us, represent, in effect, a defined feature of the Brazilian character, to the extent, at least, that patterns of human sociability formed within the rural and patriarchal milieu continue to exist.[22]

Holanda reminds us that it would be a mistake to understand cordiality as mere good manners or civility. Rather, the word *cordial* should be understood in its precise and etymological sense. Far from having a ritualistic, stylized, or formulaic attitude to social life, in their cordiality Brazilians place a high premium on what is natural and spontaneous. The author further explains that this cordiality, foreign in a certain sense to all formalism and social convention, includes not only positive feelings. On the contrary, *hostility* can be as *cordial* as friendship since both are born in the heart.[23] (The word *cordial* derives from Latin: *cor, cordis*, heart).

So cordiality is a complex phenomenon in Brazilian culture, showing two aspects: one apparent, easily seen, which flows according to social expectancy; another hidden, with strong feelings, not easily perceived, flowing underneath the surface. Among his many psychological gems, Holanda gives us a precise and vivid description of the archetype of the persona as it expresses itself in the collective psyche of present-day Brazilian society. He teaches us that "cordiality" can not only express itself as spontaneous affability but can just as easily function as a disguise for violence, rejection, a superior attitude, and most importantly, closed doors to equality in jobs and education for Blacks, mulattos, and Indians in Brazil.[24] The cordial man has difficulties in showing negative feelings of racial prejudice openly. Yet after five centuries of crossbreeding, the integration of the non-White population hasn't yet occurred, and good jobs and good salaries are still the prerogative of a social elite composed of the White population.

The racial factor is very present in the Brazilian collective psyche. Recently there was an example of this in the Supreme Court. Two judges started a quarrel that reached the press. The confrontation became more and more strained until one of them, a White man, said about the other, who is Black: "He is very unstable and fragile. He keeps asking himself whether he was chosen for this high post in the Supreme Court due to his skin color or due to his personal value."[25] This odd confrontation confirms that there is a collective guilt resulting from the repression the Black population suffered for centuries (and still suffers in a *cordial* way) and illustrates how people try to find ways to mend this cultural error in an attempt to heal the cultural complex.

A Clinical Case With Racial Prejudice

I recently saw in my practice a patient who illustrates how racism is alive in the Brazilian psyche. The patient, whom I shall call Carlos, is 45 years old, a Catholic priest, Black, extremely intelligent, and very well trained academically. A conflict with the Church started when Carlos applied to be a teacher in a widely known Catholic university in Rio. The bishop and other ecclesiastic authorities, although showing signs of friendship and admiration towards Carlos, opposed, in secret and *with cordiality*, his admission into the university. As Carlos came to find out later, their opposition was based on his activities in his parish, which were considered unorthodox. He was also "paying too much attention to the African deities of *Candomblé*." The Bishop wanted him to adhere to strictly Catholic materials by studying the tradition and values of the Roman Catholic Church according to the teachings of the present pope. Due to the strong opposition of his superiors, Carlos did not acquire a position at the university. During this difficult period of confrontation, Carlos fought courageously for his ideas and wrote an open manifesto to his superiors, affirming his rights and freedom to study and write about the African deities. He made a strong claim that this would not contradict the practice of celebrating the Catholic Mass and conducting other Catholic rituals.

When working out this situation in analysis, Carlos was seized with deep emotion. I suggested that he could draw what he was feeling, using colored pencils and crayons. Carlos drew a powerful tree, with a solid trunk and roots deep into the earth. Large fruits were hanging from the tree. He said the fruits represented his seven brothers and sisters. All the fruits were connected to each other and to the sun by a thin thread. The patient felt that the fruits, besides being connected to one another, were also connected to the strong tree which contained a huge energy that transcended their individual personalities. He had the feeling that this tree, deeply rooted to the earth, represented his ancestry and his deep values.

The image of the tree came back in a dream the following week:

Carlos is in large square, where there is a kind of meeting or festival with many people, most of them Black. It seems to be a festival with religious undertones of Black religion. Then he sees an altar, typical of the Candomblé religion, with a statue of a god. (It is not clear for him which god is present in this dream). Suddenly, he sees a powerful and numinous tree in the center of the square, and he is filled with awe. He awakes with feelings of peace and happiness.

Carlos associated this tree with a representation of the African Goddess *Iroko*, a deity associated with a powerful tree. This was the first tree to grow, through which all the *Orishas* (gods in the African Yoruba religion) descended to earth. The *Iroko* deity represents *ancestry*. I interpreted the dream (and the drawing), suggesting to

Carlos that he should affirm his deepest values and symbols by resisting any kind of pressure from his superiors in the Church. His psyche was reacting to the present crisis concerning his values by literally putting him in touch with the solidity of the African roots with which he identified. This was a very significant moment in Carlos' analysis: an encounter with his own values and traditions. He then said that he considered the Catholic Church's attitude toward him to be "racist." "By taking away these values and mythological ideas the Church is putting aside myself as an individual," he said.

Social Class, Perception of Color, and the Racial Persona

It is most difficult for a Black person to acquire a higher standard of living in Brazil. When it does happen, the *Black becomes White*, or to express it more precisely, he even perceives himself as being White. *He is considered White.* There is a strong connection between skin color and social class in Brazil, and between racial prejudice and class prejudice.

Paradoxically, Brazil's very stratified social system, in which social position is strongly related to skin color, has its origins in the time when slavery was abolished. At that time, Brazil had a predominantly agrarian or rural economy. The slave masters were the landowners. They knew that the abolition of slavery would not change social relations significantly, that they would continue holding the power. Their attitude was contrary to the Brazilian abolitionists of the time, who were more naïve in this respect and sought deep social transformations. The White slave-owning landowners had the monopoly on political, economic, and social power. The lower, less financially secure levels of the population were mostly composed of recently freed colored men, Indians, and some poor Whites. These populations were simply expected to follow orders from the upper classes. So the stratified social system that existed in colonial times obeyed a rigid ethnic pattern, which continued to exist even after the abolition of slavery.[26]

The half million slaves who were freed in 1888 entered a complex multiracial social system in which the *persona* took on the peculiarities of what I term *the racial persona*. This *racial persona* was of central importance in placing an individual in the existing social hierarchy. From the beginning, Brazil was never a biracial society like the United States or South Africa. And from the beginning, Brazil's colonizing population was created by crossbreeding. The majority of the population had Indian or Black blood. The multiracial society included all shades of colors between the White European and the Afro-Brazilian. Skin color, hair texture, and other physical signs that created one's *racial persona* determined to a great extent an individual's capacity to climb the social ladder. This happens because in a subtle way the Black population still has limited access to proper education and health. The mulattos or mestizos, being lighter, are generally considered as White. As the cynical Brazilian saying goes: "money turns things White."[27] As a person acquires money and he or she is able to go up the social scale, *his or her skin, as if by a miracle, becomes more White.*

In Brazil, in fact, it is very surprising, even dazzling to discover the extent to which social class interferes with the perception of skin color. In this context, listen to what the well-known soccer player Ronaldo Nazario had to say when asked about racial incidents in football matches in Europe and South America. Ronaldo responded that he was quite sad about the incidents, but in his words, "as he was a White man," he was not directly subjected to these racists attacks, although he could quite understand his friends' suffering.[28] In fact, Ronaldo is a light-skinned mulatto. But as Ronaldo has risen in class, the perception of his skin color has changed. Surely Ronaldo Nazario would have admitted to being a mulatto earlier, when he was a very poor boy in Rio de Janeiro's Bento Ribeiro district. But after defending Brazil's title during the 1994 World Cup in the United States, he became a world champion at the age of 18. Since then, he has become a multimillionaire by playing on professional teams in Italy and Spain. Ronaldo is no longer a Mulatto. People don't identify him as a mulatto, and he seems to agree with them.

Another interesting example of this mixture of social class and perception of skin color was reported by the anthropologist Darcy Ribeiro, demonstrating that this is a very old attitude. Ribeiro tells the story of Henry Koster, an Englishman traveling in Brazil during the nineteenth century, who was surprised to see a mulatto occupying the high rank of chief-captain. He then heard the following explanation: "Yes, he was originally a Mestizo, but now as Chief-Captain, he must be no person other than a White man."[29]

The Whitening of the Race

The unique racial prejudice in Brazil involves a powerful fantasy about the "*Whitening of the race.*" According to the American Brazilianist Thomas Skidmore, facilitating White immigration from Europe was not just an economic decision. The Brazilian intellectual elite was strongly influenced by European racist ideas and wanted a "whitening of the race" as far back as the end of the nineteenth century.[30] But the actual reality regarding color in modern Brazil is that the number of mestizos and mulattos has increased, not only by a Whitening of the Blacks but also by a darkening of the Whites.

The *Whitening* thesis maintained that White genes were stronger than Black ones and that through repeated crossbreeding, the White genes would prevail over Black or Indian genes. The theory held that, in time, a White population would predominate after various generations of Mestizos through the penetrating power of the White gene. *Brazil would reach ethnic purity through miscegenation!* These racist ideas are more comprehensible in the context of knowing that Brazil's intellectual elite looked for the prevailing ideas originating among Europeans and North Americans at the time.[31] This ideal led to the fantasy, among parts of the Brazilian elite in the years between 1889 to 1930, that "Whitening the race" would occur not by separation or exclusion but, surprisingly enough, by crossbreeding.

The first ethnologist to present this theory was Joao Batista de Lacerda during the first Universal Congress of Races in London, 1911. Often presented as a scientific formula, this theory was never adopted elsewhere.[32] This theory has been very unique to Brazil and deserves to be discussed. The *alchemical idea* of "Whitening of the race" was opposed by another sociological movement started in Brazil in the 1930s: the *cultural anthropology* and *cultural syncretism* movement, led by Gilberto Freyre, among others. Freyre strongly attacked the "Whitening of the race" idea, since cultural anthropology argued that environment and culture were the main issues and "races" in themselves were less important for sociology. From 1930 onward, with the rise of Nazi-fascism in Europe and its fanatic overvaluation of the "race" factor, Freyre's emphasis on the environment proved to be correct.[33]

The old ideas of race disappeared in Brazil, and theories of scientific racism became an anachronism in South America. But the idea of the inferiority of non-White groups still remains in the cultural unconscious, under the potent influence of the cultural complex of racism. This complex has led to the odd idea that Blacks may come to a position of social prominence only through sports or music, but not through other professional avenues.

Conclusion: Crossbreeding in Brazil Did Not Create a Racial Democracy

Contrary to what many important ethnologists and anthropologists such as Gilberto Freyre asserted, Brazil is indeed a *racist society*. As sociologist Florestan Fernandes once said, "The Brazilian is ashamed of being [racially] prejudiced," or as we would say from a psychological point of view: Brazilians have enormous difficulties in becoming conscious of their racial prejudice because it is deeply dissociated in the unconscious as a powerful cultural complex. The result of this dissociation creates a tremendous tension between the sophisticated persona of the so-called cordial man and his cordial racism that carries a shadow of anger, superiority, and a subtle scorn toward those of the lower ethnic groups in the social pyramid.

We know that the *archetype of the shadow* shows its destructive aspects not only in projection but also in its capacity to *contaminate* the collective psyche. In Brazil's large urban areas, violent riots have occurred recently, mainly in the cities of Rio de Janeiro and São Paulo. Various explanations have been offered for these upheavals, many of which are centered on the consequences of drug trafficking. Surely international drug trafficking is a main cause, but I believe that the violence will not be controlled unless other problems in this very complex multiracial society are consciously engaged. High on the list of these problems is Brazil's cordial racism, which is related to social class differences.

Notes

1 In this paper the terms "race" and "racial" will always be used with quotation marks. This because it has been proven "that the term is entirely empty as a system of categorization." Helen Morgan, "Exploring Racism," in *The Cultural Complex: Contemporary Jungian Perspectives on Psyche and Society*, eds. Thomas Singer and Samuel Kimbles (New York: Routledge, 1994), p. 212.

2 See the concept of *racial democracy* developed in Gilberto Freyre, *Casa Grande e Senzala*, "Preface" by Fernando Henrique Cardoso (S. Paulo: Global, 2009), 26th ed. American edition, *The Masters and the Slaves* (New York: Random House, 2000).
3 Thomas Singer and Samuel Kimbles, "Introduction" to *Cultural Complex*, eds. Singer and Kimbles, p. 7.
4 Andrew Samuels, *The Political Psyche* (London: Routledge, 1993).
5 See Joseph Henderson on the cultural unconscious, in Joseph Henderson, "The Cultural Unconscious," in *Shadow and Self: Selected Papers in Analytical Psychology* (Wilmette, IL: Chiron Publications, 1990), pp. 103–113. See also: Joseph Henderson, *Cultural Attitudes in Psychological Perspective* (Toronto: Inner City, 1984).
6 For a discussion of these concepts see Michael Vannoy Adams, *The Multicultural Imagination: "Race," Color, and the Unconscious* (London: Routledge, 1996).
7 For the role of the outcasts in Brazilian colonization, see Eduardo Bueno, *Náufragos, Traficantes e Degredados* [*Navigators, Traffickers and Outcasts*] (Rio de Janeiro: Objetiva, 1998).
8 Darcy Ribeiro, *O Povo Brasileiro* (S. Paulo: Companhia das Letras, 1995).
9 Freyre, *Casa Grande e Senzala*. American edition, *The Masters and the Slaves*.
10 The ethnologist Monique Augras maintains that *Candomblé* is in fact a Brazilian religion, not an Afro-Brazilian religion, because of its unique characteristics developed in Brazil. (Monique Augras, Seminar at the Jungian Institute of Rio de Janeiro (AJB) on "African Mythologies in Brazil" (July 2010).
11 Ribeiro, *O Povo Brasileiro*, p. 120, my translation. I use the expression *cultural unconscious* following Joseph Henderson: "[The cultural unconscious is] . . . The segment of the collective unconscious belonging to a nation or culture." Joseph Henderson, "The Cultural Unconscious," in *Shadow and Self*, pp. 103–113. I think this concept is central in anthropological and ethnological studies.
12 Luigi Zoja, "Trauma and Abuse: The Development of a Cultural Complex in the History of Latin America," in *Cultural Complex*, eds. Singer and Kimbles, p. 78 ff.
13 Donald Kalsched, quoted by Luigi Zoja in "Trauma and Abuse," in *The Cultural Complex*, eds. Singer and Kimbles, p. 85.
14 Luigi Zoja, "Trauma and Abuse," *Cultural Complex*, eds. Singer and Kimbles, p. 84.
15 According to Michael Vannoy Adams "there are two dimensions, not just one, to the collective: an archetypal (a natural – that is, a transhistorical, transcultural, transethnic) dimension and a stereotypical (a historical, cultural, ethnic) dimension." See Michael Vannoy Adams, *Multicultural Imagination*, p. 46.
16 Some novels by Machado de Assis have acquired worldwide recognition. Books like *The Posthumous Memories of Brás Cubas, Quincas Borba, Dom Casmurro-A Novel*, and *The Alienist* have been praised for their literary quality and psychological subtlety.
17 Salman Rushdie commented on his admiration of Machado de Assis at the FLIP 2010, the Literary Fair of Paraty, Brazil.
18 Laurentino Gomes tells an interesting story about illiteracy at that time. The king of Portugal, fleeing from Napoleon's army, came to Rio de Janeiro in 1808, staying in Brazil for 13 years. As part of his rich cultural contribution, he brought his enormous Library of 60,000 volumes, one of the largest in Europe at that time. A French voyager visited the King's Library, admiring its richness in rare books and variety of topics. But as he went through the immense Library, he saw nobody there except himself and the Library's administrator. Intrigued, he visited the library a second time and again met no other visitor. The lack of visitors had a simple explanation – the vast majority of the population was illiterate and could not read the books. *Laurentino Gomes 1822* (Rio de Janeiro: Nova Fronteira, 2010), pp. 70 and ff. The National library is still in downtown Rio de Janeiro. It is considered the largest library in South America and is one of the eight largest libraries in the world. In recent years, parts of its rich archives have been digitalized. For more information on the National Library, see the Library's website: www.bn.org.br.

19 C.G. Jung, "The Relations Between the Ego and the Unconscious," in *The Collected Works of C.G. Jung, vol. 7, Two Essays in Analytical Psychology*, trans. R.F.C. Hull (1918; repr., Princeton: Princeton University Press, 1973), § 305.
20 Folha de S. Paulo/Datafolha, *Racismo Cordial* (S. Paulo: Ática, 1998, 2nd printing).
21 I refer to cordial racism as typical of Brazil because I did not make a systematic approach to racism in Latin American as a whole. However, I would guess that the attitude to different "races" is very similar throughout the whole region.
22 Sérgio Buarque de Holanda, *Raízes do Brasil* (São Paulo: Companhia das Letras, 1936/1999), 26th ed., pp. 146 ff., my translation.
23 Ibid., p. 205.
24 Very recently the daily paper *O Globo* published social research showing inequality in the populations served by the public health system. The White population uses its services more than Blacks (*O Globo*, December 24, 2010). Cordial racism is alive and well in producing its destructive effects.
25 Daily Paper, "*O Globo*," April 21st, 2012, p. 4.
26 See Thomas Skidmore, *Preto no branco* (Rio de Janeiro: Paz e Terra, 1989), 2nd ed., pp. 54, 55. American Edition: *Black into White: Race and Nationality in Brazilian Thought* (Oxford: Oxford University Press, 1974).
27 Skidmore, *Preto no branco*, p. 55.
28 Revista Veja, Internet site, *Veja on-line*, June 1st, 2005. Quotation by Ronaldo about racism in European football teams. http://veja.abril.com.br/010605/vejaessa.html.
29 Ribeiro, *O Povo Brasileiro*, p. 225.
30 For more information about the Whitening of the race idea, see Skidmore, *Preto no branco*. p. 55.
31 The concern with the absence of White European population in Brazil goes back, in fact, to the period of the arrival of the King D. John VI and the royal Portuguese family fleeing from Napoleon's army. Already in the early nineteenth century the king authorized the immigration of many European families.
32 See the role played by the sociologist João Batista de Lacerda in the propagation of the Whitening of the race theory in Skidmore, *Preto no branco*, p. 81 ff.
33 Here we find the traditional controversy in science, the discussion of which is most important, "nature or nurture." The racist idea argues that *nature* is the unique factor, since people are born with their definitive features, virtues, and vices. The "superior race" ideology of Nazi-Fascism emphasizes *nature*. According to the cultural anthropology of Bronislaw Malinowski and Franz Boas, cultural influences are the main factor in anthropology. Gilberto Freyre was the main representative of cultural anthropology in Brazil.

Chapter 3

Non Ducor, Duco I Am Not Led, I Lead

Denise G. Ramos

I was at the Ministry of Education in Brasília, the capital of Brazil, attending a meeting of coordinators of postgraduate courses in psychology offered all over the country when, after six hours of heated debate, it dawned on me that we were getting nowhere. Each and every argument ended up in some polemic that had little to do with education or specific problems in the area of clinical psychology. The ideas proposed by the group from São Paulo were quickly dismissed by the others without our even having enough time to finish our presentation. I realized that the atmosphere was not conducive to holding a debate on a rational, logical level. Emotions had taken control of the meeting. Professors stood up finger-wagging to argue that their programs needed more money and were being jeopardized. Trying to understand what was going on, I distanced myself a little from my colleagues, and then I saw where the conflict was coming from: it was a clash between two "Brazils," rich Brazil and poor Brazil. Colleagues from the north and northeast of the country displayed their deep resentment, especially toward the coordinators of the São Paulo courses, and did not allow any consensus to be reached with regard to the decisions we needed to make about education at our respective schools, let alone the future of the postgraduate programs. The accusation was that those who represented São Paulo enjoyed more privileges and were allocated more funds from the federal government. The data which showed that this was untrue was utterly disregarded and made the meeting even more conflicted.

After two days of meetings we returned to our respective cities tired and disheartened by the unproductivity of our joint labors. We had failed to discuss the matters that had led us to come together: education and improving postgraduate studies. Nothing was achieved. It is true that the city of São Paulo is the richest in the country, but what did that have to do with the debate on the progress of education? We had gone there to talk about philosophy, psychology, and pedagogy!

Analyzing the problem later on, I came to the realization that a *cultural complex* had diverted us from the theme of the meeting and destroyed the considerable investment we had made in time and money to gather together in the capital of the country. And this is just one example among others observed by me and colleagues in similar situations. In politics, too, we see fighting and rivalry between members of parliament and senators from different states. Politicians from the south, predominantly from São Paulo, often form alliances against politicians from the north and northeast of the country.

The rivalry between citizens from other locations and those living in the city of São Paulo is known to all and is the object of jokes and prejudice, some examples of which I will offer later in this chapter. Myths and symbols referring to the formation of this city, as well as its history and the position it enjoys in the economic and social scenario, help us to reflect on the various projections of power onto its inhabitants and a possible underlying complex.

A country with Brazil's territorial size and colonized by several cultures can generate differences among its inhabitants that take the form of rivalries and prejudices. Territorial images are formed in the unconscious of a population that identifies with certain geographical and historical characteristics to shape an image of itself, an identity and cultural complex passed on from one generation to another.

In the case of the city of São Paulo, its first impact on newcomers is its sheer grandeur (Figure 3.1). Enormous skyscrapers of different shapes and heights leave little space to glimpse the horizon. The sensation is both of oppression and grandiosity. With a population close to 11 million, its history is permeated with adventures and pioneering.

In this article I shall offer a brief review of historical and cultural events that have marked the development of the city and analyze significant symbolic representations that justify the hypothesis of a *power complex* peculiar to the inhabitants of São Paulo City.

Figure 3.1 Skyline of São Paulo.
Source: Photo by Flavio Meyer

Who Is "São Paulo"?

São Paulo is the capital of the state of São Paulo and the largest city in Brazil. It is also the largest city in the western and southern hemisphere, ranking as the second most populous metropolitan area in the Americas and among the five largest metropolitan areas on the planet.[1]

São Paulo also exerts enormous regional influence on commerce and finance as well as the arts and entertainment. It shows a strong international influence and is considered an Alpha World City.[2] The nineteenth richest city in the world, with a Gross National Product (GNP) of 107 billion USD, São Paulo accounts for 20 percent of the Brazilian economy and for 15 percent of the GNP of South America. The *per capita* income in São Paulo is almost twice the national average. Its inhabitants produce 36 percent of goods and services of the State of São Paulo, and the city of São Paulo is home to 63 percent of the multinational companies established in Brazil, besides being responsible for 28 percent of all national scientific production.[3]

Given all this might, the city is seen as the engine of Brazil and is sought out by all sorts of people who come to it to try their luck. It offers great opportunities for business, interchange, and culture. Its population is made up of 152 nationalities who have brought the many different cultures and traditions that today are evident in the city.[4]

São Paulo's staggering rhythm of growth begins in the early morning. At 6:00 a.m. we can already see streets busy with pedestrians hurrying by to set the pace of the day: "Wake up, wake up! Time to get up, let's get up!" says the radio alarm clock shoving the *paulistanos* out of bed (the term *paulistano* refers to the inhabitants of the city of São Paulo).

As far as culture is concerned, São Paulo boasts the liveliest cultural life in the whole country. Each and every day there appear new opportunities for leisure, entertainment, and amusement: permanent and temporary art exhibits, hundreds of cinemas, theaters, shopping centers, and a lot more. The night life in São Paulo is so feverish that it created the myth of a city that never stops and is constantly changing. This is "a mercurial city," in the words of analyst Augusto Capello, reflecting on the speed of the territorial and cultural changes and the intense agitation of the traffic.[5] There is a kind of "dictatorship" of movement, with a constant flow of cars, buses, subways, trains, feet, and carts. To be in São Paulo is to be always in motion, coming and going to or from someplace.[6]

This basic information enables us to feel the grandiosity of the city and offers us a basis for reflecting on the sense of power felt by its inhabitants, as well as the power projected onto them by people who live elsewhere.

A brief note on the historical background of São Paulo and a description of the dynamism and symbols that marked and continue to mark this city will allow us to make a more appropriate analysis of the factors that permeate the formation of the identity of its inhabitants, resulting in a possible cultural complex based on a feeling of superiority toward the other inhabitants of the country.

Origins

The Jesuit priests came from Portugal to found the city of São Paulo in 1554 and left the stamp of their strength on the culture and the economy. The name of the city honors Saint Paul. The choice of this name already reflects a project of large scale that its Jesuit founders envisioned for what was at the time just a small town in the mid-sixteenth century.

Paul the Apostle, also called the Apostle Paul (5 AD–67 AD), was one of the most important early Christian missionaries. His influence on Christian thinking has been significant due to his role as a prominent apostle of Christianity during the spreading of the Gospel through early Christian communities across the Roman Empire, and his teachings form a considerable portion of the New Testament.

Regardless of the intentions of its founders, the choice of this saint as the city's patron seems to have inspired its inhabitants to assume the role of national leaders both in industry, science, and technology.

Symbols and Representations of Power in the City of São Paulo

Coat-of-Arms: **Non ducor, duco**

The coat-of-arms of São Paulo City is formed by a shield with an arm wielding the flag of Christ's Cross used by the Portuguese navigators, the symbol of the Christian faith (Figure 3.2). On top there is a crown with eight towers, the symbol of a

Figure 3.2 Coat-of-arms of the city of São Paulo.

state capital. The sides are adorned with coffee branches: the chief element of the *paulista* economy at the time it was designed: 1916 (the term *paulista* refers to the inhabitants of the state of São Paulo).[7]

The motto "*Non ducor, duco*" – "I am not led, I lead" – valorizes the independence of the actions taken by the city and its leading role in the state and the country. This phrase, as well as the image of an arm bearing a weapon, appears as the motto of the city's inhabitants to indicate a desire for independence and leadership.[8]

Flag

The *paulista* flag is white with the Christ Cross in red, and the coat-of-arms of the municipality in the center. Here white symbolizes peace, purity, temperance, truth, candor, integrity, friendship, and the synthesis of the races. The red symbolizes boldness, courage, value, spirit, generosity, and honor, while the cross evokes the founding of the city. The circle is the emblem of eternity, in affirmation of São Paulo's position as capital city and state leader.[9]

São Paulo's Animal Symbol

A contest held in 2011 by the São Paulo Department of Nature and Environment (*Secretaria do Verde e do Meio Ambiente*) elected the *Puma concolor* as the wild animal to symbolize the city's biodiversity. This animal is known as the *brown puma* because of its coloring. Its habits are solitary and nocturnal. It hunts and feeds on small mammals such as *coatis, catetos*, armadillos, and water dogs, or small vertebrates. Measuring between 86 and 154 cm – plus its tail, which can be as long as 96 cm – the puma weighs between 29 and 120 kilos. According to the department, it is the biggest feline recorded at present in the city and the second biggest in Brazil. Another interesting characteristic is the puma's great capacity to adapt to different environments and climates.[10]

The important thing in this context is that the puma beat out 14 other animals for this honor, especially many birds whose songs are commonly heard in the city, whereas the puma is only seen in the zoo. The choice astonished veterinarians since this animal is certainly not part of the daily life of the *paulista* community. So why this choice? Aren't we choosing here a symbol of power, this being the strongest and most dominating animal in Latin America's forests?

The Monument to the Explorers

The Monument to the Explorers (*Bandeirantes*) is a large granite sculpture 50 meters long and 16 meters high, the work of the Italian-Brazilian sculptor Victor Brecheret (Figure 3.3). It was inaugurated in 1953 during the commemorations of the 399th anniversary of the city. The monument represents an expedition of exploring frontiersmen with two men on horseback: the Portuguese chief and the Indian

Figure 3.3 The Monuments to the Bandeirantes.
Source: Photo by the author

guide. Behind them comes a group made up of Indians, Negroes, Portuguese, and Mamelukes pulling a canoe used by the explorers in their river expeditions.[11]

This monument is perhaps the most representative of the city, portraying as it does the efforts of the *paulistanos* to explore the country, an ambition that remains today, no longer as a territorial objective but certainly in the field of ideas and politics.

This image, placed in a very visible central location, in the Park of Ibirapuera, reminds everyone of the importance of the courage and daring of the first inhabitants of the city, those who faced enormous difficulties trying to tame the forest that surrounded the city. Nowadays the role of these pioneers is contested, in that they exploited the indigenous population in search of precious stones later sent to Europe. Nonetheless, the symbol of pioneering and boldness remains stamped in the unconscious of the population.

Forming Identity

The Explorers

The name *bandeirantes* (from *bandeira*, flag) is given to the men who braved the hinterland of São Paulo in the early sixteenth century, penetrating the backlands in search of mineral riches, especially silver, Indians to enslave, or *quilombos* (enclaves where runaway African slaves lived) to exterminate. They were responsible for conquering and developing the interior of Brazil, as well as for the expansion of the country in its territorial struggle against Spain. They are also given credit for discovering precious metals that would later feed the European markets.[12]

The action of the *bandeirantes* was of the utmost importance for the exploration of Brazil's interior, as well as for maintaining the economy of the colony, whether because of the consequences for trade or for the capture of Indians to supply the labor-force for agriculture, especially sugar cane. Known for their aggressiveness, these explorers would attack the Indians who were being catechized by the Jesuit priests and then sell them as slaves to work on the big farms. They did so in defiance of the law and the kings of Portugal, who had forbidden such practices.[13]

Many reports illustrate the behavior of these pioneers. In the first half of the seventeenth century, Montoya proclaimed that the entire town of São Paulo was inhabited by soulless, aggressive people with no regard for the law. Their assaults on the houses of the Jesuits who sheltered the Indians gave the *paulistas* the reputation of being the most unsubmissive subjects of the kings of Portugal.[14] Auguste Saint Hilaire, in his second journey to São Paulo in the eighteenth century, described the *paulistas* as follows:

> When one knows from personal experience how much fatigue, privation, and danger still lie ahead for the traveler who ventures into these distant regions, and when one learns the itinerary of the endless expeditions of the first *paulistas*, one feels a kind of awe, one has the impression that these men belonged to a race of giants: the *paulistas* were never a submissive people.[15]

Despite the historical revision of the role of these adventurers in the development of the country, their descendants are extremely proud of their origin and give themselves the title "the four-hundred," distinguishing themselves especially from the other inhabitants who descended from European immigrants, whom they consider to be people of a lower "class."

The Four-hundred

"Four-hundred" is a term coined in the middle of the twentieth century, in 1954, to refer to the celebration of the four hundred years of the founding of the city of São Paulo, the so-called "Fourth Centenary." The term designates the traditional *paulistano* elite, the old families of São Paulo, the descendants of the early colonizers, thus distinguishing them from the so-called "*nouveau-riche*," the relatively newly arrived descendants of immigrants of various nationalities who tried to form a new social category.[16]

As a result of globalization and as a sign of the cosmopolitanism of the *paulista* metropolis, little by little the term "four-hundred" has lost its original meaning of "citizen belonging to an old, powerful and traditional family," since many members of these families have been joined through marriage to immigrant families.

However, in spite of globalization and cosmopolitanism, the "four-hundred" lives on in remembrance of the pioneering, populating explorers. At first the *paulistano* elite tried to make themselves special by separating from the immigrants through exclusive schools and clubs for themselves and their descendants, in this way creating an image of proud and haughty snobs.

The fact is that the *bandeirantes* movement has left such profound marks on the *paulista* psyche that some people consider São Paulo as the focus of the history of Brazil on account of its being the "home of the civilization of the *bandeirantes*." This is one of the factors that has contributed to the rivalry between this city, considered the seat of "pure and integral Brazilianism," and the other capitals, especially the city of Rio de Janeiro, as we shall see further ahead.[17]

Ideological Bases of the Identity of São Paulo Inhabitants

The idea that São Paulo was to fulfill a superior, leading role in the country was already foreseen by the *bandeirante* Amador Bueno in 1640, when he said that São Paulo should play vis-à-vis Brazil the same role that Paris played for France, or using another metaphor, that São Paulo would be the brain that thinks and the rest of the country the arm that executes.[18]

In the early twentieth century there was a clear revival of these ideas with the appearance of the term *"paulistanity"* to express the feeling that takes hold of *paulistas* due to increasing conflicts with the federal government.

Paulistanity is the ideology that informs a series of values and characteristics that are peculiar to the status of *paulista*. In order to validate this condition, the *bandeirante* is seen as the ancestral, civilizing patriarch. *Paulistanity* is then defined as being based on two essential functions: as self-affirmation/identification of a social group on the rise economically and socially, and as an instrument of this group to attain its objectives of social hegemony and control over the other segments of Brazil's dominating class.[19]

For instance, the coffee-growing elite began to identify themselves with the *bandeirantes* as a way to establish for themselves a historical and psychological status:

> For half a century, few educated *paulistas* were in any doubt that their collective psychology had been inherited from the *bandeirantes*, yet most authors and apologists emphasized the positive aspects: the *bandeirante* had expanded the frontier (the "frontiersman" proper), had lent all his energy to productive ends, had envisaged opportunities and made good use of them, and had shown the path of the future of the Brazilian nation. It was up to their modern descendants to accept the destiny of leading the *paulista* country.[20]

The 1920s saw the systematization of this political ideology, strengthened by the so-called "modernist movement." This was a wide-sweeping cultural movement that had strong repercussions on the artistic scene and Brazilian society in the first half of the twentieth century, above all in the field of literature and art. Its main concern was to explain the singular nature of Brazil.

The "green-and-yellow group" (the colors of the Brazilian flag) that constitutes the conservative perspective of the movement lent strength to the ideology of superiority. This group built its arguments with the objective of electing São Paulo as the nation's center, thereby disqualifying Rio de Janeiro (at that time the capital of Brazil) from fulfilling that role.

Several arguments were used to prove this superiority, including that São Paulo was the cradle of the nation due to its geographical configuration. Unlike other regions, in São Paulo the hydrographic network runs in the direction of the interior, which leads its inhabitants to follow the course of the rivers to brave the hinterland. While those who live on the coast look abroad, dreaming and fantasizing about Europe, the people who live in São Paulo prefer to explore the interior of the country in search of precious stones and territorial expansion. This leads one to the conclusion that São Paulo should assume the role of guardian of the nation's traditions.[21]

It is based on this paradigm that the residents of São Paulo defend their right to command the country: if the *paulista*, by dint of geographical circumstances, became the national hero – that is to say, a *bandeirante* frontiersman – the opposite occurred with the *carioca* (as the inhabitants of Rio de Janeiro are called), who just sat there on the beach eyeing the "mermaids." Since the first exploring expeditions date from the sixteenth century, the idea remains that it was the *bandeirante* who mapped the vast expanse of the country.[22]

Accordingly, the modernist movement, responsible for reviving the national aesthetic and the movement against imported culture, revives the myth of the original *bandeirante* explorers. Just like their ancestors, today's *paulistas* also feel invested with a mission: to carry their avant-garde ideals to the rest of the country, thus guaranteeing Brazilian borders. Always present in the group's argument is the idea of the *paulista* being ahead of the rest of the country. The other states are looked down on as "poor, backward brothers." Hence the well-publicized image of São Paulo as the locomotive hauling behind it a line of empty wagons.[23]

More than ever before, this feeling of power and innovation was reinforced in the revolution of 1932, the biggest military conflict in twentieth-century Brazil.

The Revolution of 1932

On two occasions the inhabitants of São Paulo rose up against the federal government to lead movements opposed to totalitarian federal power. The more significant of the two was what is known as the Revolution of 1932 or the Paulista War, an armed movement that took place in the State of São Paulo between the months of July and October 1932, its express purpose being to overthrow President Getúlio Vargas' dictatorial, provisional government and to promulgate a new constitution for Brazil.

This armed conflict was also the largest popular mobilization in the history of the city. Men and women – students, politicians, and industrialists – participated with enthusiasm in the hope of defeating the central government located in Rio de Janeiro. Of course, just beneath the surface, there was also a separatist desire, strong enough for the Paulista Republican Party to propose that São Paulo should break away from the rest of the country and constitute what at the time was called the Paulista Fatherland (*Pátria Paulista*).[24]

Here is not the appropriate place for delving deeper into the context that led to this revolution. Its importance for our thesis is to know that in the first half of the twentieth century the State of São Paulo experienced an accelerated process of industrialization and prosperity due to profit from its coffee plantations. Nevertheless, amidst a serious economic crisis caused by the Great Depression of 1929 that made the price of coffee plummet, an inhabitant of São Paulo, Julio Prestes, was elected president of Brazil in 1930 with 91 percent of the votes. However, dissatisfied with the political supremacy of São Paulo, an alliance was formed among other States to prevent the President elect from taking office and to replace him with a politician from another State: Getúlio Vargas. This president immediately installed a dictatorship: he suspended the constitution, dissolved the National Congress, the State Congresses (State Houses and Senates), and municipal chambers.[25]

Many denunciations were made against what was considered an attack on São Paulo. One such denunciation was made by a Senator in the following terms: "This undying envy of our amazing progress should rather be pride for the whole of Brazil! Instead of thanking us and embracing us like brothers, they offend and threaten us with their spears and their horses' hooves!" (Speech made by the senator Cândido Nogueira da Mota, Senate of the Legislative Congress of the State of São Paulo, September 24, 1929).[26]

On the anniversary of the founding of the city in 1932, the first of several mega-rallies was held against the dictatorship. In February 1932, some political parties joined together in a United Front (*Frente Única*) to demand the end of the dictatorship under the "Provisional Government" and the drafting of a new constitution. This showed that the whole of São Paulo was against the dictatorship.

The *paulistas* believed that their State was being treated by the Federal Government like some land that had been conquered and that they were not being recognized for the importance that they deserved.

What triggered the revolt was the death of five young men in the center of the city of São Paulo, killed by shots fired by supporters of the dictatorship during a demonstration. These deaths gave rise to an opposition movement that came to be known as *MMDCA*, the initials of the five young victims.

The poster of the *paulista* movement against the dictatorship shows a São Paulo inhabitant dressed like a gigantic frontiersman (*bandeirante*) smashing in his hands the then-president of the republic (Figure 3.4).

The *paulistas* then began to plot an armed movement aimed at overthrowing the dictatorship, under the banner of the proclamation of a new constitution for Brazil:

> São Paulo rose up in arms on the 9th of July 1932 to deliver Brazil from a government that had taken power after a revolution ... and was perpetuating itself indefinitely, crushing the rights of a free people ... and stamping on the ever-glorious São Paulo with the boots and whips of a slave-master.[27]

Figure 3.4 The *Bandeirante* (explorer) smashing the president of the republic.

Figure 3.5 Pro-Brasilia Fiant Eximia.

On this occasion was created the coat-of-arms of the State of São Paulo, bearing the Latin expression: "*Pro Brasilia fiant eximia*" ("Let great things be done for Brazil") engraved in silver on a red sash (Figure 3.5). Graphically, the coat-of-arms is composed of a red Portuguese shield on which sits a Roman sword, the symbol of justice that here also represents Paul the Apostle.[28]

During this period, in addition to the coat-of-arms, numerous songs and marches were written paying homage to São Paulo. Many texts were published exalting the spirit and glory of the *paulistanos*: one of the headlines reads "São Paulo rises up for Brazil."[29]

São Paulo also created its own money with images of the principal frontiersmen-explorers and which was supported by the residents, who donated jewels and even their wedding rings to the campaign called "Gold for the good of São Paulo," which also went by the name "Gold for victory."

Such enthusiasm could only be based on the deep emotion provoked by a revival of the *bandeirante* traditions. Deep in the hearts of the *paulistas*, there was the desire expressed by the famous writer Mario de Andrade: "At the moment, I would do anything to separate São Paulo from Brazil."[30]

Thousands of volunteers enlisted to form columns and all sorts of campaigns, but although it counted on more than 40,000 soldiers, São Paulo found itself at a disadvantage militarily and economically because it was fighting practically alone against the entire country. With the advance of the federal government troops and its economy asphyxiated by a blockade on the port and roads, it was forced to surrender. Extra-official estimates reckon that over a thousand *paulistas* died in the uprising.

For the *paulistas* the Revolution of 1932 became the ultimate symbol of the struggle for a constitution to guarantee the right of freedom and equality for all. Losing the war did not destroy the morale of the people, who saw the revolution as a valid sacrifice, which two years later led to the longed-for change in the constitution:

> Often, feats of this grandeur fail to triumph with arms. The triumph comes with time, after the seed of repulsion is sown to redeem and save a people. The rising came to an end after ninety days of heavy, endless fire. But the example, if not the proof, remained that in the zeal of nationality sat latent and indomitable the spirit of freedom and democracy.[31]

Today the revolution is still enthusiastically commemorated in the city of São Paulo, where the destruction and deaths caused by the rebellion are still remembered. Numerous books and articles have been written to celebrate this movement, which also served to inspire poets, authors, and commentators both here and abroad.[32]

In synthesis, the Revolution of 1932 is a mark in the molding of the identity of the people of São Paulo, according to whom the process of redemocratization would not have taken place were it not for this struggle. The residents of the city pride themselves on their past and feel superior for having fought all alone against the dictatorship. Among those who participated in this event, as well as their descendants, one notices even today a feeling that it would have been very good if São Paulo had managed to free itself from the rest of the country. Many imagine that São Paulo would be a rich, prosperous nation, "if it didn't have to carry all the other compatriots."

In honor of the Revolution of 1932, at the beginning of July a group of *paulistas* participate in the "9th of July Walk," covering on foot the 927 kilometers through the state of São Paulo where the conflicts took place. The organizers of this civic walk aim to enter the walk in the *Guinness Book of World Records* as the world's longest civic walk.[33]

Another tribute paid to the heroes of that revolution is the Obelisk erected in the center of the main park in the city, today a symbol of power and pride for the *paulistanos*. Called the Mausoleum of the Constitutionalist Soldier, this monument preserves the memory and the ideals of 1932.

Stereotypes

Another excellent source of data for analyzing the underlying subconscious contents of the identity of the *paulistano* and their superiority complex is a survey on the most common stereotypes concerning the city and its inhabitants. We have chosen three sources: epithets, ethnic anecdotes, and sociocultural rivalries.

Epithets

A search among different popular sites on the Internet came up with the most common epithets related to São Paulo. As can be seen, they all reveal an image of power:

"São Paulo, powerful São Paulo, the Brazilian locomotive, the locomotive of Brazil."
"São Paulo, the pride of Brazil! The pride of this immense mixture of Portuguese, Italian, Arab, Japanese, French and African, among others, that makes the *paulista* people incomparable."
"A State that is so big, rich, gastronomically varied, cultural and beautiful that it arouses the envy of the other States that try to be like us – but always fail!"
"São Paulo is complex, gigantic, and contains many 'worlds within worlds,' beginning with the actual mentality of each *paulista*."
"*Paulistanos* are folk with guts, strength, fighters who each and every day fight the battle of life, always with a smile on their face."
"Those who speak badly of São Paulo are envious or else so alienated from their own base that they don't let themselves see the world, it's like wanting to blame your failure on the success of others."
"São Paulo will always be the heart-beat of Brazil."
"Sao Paulo, the rough Colossus." "In the superlative metropolis, that threatens to kill of fright the newcomer, nobody dies of boredom."[34]

Innumerable other epithets always reflect the same idea of power, vibration, and being the center of the country. The inhabitants of São Paulo describe themselves as being proud of their citizenship and superior to other Brazilians because they are the ones who lead the rest of the country – "the locomotive force."

Ethnic Anecdotes

Another source of information about the image of the city and its inhabitants is the ethnic anecdote. Some jokes depreciate and treat others as inferior, principally the residents of São Paulo who originally came from the north and northeast of the country and who are seen as being less intelligent and incapable of learning.

According to Conde, the joke as a phenomenon of language equipped with technique and form uses stereotypes and generally serves as a vehicle for some frowned-upon discourse.[35] Accordingly, from the analytical point of view, the clashes between *paulistanos* and "the other" Brazilians underline an envy and contempt that is mutually felt.

The following anecdote is a typical example:

> A poor immigrant travels down to São Paulo. During the journey he meets a *paulistano* leg-puller who has some fun with him by telling him that in São Paulo money grows on the ground. After hearing this marvelous story, the northeasterner gets off the bus in São Paulo, together with another friend who has also come south to look for a job. Right outside the bus station, a bank is being robbed, and in their flight the robbers, not to be caught *in flagrante*, toss a bag of money on the ground. The northeasterner passes by right after the bank-robbers have thrown the money away, and when he sees the bag lying there, he comments to his friend: "Hey, that fellow was right, money here really does grow on the ground, but today is Sunday so I'll just wait till tomorrow to come back and gather it up."[36]

Another example:

> Three o'clock in the afternoon. Two poor immigrants are leaning against a tree at the side of the road. All of a sudden a car shoots by at top speed and a 100-Real bill flies out the window and lands on the other side of the road. Five minutes later, one of them says to the other: "Hey, man . . . if the wind changes, we're made!"[37]

The two jokes clearly express contempt for the immigrants from other cities and, above all, for those who hail from less-developed places and are considered slow-witted and naïve.

Sociocultural and Typological Rivalry

Among the various stereotypes projected on the inhabitants of São Paulo, special mention should be made of the rivalry with the *cariocas* (the inhabitants of the city of Rio de Janeiro). These stereotypes could be summed up in the popular concept: "While São Paulo is the city of progress and work, Rio is a place for tourism, Carnival, and fun. The solution would be to work in São Paulo and enjoy oneself in Rio de Janeiro!"

In other words, São Paulo is an Apollonian city, whereas Dionysus or Bacchus rules over Rio de Janeiro. This notion reveals the desire of the inhabitants of São Paulo to show themselves as superior beings, since it is "Apollo" who builds the country, while "Dionysus" is only concerned with having a good time.

As a reflection of this stereotype, a famous *carioca* author asks: "Why are the women in São Paulo never game?" And answers: "Because their husbands are such boars!"[38] Or else "The worst kind of loneliness is being in the company of a *paulista.*"[39]

In the vast majority of cases the *paulista* is satirized as a prejudiced and boring worker, whereas the *carioca* has the reputation of being a crafty *bon vivant*. This ideology that places São Paulo and Rio de Janeiro at opposite poles is widespread in the popular imagination. It is present in the theater, cinema, literature, music, comic-strip characters, and so on and is even incorporated as a legitimizing dimension of power.

Velloso analyzes this question using the figure of Zé (*José or Joe*) Carioca, the cartoon character created by Walt Disney in the days of the good-neighbor policy between Brazil and the United States (under President Roosevelt).[40] Designed as a crafty, good-humored liar who tends to resolve everything with a joke, this character definitively popularized the cliché created around the figure of the *carioca*. In turn, the stereotype of the *paulista* was enshrined in the caricature of Juca Pato created by the journalist Belmonte. An irascible and distrusting sort of man who was always moaning about something or other, Juca Pato moves in the opposite direction from pleasure and leisure. Always dressed in a dark suit and wearing glasses, he is the personification of seriousness and sobriety, in contrast to the zanily exuberant humor of the colorful Zé Carioca.

The rivalry between the cities of Rio de Janeiro and São Paulo remained even after the capital of Brazil was removed to the center of the country, in Brasília. Several factors contribute to this rivalry, which is present in both the economic and cultural areas. "How can one possibly think under a blazing heat on a beautiful, inviting beach?" While Rio de Janeiro is a colorful place famous for its Carnival parties, the image of São Paulo is gray, sober, and dresses formally. According to the inhabitants of São Paulo, that is why "Rio de Janeiro is a place for visiting, whereas down here we work." From this angle, São Paulo would be a thinking, reflective city that scorns the Dionysian extraverted-feeling type personified in the *carioca*, who "only thinks about Carnival." Could one city be the shadow of the other? Does Rio de Janeiro represent the extraverted type, while São Paulo represents introverted thinking? The important thing in this typology is that one type disdains and sees the other as inferior, without perceiving their own shadow. Today these stereotypes, still present in our culture, are the source of projections and conflicts.

Conclusion

The historical facts described here, as well as the myth of identity of the inhabitants of São Paulo, help us understand certain frequent modes of behavior in the daily life of the city. This behavior contributes to the thesis of the existence of a cultural complex based on the feeling of superiority of the inhabitants of São Paulo vis-à-vis other Brazilians.

The myth of the *bandeirante* frontiersman is reproduced by reintroducing every day a differentiation on the national level between "us" and "them" opposites that repel one another: on one hand a progressive mentality, on the other hand a backward mentality.[41]

According to Cerri, in the mind of the elite, the *bandeirante* atemporally associates the *paulista* with a vocation for building the wide borders of Brazil's territory and preserving the national grandeur.[42] This myth, however, creates a feeling of superiority that can be seen in the endless jokes, stereotypes, and prejudices that permeate the day-to-day affairs of the inhabitants of São Paulo. There is a notable discrimination against the immigrants from the northeast and other less privileged regions of the country, poor people who make every effort to lose their backlands accent as quickly as they can.

> At present, even with the regression witnessed in the indices concerning population flows from the northeast to the southeast, the opposition expressed as discrimination remains. Furthermore, it is odd that in the course of a period considered as one of expanded capitalism and material progress in Brazil, it is becoming increasingly more intense to publicly express feelings of superiority and contempt toward those who are supposedly relatively backward.[43]

This ideology emerged again in 2011, right after the elections for president of the republic, when there was great mobilization in the media (newspapers and the Internet) showing the distribution of votes across the country. While the candidate-elect Dilma Roussef had the majority of votes in the north and northeast, the São Paulo-born candidate José Serra won in the south and southeast. Abreu analyzed Internet sites that demonstrated how exacerbated were the separatist desires expressed in messages over the social network, denigrating the image of the northeastern Brazilians: the situation reached its peak when a *paulista* law student wrote: "northeasterners aren't people, so do São Paulo a favor and drown a northeasterner!"[44]

These current facts show us how intensely the inhabitants of São Paulo feel both that they are jeopardized by their compatriots and that if they had the political power, the country would be a far better place: it would be more cultured, more developed, and more dynamic. Of course, most times such sentiments lie unconscious, only to reappear at critical and conflicted moments for the country, when negative projections serve as arms of destruction (such as at the national psychological meeting described at the beginning of this article).

What suffers most is self-esteem, shaken as it is on both sides: you are either superior and disdain the "other" (the other Brazilians), or you feel impotent and inferiorized by the snobbism of the inhabitants of São Paulo who, even without expressing it, carry inside them the "pride of being a *bandeirante*." Other expressions of this complex appear in the motto of the city, in its coat-of-arms, and its symbols. Even the bizarre choice of an animal alien to the city, the puma, reveals the desire for a powerful force to represent its people.

At this point we might also consider whether this power complex is not some unconscious defense against the feeling of having been colonized. The fight of the modernist movement for Brazilian art and thought to be given their due status vis-à-vis their European counterparts could be concealing resentment for having been colonized and the desire to be seen as equal to the European colonizers. Accordingly, the projection of inferiority is transferred to the inhabitants of the poorer regions of Brazil to make them feel the same sense of worthlessness that the *paulistanos* once suffered.

As a result of this complex, so ingrained in the core of the collective psyche, there appear inexplicable conflicts, resentment, and complications when it comes time to make collective decisions, to the detriment of a broader and more balanced view of the country. Awareness of the shadow of this complex – the shadow of power – would allow the *paulistanos* to adopt a more comprehensive position, one less all-important and certainly more in harmony with their fellow Brazilians. With this in mind, political solutions would probably be better balanced, rid of the present polarization of the "two Brazils" that has been such a hindrance to national development.

Notes

1 Gustavo Barcellos, "São Paulo: Harlequin City," in *Psyche and the City: A Soul's Guide to the Modern Metropolis*, ed. Thomas Singer (New Orleans, LA: Spring Journal Books, 2010).
2 A team called Globalization and World Cities (GAWC) Study Group & Network at Loughborough University in the UK created an Inventory of World Cities based upon their level of advanced producer services. Global service centers are identified and graded for accountancy, advertising, banking/finance, and law. There are 47 Alpha Cities in the world.
3 "SP 457 anos. São Paulo em números," *Jornal o Estado de São Paulo* (25 January 2011), pp. H10–11.
4 Gilberto Dimenstein e Okki Souza, *São Paulo, 450 anos Luz. A redescoberta de uma cidade* (São Paulo: Editora de Cultura, 2003); Augusto Nunes, "O áspero colosso," *Revista Veja* (25 de janeiro de 2012), pp. 92–96.
5 Augusto Capello. Personal communication. Campos de Jordão: Moitará, 2010.
6 Raquel Rolnik, *São Paulo* (São Paulo: Publifolha, 2001).
7 Milton Luz, *A história dos símbolos nacionais: a bandeira, o brasão, o selo, o hino* (Brasília: Senado Federal, 1999); Tiago José Berg, "A história dos símbolos paulistas," *Jornal O Estado de S. Paulo* (9 de julho de 2009).
8 Clovis Ribeiro, *Brasões e bandeiras do Brasil* (São Paulo: Editora São Paulo Ltd, 1933).
9 A. Freitas, "A Bandeira Paulista," *Revista do Instituto Histórico e Geográfico de São Paulo*, no. 51 (1953): 211–214; Milton Luz, *A história dos símbolos nacionais: a bandeira, o brasão, o selo, o hino* (Brasília: Senado Federal, 1999).
10 Marina Franco, "A onça venceu o concurso," *Planeta Sustentável* (26 November 2010).

11 *"Monumento às Bandeiras,"* Dep. do Patrimônio Histórico. Secretaria Municipal de Cultura. Available at www.prefeitura.sp.gov.br/cidade/secretarias/cultura/patrimonio_historico. Accessed on April 2011.
12 Gilberto Dimenstein e Okki Souza, *São Paulo, 450 anos Luz. A redescoberta de uma cidade* (São Paulo: Editora de Cultura, 2003).
13 Franco Carvalho, *Dicionário de Bandeirantes e Sertanistas do Brasil* (São Paulo: Editora Itatiaia Limitada. Editora da Universidade de São Paulo, 1989); Laerte M. Ribeiro, *20 gerações de João Ramalho e Bartyra* (São Paulo: Grafica Editora Ltd, 1989).
14 Afonso de Taunay, *São Paulo nos Primeiros Anos, São Paulo no Século XVI* (São Paulo: Editora Paz e Terra, 2004), p. 418; Afonso de Taunay, *Ensaios Paulistas* (São Paulo: Editora Anhembi, 1958).
15 August Hilaire, *Segunda viagem a São Paulo e quadro histórico da Província de São Paulo* (Brasília: Senado Federal, Conselho Editorial, 2002), p. 153.
16 Raimundo Faro, *Os donos do poder. Formação do Patronato Político Brasileiro* (Rio de Janeiro: Globo, 1958).
17 Lucia Lipp Oliveira, *Ilha de Vera-Cruz, Terra de Santa Cruz, Brasil. Um estudo sobre o nacionalismo brasileiro* (Ph.D. diss., São Paulo: USP, 1986).
18 Joseph Love, "O Poder dos Estados: Análise Regional," in *História Geral da Civilização Brasileira*, ed. Bóris Fausto, 1° vol. (São Paulo: Difel, Tomo III, 1975), p. 55.
19 L.F. Cerri, "Non ducor, duco: A Ideologia da Paulistanidade e a Escola Revista Brasileira de História," *Revista Brasileira de História*, vol. 18, no. 36, São Paulo, 1998. http://doi.org/10.1590/S0102-01881998000200007. Accessed on April 2011.
20 Love, "O Poder dos Estados: Análise Regional."
21 P. Monica Velloso, "A cidade-voyeur: O Rio de Janeiro visto pelos paulistas," *Censo 2000-IBGE*. LPP, Laboratório de Politicas Publicas, no. 8, Rio de Janeiro (2002).
22 Ibid.
23 Love, "O Poder dos Estados: Análise Regional."
24 Alberto Sales, *A Pátria Paulista* (Brasília: Editora da Universidade de Brasília, 1983).
25 Ibid.
26 Jacqueline Melo, *A família Prestes de Albuquerque na história de São Paulo*, 2007. Available at http://julioprestes.wordpress.com. Accessed on June 2010.
27 Adhemar de Barros, 1932. Available at www.portalviva.com.br/index. Accessed on May 2010.
28 Hilton Federici, *Símbolos Paulistas: estudo histórico-heráldico* (São Paulo: Secretaria de Cultura, Ciência e Tecnologia, São Paulo, 1980).
29 *Correio Paulistano*. São Paulo, p. 01, 15 out. 1930. "São Paulo levanta-se pelo Brasil." Available at http://memoria.fundap.sp.gov.br/memoriapaulista/publicacao/revolucao-de-1930/sao-paulo-levanta-se-pelo-brasil. Accessed on April 2011.
30 Mario Andrade, 1932. Available at www.controversia.com.br/index.php. Accessed on May 2010.
31 Nagiba Maluf, *Revolução de 32* (São Paulo: Global Editora, 2009), p. 141.
32 Marco Cabral Santos, *O espírito que não descansa*. Available at www.cartacapital.com.br/carta-na-escola/o-espirito-que-nao-descansa. Accessed on May 2011.
33 *Canção Nova*. Available at http://noticias.cancaonova.com/noticia. Accessed on April 2011.
34 Augusto Nunes, "O áspero colosso," *Revista Veja*, 25 January 2012, pp. 92–96.
35 Gustavo Conde, *Piadas regionais: o caso dos gaúchos* (M.A. diss., São Paulo: Unicamp, 2005).
36 http://estereotipos.net/tag/anedotas-etnicas. Accessed on May 2010.
37 Ibid.
38 Nelson Rodrigues, *A Cabra Vadia* (Rio de Janeiro: Eldorado, 1969), p. 168.
39 Nelson Rodrigues. *Flor de Obsessão*, 1997. Available at www.releituras.com/nelsonr_flor.asp. Accessed on May 2010.

40 P. Monica Velloso, *A "cidade-voyeur": O Rio de Janeiro visto pelos paulistas. Censo 2000-IBGE*. Rio de Janeiro, no. 8, LPP, Laboratório de Politicas Publicas, Rio de Janeiro, 2002.
41 R. Abreu, "O mito bandeirante e a escalada da intransigência no mundo virtual," *Laboratório de Estudos Hum(e)anos*, UFF, no. 18 (2011).
42 Cerri, "Non ducor, duco."
43 Abreu, "O mito bandeirante e a escalada da intransigência no mundo virtual."
44 Ibid.

Chapter 4

São Paulo and the Cultural Complexes of the City
Seeing Through Graffiti

Liliana Liviano Wahba

Translated by James Mulholland

This chapter is the result of research carried out at the Catholic University of São Paulo in 2009 and 2010 on graffiti in the city of São Paulo. The analysis of the graffiti images is based on concepts regarding the significance of art in analytical psychology, the cultural complexes arising in megalopolises, and postmodern and hypermodern culture.

About the meaning of art, Kandinsky considers it to be spiritual in the sense of holding the potential of the future and having the power of a prophetic awakening.[1] Vygotsky criticizes Freudian psychoanalysis in its assertion that the creative process derives from the wish to satisfy desires, and serves as a means of removing conflict within the unconscious.[2] Vygotsky published *The Psychology of Art* in 1926, at a time when Jung was delving into a similar theme in texts dating from 1922 and 1930 in the volume *The Spirit in Man, Art and Literature*. Both thinkers agree about the fundamental role of art in culture and human development.

The "trembling," as Vygotsky puts it, provoked by art is the same as the *numinous* referred to by Jung when we are moved, even overwhelmed, by the vigor and depth of a work of art.[3,4] The artist conveys what is timeless in images of the present "and so makes it possible for us to find our way back to the deepest springs of life" (Jung),[5] "revealing and exploding the [hitherto unknown] immense potential of life" (Vygotsky).[6] Aesthetic emotion, even if its effect over time is to motivate behavior and change attitudes, rarely produces immediate action. Rather for Vygotsky[7] it induces "a guide to the future," just as for Neumann[8] "the artist expresses and shapes the future of his time."

The period in which we live is called postmodernity by Bauman,[9,10] late modernity by Giddens,[11] and hypermodernity by Lipovetsky.[12] These authors converge in their description of man's place in society and how society is constituted. Individuality and autonomy are emphasized through the multiplicity of points of view and lead to a reorganization of the experience of time and space in an interconnected world. This results in fragmentation, dispersion, and a climate of uncertainties. Inconstancy and an emphasis on values such as freedom and immediate satisfaction pervade. The increasing speed of economic, cultural, and technological change becomes most highly valued and renders useless whoever fails to adapt. The result

DOI: 10.4324/9781003400820-7

is a climate of risk and uncertainty which is felt in the paradoxical experience of "euphoria and vulnerability," raising also ethical questions.[13]

In the nineteenth century, the sociologist Simmel already noted in Germany that the city makes inhabitants insensitive to the qualitative changes around them through the intensive bombardment by daily stimuli, which cultivates in the metropolitan resident an attitude of notorious indifference to conflict, a blasé attitude.[14]

Psychoanalytical studies have investigated the psychic consequences of the modern urban milieu and how it shapes the experience of meaning through the internalization of the maladies that beset modern cities.[15,16,17,18,19] In other words, the city extends itself into the human psyche, being at one and the same time an internal object and a "geographical metaphor." Experiences of being uprooted, of exclusion and violence, become referential experiences for today's urban culture. A culture of excess, fragmentation, and associated paradoxes has its own psychopathology sheltering and nourishing the psychopathology of the individual.[20]

The city of São Paulo has experienced extraordinary and uncontrolled growth driven by financial interests rather than an organized and collective search for quality of life. In this context the symbols of graffiti and the trauma to which they refer are revealing. This chapter investigates the symptoms of cultural distress as they are mirrored in the symbolic images of the city's graffiti. In particular, we identify a sense of rootlessness and instability that results in a fragmentary and fluid self. In addition, we detect the potential for creative renewal coming through art.

Cultural Complex and Dissociative Defenses

According to Jung, "the complexes arise from the clash between a demand of adaption and the individual's constitutional inability to meet the challenge."[21] Although they can originate in adult life, the typical primary forms are built in childhood.

A cultural complex is built by repetitive traumatic experience: an "intensive collective emotion is the hallmark of an activated cultural complex at the core of which is an archetypal pattern."[22] A healthy cultural identity can be contaminated by the negative aspects of cultural complexes. Ramos has investigated the symptomatology shared by a group around an underlying complex,[23] and Weisstub has emphasized that external trauma may undermine the "authority of the good Self," when previously adequately functioning individuals become nonfunctional, losing motivation for life, as in post-traumatic stress disorders.[24]

Wilkinson studies the detrimental long-term effects of exposure to traumatic stress sustained over a long period.[25] She analyzes dissociative defenses that result from overwhelming affect in early childhood. Unintegrated affect generated by trauma threatens the experience of self-coherence, self-cohesiveness, and self-continuity resulting in a dissociated self-state manifested by defenses such as "splitting, projective identification, idealization or diabolization, trance-states, switching among multiple centers of identity, depersonalization, psychic numbing, etc."[26]

Depersonalization robs an individual of the experience of feeling real and fully alive, and trauma causes the self to retreat, hidden by protective defenses.

Neurosciences investigate how the brain reacts to excessive emotions of fear. Freezing and avoidance are responses to danger which are mediated by the amygdala. "The fear system can learn and store information about stimuli that warn of impending bodily harm or other dangers."[27] The repeated exposure to actual or imagined fear situations can create the conditions for the release of fear emotions even when there is no real danger. Activating such emergency responses causes the release of neurochemicals in the brain that retraumatize the person.[28,29]

São Paulo is a city that offers multiple cultural and business stimuli, with all its enriching and varied cultural activities. However, it is also an environment of intense urban violence, with car accidents and burglaries, not to mention cutthroat competitiveness. All this provokes reactions of fear and insecurity, which when hyper-activated become pathological anxiety.

> Most of the time the brain holds the self together pretty well. But when connections change, personality too, can change. That the self is so fragile an entity is disconcerting. At the same time, if the self can be disassembled by experiences that alter connections, presumably it also can be reassembled by experiences that establish, change, or renew connections.[30]

Wilkinson stresses the importance of the right brain for the capacity for repair and reconciliation, helping to drop defenses that have become life-denying. The human mind has evolved to the point where it is able to bypass and overcome dysfunctions in the physical organ upon which it depends: the brain.[31] According to Fonagy the ability to symbolize an affect is crucial in the achievement of control over overwhelming affect.[32] We postulate that street art expresses and may even have an integrating effect on the negative emotions of the cultural complexes that arise from fear and trauma in the stressful, menacing feelings of everyday life in the city.

Street Art

Graffiti is a combination of an individual means of expression and a modern, creative art form that reflects sociocultural realities with archetypal undercurrents that fuel images which are set in a particular historical moment. Graffiti can be thought of as a portrait of the archetypal situation of a contemporary urban society. It offers us the opportunity to analyze symbolically major cultural complexes of our epoch. The research shows that most citizens see graffiti as an art form that compensates for the chaos and degradation of public property.[33] Although sometimes aggressive, it is a creative answer that denounces the misuse of public space.

Graffiti communicates an important history of its own that has been winning more and more space in museums and the streets through partnerships between artists, governments, and corporations. It is used in social projects as a way of bringing young people back into the work market and even as an auxiliary therapeutic tool.

Returning to Jung's idea that art embraces both the problems of an era and the proper archetypal images to elaborate them, we assume that this growth of graffiti – both in quantity and in the space it has won in society – contains some message for us today.

The graffiti of a city shows us its skin marked by scars and sores. In its cluster of forms, colors, and styles, graffiti reveals through its imagery a web of associations that are the stuff of personal and cultural complexes. When trying to decode the language of the pulsating psyche of the megalopolis, we end up attracted to the images of graffiti.

What Do the Images Say?

Symptoms of Dissociative Affects

Suffering and dehumanization are featured in graffiti images of fragmented, mutilated, and lacerated bodies that can be represented as liquid-like or robotic. There is a prevalence of distorted faces instead of whole bodies. The women have inexpressive eyes and sensual lips that suggest orality in a fragmented figure. The men's mouths are filled with teeth, and their aggressive orality is marked by shouting, rage, and voracity. Other mouths often appear in locked silence refusing to dialogue. When they do express themselves, they shout or bite. These representations suggest bodily and psychic dissociation and deep regression that are characteristic of primitive defense mechanisms that have arisen in response to trauma.

The graffiti also portrays isolated parts of the body. The heart appears most frequently, but as a rule it is drawn schematically or out of place. Some of the graffiti with hearts are abstract drawings with cold colors and thick edges. Other hearts are held in human hands, as if they had to be secured or given some support to prevent them flying away or falling to the ground. The metaphoric meaning is "to have one's heart in one's hand" (the Portuguese equivalent of "to have one's heart in one's mouth"), that is to say, to feel fear and anxiety (Figure 4.1). As love, the heart appears in conflict, with a man holding a heart outside his body in his left hand and embracing a feminine silhouette in his right, while another man holds a heart on high in his left hand and a tower in his right. This could be the opposition between love and power. A black man has hearts in an oven instead of a chest: a calcinating or calcinated love. An extraordinary image of a bright-red heart crowned with diamonds transmits all the strength of the heart.

Besides hearts, the hands and eyes are other parts of the body that show up frequently in the graffiti images. The eyes in the graffiti transmit several impressions: some seem mythical, as if they are the eyes of the unconscious; others have more harmonious colors and shapes; some are aggressive and deformed; some are anthropomorphized and carry war devices; it feels as though the eyes of the city seem to be paranoically stalking the viewer.

Figure 4.1 Man holding a heart.

The hands in the graffiti are active and display attitudes that seem to signal something special, either through the specific objects they hold or the signals they emit. However, the hands do not appear in such a positive and significant manner when they are connected to the body of a human being. And often the characters in the graffiti images do not even have hands, communicating a sense of dissociated or nonintegrated action.

Defensive Persona and Aggressiveness

Among the objects of daily use pictured in the graffiti, there is a prevalence of hats, especially on masculine figures. There is also a significant number of figures wearing dark glasses and masks. The head is often prominent and protected. Most of the masculine figures are passers-by in the big city, walking and running all over the place without any apparent aim. The men show more action and movement than the women and wear stronger colors than the feminine figures. Their senseless acceleration appears aimless and at the same time is intense and totally absorbing. The predominance of large heads, or heads without bodies, reveals a dissociation between action and its meaning.

Weapons are the second most prevalent category of objects worn or carried by the graffiti figures. The men mostly wield swords, presumably due to the strong influence of Japanese culture in Brazil. Bombs found in the graffiti images are handled by monkeys, pointing to an instinctive aggressive nature. Protective appearance and persona seems to compensate for the risk of instinctive explosiveness. Stereotypes of social roles appear frequently. A man waves a mask in front of himself to expose a dark, empty face. Another shows just a face, smiling sarcastically and smoking, placed next to a man wearing a mask of a pig's face: a spoiler figure. Others wear fancy dress masks or somber black ones. A couple is dressed in casual, undifferentiated clothes, "just doing their thing," looking cool.

To make up for an underlying sense of fragility, there is a sense of struggle between warriors, fighter figures, or brute-like figures of powerful men (Figure 4.2). Some of these are convincing and resemble hero models, but most are

Figure 4.2 A "mocking" fight.

just inflated in their posing, which may be intended to intimidate us. We see the artist playing sardonically with this bellicose spirit in an image of a fight between a masked, scythe-wielding *ninja* and a *ninja* goose sporting a ribbon on its head. We also see mythical warrior heroes as bird-men. There are truly heroic fights portrayed as well as ridiculous fights whose effect can nevertheless be quite dramatic.

When the feminine figures face the viewer, they often do so in a cold and sometimes angry manner (Figure 4.3).

Figure 4.3 A woman staring.

São Paulo and the Cultural Complexes of the City   65

A few appear happy, taking actions that are engaged in fantasy, sexuality, or work. Leisure is portrayed more often than work. The city portrayed in graffiti offers parties, drinks, and nightlife, but somehow one is left with the idea that this is more about endless sensual stimulation than about forming relationships through social activity. Contact with the earth, the ground, is often lacking, as is the capacity to manage or make contact. It seems that these figures may be waiting for someone to rescue them.

The images of mysterious, seemingly inward-looking women in the graffiti make us wonder what they want, what they dream about. They appear oblivious, or perhaps in denial, as to what is going on around them. Many hover in a sensuality that is tinged with illusion, the ephemeral and intangible. Others look distracted, without surrendering to the surrounding eroticism: how do you dance with a ballerina without arms? Sexuality exists in the shallow figure, equally ephemeral and infantilized, although she offers herself so openly (Figure 4.4). Or the sexuality is mysterious and vengeful, as in an image which shows a woman sword in hand, wearing a sadomasochistic costume, or another image displaying a feline, sensual eroticism.

Negative Emotions, Freezing, and Numbing

The feminine figures exhibit hardness, indifference, and/or suffering. Perhaps waiting for a redemption of their destiny, they appear bitter. Others are locked into

Figure 4.4 Shallow sexuality.

Figure 4.5 Woman freeing bird.

themselves. The longing for freedom stands in contrast to sadness and confinement: free a bird from its cage, let your hair blow in the wind, and float in the sea with dragons, oblivious to danger (Figure 4.5).

Failure, however, is devastating. The cruelty of death seen in images of calcinated children represents a tragic end to a fate announced in the figures' disillusioned expressions: chains, agony, and pain, no chance of salvation. Religion with its rosary beads is ineffective in prayers of despair. Perhaps there is protest, but against whom?

Many masculine figures reveal an emptiness as if all vitality had been drained from them. When energy appears, it is more in the form of sensate hedonism, revealed by unresponsive facial expressions. Most figures show sadness, awe, aggressiveness, or rage. Some of them seem to be appealing to a magic power in menacing tones. The motto seems to be everyone for himself. Now a man appears carrying the weight of a house on his back, with another man encapsulated inside: the metaphor of a beast of burden, an existence laden with imprisoning obligations.

There are also introspective figures, absorbed in an inner world and oblivious to everything around them. Their smile is smug or peaceful, but nonetheless belied by prominent, desperate mouths. Communication is precarious. Words are locked inside. The figures shut their mouths or shout and argue. Gaping mouths call our attention (Figure 4.6). We see teeth grinding and a bottomless well opening up to bite. In many of the images of stout figures, a primitive orality appears, suggesting

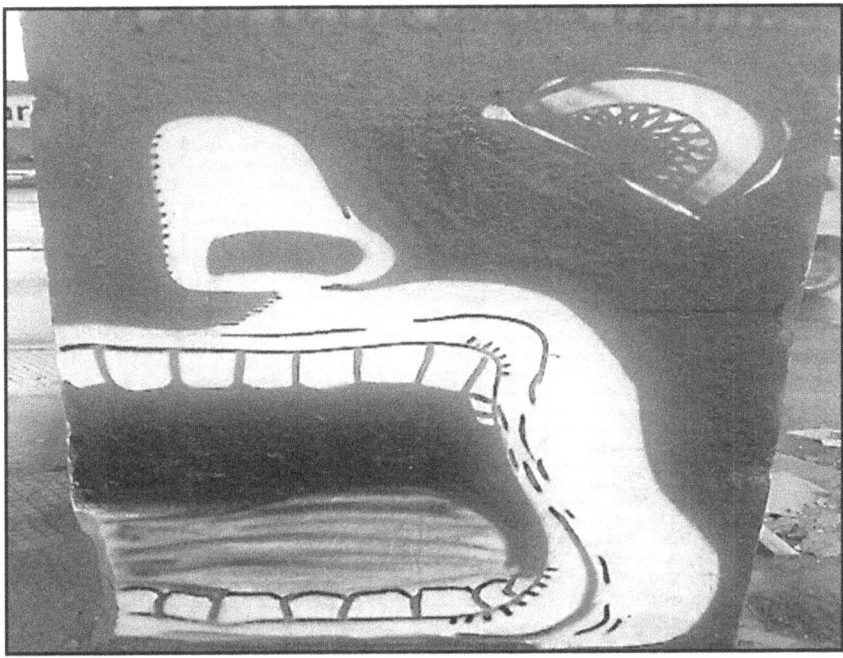

Figure 4.6 Gaping mouths.

that they are starving for psychic food as they devour and protest the world indiscriminately. They swallow more than they should and explode, unable or not knowing how to talk.

Smiles are lost amidst the menaces. There is good reason for even the clowns found in the graffiti to be somber and sinister. Their spirit seems severed from their bodies; heads are open, detached, some even float. The image of acculturated Indians preserve certain activities peculiar to them, but they are blue, cyanotic, and their arms and legs are too weak to support them. Rituals seem to exert a powerful influence in their revealing the opposites of life and death: a man holds a knife with a skull, while a butterfly is poised on his finger.

One scene shows a desperate-looking man, screaming at an extraterrestrial-looking creature, with a heart throbbing between them (Figure 4.7). The four-eyed alien creature is shouting, connected to the wires of some electrical machines with headlights like traffic lights. The scene suggests a state of shock in the daily life of a city full of stress, where fights take place, people go crazy for no reason at all, and hearts are as detached as a balloon hovering in the air, without any space for them in the chest. Or there is an ironic tone as portrayed in an image of a fellow in a suit and tie who waves, smiling and looking silly with a beam and a black cloud above his head, all mixed in with the confusion and chaos of the background. A happy fool, struck down without knowing why.

Figure 4.7 Shouting in shock.

With no sense for life, death loses its existential significance, tragedy becomes trivial, and heroic death disappears, leaving in its place tedium and the indifference of destiny.

Relationship and the Family – Parental Complexes

The capacity for contact in the masculine figures appears precarious: thin arms, bodies hidden so as not to reveal fragility, a shapeless person wearing a necktie. Sympathetic, relating persons are few in number. It is notable that musicians play their instruments all alone and seem to find it hard to share positive emotions. Schematic hearts, as seen earlier, would indicate a superficial, fleeting quality of relationships.

In short, everyone is for himself; there is no solidarity. This is poignantly displayed in three figures at the "party": the woman and the two men playing instruments but wearing dark glasses and each looking sideways.

Mass anonymity is shown in groups, agglutinations *en bloc* without any focus on interaction (Figure 4.8). Interaction is seen in collective action based on indigenous traditions like fishing.

The relationship between men and women is ambiguous. A photographer seems a distant voyeur who does not approach an indifferent woman (Figure 4.9). A man points his accusing finger at the face of a woman who resembles a severe, maternal sphinx. Another man embraces a heart outside his body with his left arm and the

São Paulo and the Cultural Complexes of the City   69

Figure 4.8 Mass anonymity.

Figure 4.9 Photographer and woman.

silhouette of a woman dancer with his right arm. The image conveys a stiff, severed affectivity with a fleeting, anonymous, unknown anima and the illusion of trying to possess the woman. We see a couple of outlaws from the slums, the man suffering with a bandage on his belly, weeping and embracing his female partner, who also seems to hold him prisoner. The traditional roles are inverted, the macho made fragile with all the power in the maternal, feminine figure. This signals regression fixed in dependent feelings.

The power of the father seems to have crumbled. In the family triad, the patriarch looks sad and alienated. The figure holding a child by the hand is fragile and tearful. Symbolizing this loss of power are the figures of kings who look ridiculous and tiny although their expressions can be evil. They might have lost their power, but they are still scheming. As Weisstub puts it: "Failure to maintain a sense of collective confidence and belief in the central authority of the cultural superego may result in collective depression."[34]

The family, the eternal triangle, looks desperate. A sad, alienated patriarch stands behind the *mater dolorosa* who leans to the side, to the past, while the child seems isolated and scared. All of them are unhappy and unprotected. Another likely father figure portrays an aimless man with an imagined or remembered barely sketched child.

There are more women with children than men, indicating the reality of the fragmented family composition without men in the picture. Family figures are few, and when they appear, they are not very caring. In fact, only two are cared for by the maternal figure; one woman feeds the child, while another, with the city in the background, offers an earphone that comes out of her solar plexus, an organic, interior listening device in opposition to the external one, perhaps to protect the child (Figure 4.10).

The dramatic nature of the collapse of the maternal figure is portrayed by the deformed woman with a child on her back, both with liquefying masks. They lean on a tree, undoing themselves in the open air. The literal destruction of the family appears in an image portraying the murder of a woman with her children, tied up and tossed in the fire, one child calcinated beside the buildings (Figure 4.11).

Life in the City

A robot-man meditates under a set of gears, suggesting that the deification of technology brings order to the current confusion but at the cost of spiritual alienation.

An image of the crown draws our attention (Figure 4.12). When worn by men it shows them to be weakened or grotesque rather than powerful or noble. One of the kings is shown with the crown having fallen from his head, and he appears small and childish with a humanoid, half-animal, half-robot standing behind him. Mechanization itself appears as the child king's monster shadow. The queens are fragile, and only the emblematic crowns are strong and colored. One gets the feeling that power has been wrongly asserted and that kings and queens need to be renewed.

In another image, next to a smoke-spewing factory we see a man with his mouth wide open apparently shouting to someone, his head displaced from his body and behind him shapeless beings carrying a ladder and a painter's roller: dehumanized

São Paulo and the Cultural Complexes of the City 71

Figure 4.10 Woman and child with earphones.

Figure 4.11 Falling woman with children.

Figure 4.12 Meditation of the robot-man.

workers. All of them are bizarre, seem out of the world, unable to determine their *dasein*.

Seven buildings appear in the graffiti depicted in Figure 4.13. One is presided over by a sad *ninja*, in a death scene of a woman and children. There is a dark factory with an extraterrestrial-looking worker and two houses in compressed images. The other four buildings are more pleasing, one of them integrated with landscape and ballerinas, another with women at night, another with a woman and a child in a healthy, caring situation, and yet another with a man and a heart. The architecture of the city, the human construction of the space we inhabit, shows its contrasts and possibilities.

This seems to be how the city is portrayed: in the middle of the buildings appears the face of a man wearing a black mask, scared and threatening, while in another a face is in profile with tough features and a tightly closed mouth; there is a cat too, those animals that wander the streets indifferent to reason. Cats, but no dogs, are depicted: they seem to be docile, though some of them have a malicious expression. They represent sensuality, rhythm, the freedom of nighttime, and the laziness of daytime. Rational control seeks power over the natural rhythm, and the revolt against this, represented by the cat, instead of being aggressive is more scornful, even cynical, as if saying: "just you wait and see."

In a city like São Paulo, with all its traffic, only one car is portrayed in the graffiti; there are other vehicles, tractors, and boats, suggesting a desire to return to

São Paulo and the Cultural Complexes of the City 73

Figure 4.13 Angry-faced buildings.

Figure 4.14 Graffiti in the city.

a slower, more rural time. There are also war vehicles, which could denote the aggressive feelings evoked in city traffic, and unfortunately also the real possibility of becoming a victim of some machine run amok.

A metaphor of the city appears in a scene symbolizing the act of making graffiti (Figure 4.14). The graffiti artist, dressed in camouflage, represents the illegality of the act. From the can of spray paint emerge letters and a face with the brain exposed. Behind it a terrible scene unfolds: a man with Indian features runs in anguish, and a red-faced devil figure bites his arm. On his legs he carries animated stones with eyes. In the forefront, as if oblivious to all this horror, two girls play innocently with the animated stones. This might be a representation of innocence that maintains some animation, some potential of building with the stones in a unique, naively playful way. A demon-like face appears behind the girls. Here the infantile anima plays in the face of destructive, demonic evil.

The animated stones of our city are telling a terrible tale which seem to be emerging spontaneously from the cultural and collective psyche.

The Child

Do these images of the child represent the real child in our society or do they symbolize the traumatized, inner child or both? However one reads them, they exude the feeling of loneliness and vulnerability to great danger.

The children who look out at the spectator smile with their eyes closed or else seem sad (Figure 4.15). There are signs of abandonment and isolation. Most of them are curled up or hunched down; some are leaning or mounted on something

Figure 4.15 Lonely child.

or someone. This suggests a search for support, something to prop them up. Active game-playing does not appear, and there is little open aggressiveness. An angry-faced boy with no arms, dressed in black with a *ninja* mask, can be interpreted as marginalized, defensive rage. In general, heads are larger than bodies, and game-playing is fantasized rather than active. An introverted attitude is pronounced. There is no jumping or running or any of the expansive movements expected of children. Some of those who smile do so unnaturally or shyly. Some smile to themselves, but in fantasy, rather than in engaged play with others. They are mostly alone.

A girl is seen at play, inviting discovery and promising future seduction like long-haired little Iara, a figure of the rivers from folklore[35] (Figure 4.16). Another girl gives a big smile, posing like her parents' little doll. The same impression is given by the children in the realistic photo of the figures who appear at the base of

Figure 4.16 Little "Iara."

the blown-up face of the "mother" as if they were her object of desire, idealized, controlled, and smiling in embarrassment. A little boy is handless and wears a hood with an electric plug in it. Little girls, without arms and legs, fly loose in the air like balloons tied to a wire. One of them wears a princess' crown. They look like the portraits of children who have become objectified, without any identity of their own. They exist by virtue of the projections of the amorous need of others. The diamond on the girls' breasts indicates a precious value to be reclaimed. The plug in the wall suggests technology without contact, solitude in front of the TV or computer, and artificial excitability, emptied of natural energy. A child floats around in circles in the air and seems to fade away, deprived of affection, lost.

The smile of a boy suggests some heroic representation such as the dragon-slaying theme, and there is a girl with a giant fish emerging from the water. Yet she seems more carried away than active. Such heroic acts appear only occasionally in the images. What is most notable is the coexistence of innocence with horror. The girl, mounted on an animal with a shapeless arm, approaches a man with an enormous arm carrying some poisonous creature. She seems to be calm. Another scene shows two innocent-faced girls playing with pebbles, while behind them a scared man runs away from diabolical heads. These opposites of child/purity and grotesque/violence live close together in these images. Perhaps it is a way of materializing the psychic monsters that assail city life. The innocence that is oblivious to destruction seems frighteningly unreal or disassociated.

A mythical child appears as a boy in the sea at risk of drowning. An exposed, child hero coexists in a scene in which the feminine figures are standing with their backs to him, playing erotic games with an equally mythical man. The small hero who would slay the dragon, the river-girl who would invite discovery, and a bigger girl in a scene suggesting the fisher of dreams – all these characters offer the hope of a change in action and mood in which the hero, creatures of nature, and the power of dreams stand in contrast to the prevailing pain, insecurity, exposure to danger, and lack of a safe container.

The Coniunctio – Traumatic Unconscious and Restoration

The somber side as well as the transforming *coniunctio* appear in three large images. A fertilizing, phallic mythic being plays erotically with women in the scene where the hero child is exposed. It suggests a potential for rebirth as well as the hedonism of a culture designed to consume every moment of the present for its own pleasure.

There is a hideous and somber side – a liquefied man is mounted on a gigantic, deformed ogre-woman, and from her legs there seems to emerge a monstrous hybrid of pig and rhinoceros. The next image, an enormous, petrified face with smoke coming out of its ear, suggests a perversion of relationship and causes us to wonder what we are doing with our capacity for union and love (Figure 4.17). Brutality erupts from a hardened man like a volcano, unable to hear, to pay attention to himself and to others.

On occasion a positive compensation appears in the spiritualized conception symbolized by winged beings such as the eagle man and the winged, pregnant

Figure 4.17 Somber *coniunctio* and petrified face.

woman in a flower bud. This represents the possibility of spiritual fecundity that exists in the unconscious. The unconscious symbols are brought to the ego as new possibilities for choice.

Repair Through Imagination

Diversified religious content appears as an alternative to the failure of the Christian religion to contain pain. Those who pray with their rosaries do not seem to receive spiritual nourishment, and the masculine saints are deformed or fragile. On the other hand, a feminine saint appears with animals, and an oriental feminine entity evokes a sense of the most primitive great mother protector. African masks representing black culture and an indigenous priest's rattle suggest religious inspiration from non-Western sources. In the graffiti images, spiritual energy seem to come from the East, from the indigenous tribes, and from African culture.

A significant number of graffiti images are of birds and winged insects, mostly small birds and butterflies (Figure 4.18). Few birds are of an aggressive or destructive nature, such as the crow, which is associated with death in the images. Unlike most of the other categories of graffiti images, the birds and butterflies fly freely in the air in a peaceful environment, suggesting the possibility of a healthy psyche in its natural grounding (Figure 4.19).

Figure 4.18 Conception of winged beings.

Figure 4.19 Butterflies.

São Paulo and the Cultural Complexes of the City 79

Water creatures are frequently represented – mostly fish. They symbolize the link with the deepest unconscious, revealing the double symbolism of regeneration (such as in the whale or swimming turtles) and wounding. Some of the sea-born creatures are mythical. For instance there is a fish that has been split down the middle, sewn up, and is carrying a house (Figure 4.20). It recalls an animal carrying the world on its back, wounded, perhaps like the wounded healer. This suggests that the theme of the resilient capacity to overcome traumatic injury and conflict is present and alive.

Looking at all the animals, it seems that the instinctual world of nature has, in large measure, been preserved. Despite all the threats of dismemberment and destruction, the creative imagination that expresses itself in fantasy is vigorous and free.

Even when fragmented bodies appear, vegetation emerges from them. This suggests the possibility of renewal at the neurovegetative level – a kind of self-preservation of very rudimentary life. Sprouts come out of heads, ears, and mouths as a vestige of preserved vitality. These images can be viewed as an attempt to restore the cycle of life and its most basic and regulatory functions: sleep, the circadian cycle, body temperature, hunger, thirst, and sexual activity. It also suggests neurovegetative psychosomatic symptoms.

Figure 4.20 Sewn fish carrying house on its back.

In the graffiti images, the waters, rivers, and sky are clear and transparent. Vegetation appears preserved and vital, mostly as foliage. Symbols of the natural realms suggest health and well-being, perhaps less flowery than one might desire, but nevertheless indicating the possibility of growth, regeneration, and resilience.

Positive emotions and feelings appear in the feminine figures who can be generous to the vulnerable, embrace their companions in tears, offer nourishment, and share their emotions with a child. A woman who liberates herself in a flower waves to freedom and to the expansiveness associated with nature (Figure 4.21).

The matriarchal force lies in the anonymous African figures, mostly by night, that provide a generating energy: pregnancy, the collective tribal chores, carrying food and water (Figure 4.22). Some masculine figures offer to those who can receive them the flowers of poetry rendered in a delicate, dreamlike quality.

The help of the imagination is called for in difficult times – whether in fairy tales, myths, or art in general: the poets (Pablo Neruda), the musicians (Adoniran Barbosa), the filmmakers, and the graphic artists who enrich the world by spiritualizing and animating the symbolic language that inhabits us and our world. Art is the vehicle of inspiration and freedom, as exemplified by two figures who can be thought of as the mercurial spirit of imagination itself: the first flies in delighted spiritual expansion, inspired by the flute played under Indian totems; and the second, like a trickster, an Earth figure from folklore, sports a top hat and a big smile while leaning on a mushroom that opens its psychedelic seed behind him in the spirit of life itself (Figure 4.23).

Figure 4.21 Woman liberating herself.

São Paulo and the Cultural Complexes of the City 81

Figure 4.22 Women by night.

Figure 4.23 Trickster figure.

Conclusion

Graffiti is a vehicle for the symbolic expression of the life of the city and of those who live in it, their relationships to one another, and to the environment that contains them.

The act of creating graffiti is both a denunciation and an appeal. In its subversiveness graffiti follows the flow of the imagination in the energizing capacity of the spirit to expand and to project. It reveals the psyche of the place and its people and creates a vision that is transitory, ephemeral, essential, and lasting. Its time measures a moment – or an eternity.

The spray paint is animated by the artist's hand, and the gas that propels it comes together with color in an image whose authorship may or may not bear a signature: the graffiti artist is all in one, and he shows the world what goes on in everyone (Figure 4.24). And "everyone" is "one" as both an individual and as a collective. The graffiti artist depicts whatever happens in the city, mirroring how we are seen, how we see ourselves, and who we are in the midst of chaos and organization.

The images on the wall expose our pain and our complexes. They jolt us out of our stiffened defenses and demonstrate to us our stereotypical, repetitive emotionality. There are images that point to the capacity for resilience and the respect for values of a humanist tradition. Some of the images seem to come straight from the depths of the unconscious, of our most fundamental human nature in which the possibility of renewal is revealed to us in pure air, clear waters, lush vegetation, and vital animal life. It is here where we discover the compensatory message of our

Figure 4.24 Making graffiti.

Figure 4.25 Symbolic fertilization.

unconscious, proclaiming that the essential nature of the psyche is healthy. It cries out to be activated in everyday life; it lies waiting, latent, and up to a point, patient.

Even as humankind in the city seems to be pursuing a path of destruction, powerful forces of renewal exist that are there to be channeled. One graffiti image, for example, projects a promising future of regeneration through the opening of a lock (Figure 4.25). The image shows an invitation extended to a throbbing, fertilizing spirit to penetrate in a *coniunctio* the feminine container that offers herself. Her tubes are animated with wings, flowers, birds. She is all poetry and sexuality, body and soul. She is psyche herself, vitalized and fertilized, ready to give birth to the coming generation and to renew the present. It is the symbol of the integrative power of the psyche striving to heal the painful complexes arising from the fear of destroying our humanity.

Notes

1 Wassily Kandinsky, *Du Spirituel dans l'Art* (Paris: Denöel, 1954).
2 Lev Vygotsky, *Psicologia da arte* (*The Psychology of Art*) (São Paulo: Martins Fontes, 1926/2001).
3 C.G. Jung, "On the Relation of Analytical Psychology to Poetry," in *The Collected Works of C.G. Jung, Vol. 15, The Spirit of Man, Art and Literature*, trans. R.F.C. Hull (Princeton: Princeton University Press, 1922/1978).
4 C.G. Jung, "Psychology and Literature," CW 15.
5 C.G. Jung, CW 15, § 130.

6 Vygotsky, *Psicologia da arte*; Jung, CW 15, p. 319.
7 Ibid., p. 320.
8 Erich Neumann, *Art and the Creative Unconscious* (Princeton: Princeton University Press, 1959), p. 94.
9 Zygmunt Bauman, *O mal estar da pós-modernidade* (*Postmodernity and its Discontents*) (Rio de Janeiro: Jorge Zahar, 1998).
10 Zygmunt Bauman, *Vidas desperdiçadas* (*Wasted Lives: Modernity and Its Outcasts*) (São Paulo: Jorge Zahar, 2005).
11 Anthony Giddens, *Modernidade e Identidade Pessoal* (*Modernity and Self-Identity. Self and Society in the Late Modern Age*) (Oeiras: Celta, 2001).
12 Gilles Lipovetsky and Sébastien Charles, *Os tempos hipermodernos (Hypermodern Times*) (São Paulo: Barcarolla, 2004).
13 Ibid., p. 65.
14 In Ricardo F. Freitas, "Simmel e a cidade moderna: uma contribuição aos estudos da comunicação e do consumo," *Comunicação, Mídia e Consumo*, São Paulo, vol. 4, no. 10 (July 2007): 41–53.
15 James Hillman, *City & Soul* (Putnam, CT: Spring Publications, 2006).
16 John Hill, "At Home in the World," *Journal of Analytical Psychology*, vol. 41, no. 1 (1996): 575–598.
17 Bernardo Tanis, "Cidade e subjetividade," in *A psicanálise nas tramas da cidade*, eds. Bernardo Tanis and Guimarães K. Magda (São Paulo: Casa do Psicólogo, 2009).
18 Alcira M. Alizade, "La Ciudad interior y los Otros (diferencias e indiferencias)," in *A psicanálise nas tramas da cidade*, eds. Bernardo Tanis and Guimarães K. Magda.
19 Claudio Eizirik, "A presença da cidade no analista," in *A psicanálise nas tramas da cidad*, eds. Bernardo Tanis and Guimarães K. Magda.
20 Hillman, *City & Soul*.
21 Jung, CW 6, § 926.
22 Thomas Singer and Samuel Kimbles, eds., *The Cultural Complex: Jungian Perspectives on Psyche and Society* (London: Brunner-Routledge, 2004), p. 6.
23 Denise G. Ramos, "Corruption: Symptom of a Cultural Complex in Brazil?," in *Cultural Complex*, eds. Thomas Singer and Samuel Kimbles, pp. 102–123.
24 Elie Weisstub and Estie Galili-Weisstub, "Collective Trauma and Cultural Complexes," in, *Cultural Complex*, eds. Thomas Singer and Samuel Kimbles, p. 160.
25 Margaret Wilkinson, *Coming into Mind: The Mind-Brain Relationship: A Jungian Clinical Perspective* (London: Routledge, 2006).
26 Donald Kalsched, *The Inner World of Trauma* (London: Routledge, 1996), p. 2.
27 Joseph LeDoux, *Synaptic Self: How Brains Become Who We Are* (New York: Penguin Books, 2002), p. 8.
28 Wilkinson, *Coming into Mind*.
29 LeDoux, *Synaptic Self*.
30 Ibid., p. 307.
31 Peter Fonagy, "Psychotherapy Meets Neuroscience," *Psychiatric Bulletin*, no. 2 (2004): 357–359, 358.
32 Peter Fonagy, "Thinking About Thinking: Some Clinical and Theoretical Considerations in the Treatment of a Borderline Patient," *International Journal of Psychoanalysis*, no. 76 (1991): 639–656.
33 Liliana L. Wahba, et al., *O grafite e os símbolos culturais na cidade de São Paulo: uma leitura junguiana* (Pesquisa de Iniciação Científica: PUC-SP, 2010).
34 Weisstub and Galili-Weisstub, "Collective Trauma and Cultural Complexes," p. 161.
35 Iara: Iara, also spelled Uira or Yara, is the name of a figure from Brazilian mythology based on ancient Tupi and Guarani mythology. The word derives from Old Tupi *yîara* = *y* + *îara* (water + lord/lady) = lady of the lake (water queen). She is seen as either a water nymph, siren, or mermaid depending upon the context of the story told about her.

Chapter 5

The Cultural Skin in Latin America

Brian Feldman

I would like to present the idea that culture provides a form of social containment, a kind of cultural skin, in which we are able to create shared meanings that in turn provide both a scaffolding and structure to both our individual and group life. The cultural skin mediates experience between the subjective and symbolic realm of images and the intersubjective dialogues which take place in the social spaces between self and other. I will explore the cultural skin as it emerges in Latin America through my immersion in Brazilian culture in which I was guided by Brazilian anthropologists, Jungian and Lacanian psychoanalysts, as well as by my experience in utilizing the infant observation method to study in depth the development of a Mayan/Hispanic infant within the context of her home over a two-year period. My infant observation research was guided by the work of Esther Bick, Mary Ainsworth, and Michael Fordham.[1]

I have been able to study Brazilian culture with the help of anthropologists from the Museu do Indio in Rio de Janeiro, which is an administrative center for education and research and for anthropological work conducted in Brazil with indigenous peoples. With their aid, I studied the culture of the indigenous peoples of the Amazon, especially those aspects related to the skin and skin painting. I have also worked as a primary school teacher in an indigenous school in Arequipa, Peru, a beautiful city nestled high in the Peruvian Andes.

My research has had as a focus the development of sensory and symbolic experience in infancy, childhood, and adolescence, and the impact that these experiences have upon shaping our identity in adulthood. Through my field experiences I encountered the Andean and Amazonian (other), and this, in addition to academic work in anthropology at the University of Mexico, helped to forge an interest in Latin American anthropology, which continues through the present.

I was also helped in this project by my two teachers of Portuguese with whom I studied while they were on sabbatical at Stanford University in California and then later in Brazil. Jose Luis Jobim is a professor of Brazilian culture and literature at the National University of Rio de Janeiro, and his wife, Bethania Mariani, is a professor of linguistics and a practicing Lacanian psychoanalyst in Rio de Janeiro who has conducted studies of the language of the indigenous Amazonians. I am grateful to them for introducing me to the richness and depth of language and culture in Brazil. Both have taught me much about the nuances and meanings of the Portuguese language and its impact upon the evolution of meanings within the Brazilian cultural framework.

I have also been especially influenced by the Brazilian anthropologist Sergio Buarqe de Holanda, who describes the concept of *homen cordial*, the cordial and friendly aspect of interpersonal interaction which is highly valued by Brazilians.[2] He describes this as a kind of cultural skin which helps to modulate and choreograph interactions between self and other in Brazil and which provides a scheme of interpersonal attachment which preserves, protects, and regulates social interaction. I have also found enormously helpful Gilberto Freyre's seminal work *The Masters and the Slaves* (*Casa Grande e Senzala*), in which he traces the dialogic interactions between the colonizing Portuguese, the indigenous Brazilians, and the arriving slaves from Africa who, over time and through the ever-increasing mixture of cultures and genes, has led to the unique transformation that is the contemporary Brazilian identity and soul.[3] Freyre provides one of the first postcolonial views of Brazilian culture and helps us to understand the importance of sexuality, the body, ritual, and spirituality in the emergence of a Brazilian cultural skin.

I have also been influenced by Jungian analyst Roberto Gambini's study of Brazilian culture, *Indian Mirror: The Making of the Brazilian Soul*.[4] In this book Gambini looks at letters written by Jesuit priests in Brazil to their superiors in Portugal during the colonial period, correspondence which details the relationship between the colonizing Portuguese and the indigenous other. From an analytical perspective Gambini shows how these letters give us insight into the shadow side of the Portuguese, especially their repressed sexuality and aggression, which they projected onto the indigenous other. In the colonial discourse which Gambini examines, the indigenous peoples of Brazil were conceptualized as exotic (sexual) and pathological (cannibalistic), the antithesis of what the colonizers thought themselves to be. This image of the exotic/sexual and deviant/cannibalistic other represents, I think, the disavowed internal other of the colonizing Europeans.

In the Americas, the indigenous peoples were treated by the colonial Spanish and Portuguese as alien others, to be objectified and studied at a distance. They were seen as "primitive" and uncivilized, as lacking a soul. According to Gambini, Brazil – on the other side of the earth from Portugal – was the land of the unconscious for the Portuguese precisely because it was outside the realm of any knowledge, faith, or power. The view of the colonizers was that Brazil had to be conquered, integrated, and identified with mother Portugal as soon as possible and hopefully at a profit. The Portuguese sought to expand their territory and riches, yet at the same time not change their identity through contact with the indigenous Brazilians. They would not allow for an intersubjective interchange with the indigenous other. They would not protect, preserve, or relate to the indigenous other on equal terms. Rather, the main aims of the Portuguese were to colonize the land, strengthen and enrich the Crown, and convert the natives to Catholicism.

The Jesuits, as portrayed in their letters from Brazil to Portugal, projected onto the indigenous Brazilians all of their own dark and suppressed impulses and feelings.[5] The native Brazilians were viewed as containing the shadow of the Jesuits: sensuality, unbridled sexuality, and a natural pleasure in the body. The Indians were seen as polygamous pagans who had little understanding of Christian morality. The Jesuits were incapable of accepting that Brazilian Indians who, as a result of their long heritage in the tropics, tended to follow their natural, animistic, spiritual, and sensual/sexual inclinations. The Jesuits judged such a disposition as an unspeakable wickedness, akin to being influenced by the devil. The Jesuits felt that pursuits such as singing, dancing, and expressed sensuality and sexuality would damage the soul. What was expected of the Indians was that they behave as soft clay, allowing their obscure and chaotic nature finally to be shaped into human (or Portuguese) form. The Jesuit was the mirror in which the Brazilian Indian had to look, as if saying, "Teach me, let me be like you, make a decent human being out of me." The conversion of the Brazilian Indians was seen as a holy war against the devil, the dark other. The missionary motto was to deliver the Indians from the powers of hell. In this attitude we can see that the repressive tendencies of the Portuguese led to the destruction of the cultural skin of the indigenous other as the shadow elements were disavowed and had to be controlled or destroyed, or else they could contaminate and undermine colonial power.

In Brazil, the Portuguese found not the pious, submissive, and perhaps restrained women they knew in their homeland, but new, different, and to their eyes amoral, seductive, and above all available and naked females (and males) at their total disposal with whom they could live out all of their erotic fantasies. A married man, leaving his wife in Portugal, could have Indian woman slaves and make use of them as sexual objects. While there is little mention of homosexuality in the letters of the Jesuits, Freyre notes that homosexuality and bisexuality were accepted and practiced among the indigenous Brazilians and that shamans (*pajes*) and creative artists were often homosexual and bisexual and were seen to have a deeper relationship to the unconscious at both the individual and collective levels.

The sensuous and sexual metaphors which involve transactions with the skin of the self and other is an image from the Brazilian cultural unconscious which emerges with much frequency in Brazilian literature, music, and film. Brazilian culture has a primal scene invoking both sensuous and sexual desire: a Portuguese/indigenous coniunctio with all of its tropical "juissance" at the center of its cultural identity. Tom Jobim gave voice, rhythm, and shape to this distinctly Brazilian coniunctio in his bossa nova ballads.

Jungian analyst Gustavo Barcellos has commented on this aspect of Brazilian culture quite sensitively in his work on *saudade*.[6] *Saudade* is a Portuguese word that has no exact equivalent in English. *Saudade* means yearning, longing, and desire triggered by separation and absence. To experience *saudade* is to experience an emotional state filled with a melancholic sweetness that fills the soul with longing, desire, and evocative memory. *Saudade* pervades Brazilian culture and thought. It is depicted with great depth and sensitivity in Brazilian music, literature, and film, as well as in its psychology.

Bossa Nova, a new wave music that began to be recorded in Rio de Janeiro in the late fifties, expresses *saudade*, this emotion of yearning, longing and desire, in internationally known classic songs such as "Chega de Saudade" ("No More Blues"), "Desafinado" ("Tuneless"), and "Coracao Vagabundo" ("Vagabond Heart"). These songs, recorded by Joao Gilberto, express the torment, sadness, and longing of one who yearns for connection, intimacy, touch, and holding, which has been lost and cannot be found again. *Saudade* is a longing for a kind of emotional paradise, for an immersion in the softness and tenderness of intimate moments and connected states of being, much like the state of mind of the infant in the arms of a secure and loving caregiver, as well as the tender and erotic embrace of lovers in states of quiet passion. In "Chega de Saudade," the most famous of the bossa nova songs recorded by Joao Gilberto, the essence of *saudade* is expressed in the intimacy of the dialogue between voice and guitar. These songs celebrating *saudade* were created by the *santissima trindade* (holy trinity) of bossa nova: Vinicius de Moraes (lyrics), Antonio (Tom) Carlos Jobim (music), and Joao Gilberto (singer). Bossa nova has its roots in the Copacabana and Ipanema districts of Rio de Janiero, districts that grew up and flourished around Rio's scenic beaches and in view of its dramatic landmarks: Corcovado mountain, topped by the enormous statue of Christ the Redeemer who overlooks the city with arms held out as if initiating an embrace, and Pao de Acucar, the mountains that emerge like the two enormous and beautiful breasts of a great goddess from the calmness of the waters of Guanabara Bay. In "Chega de Saudade" sadness and melancholy provide the emotional backdrop of a man musing about his absent lover. His desire for connection, for an embrace that will erase the sadness, an embrace that will bring pleasure and forgetfulness, is the *saudade* that is experienced with an intensity that nourishes his imagination and soul. In "Chega de Saudade," the synergy of the music, lyrics, voice, and guitar lead to such a profound experience of aesthetic beauty and emotional depth that the song can also be viewed as an expression of the Brazilian unconscious, of the Brazilian soul. This feeling of *saudade* pervades Brazilian culture and is one of the deeper components of its collective soul.

Lévi-Strauss and the Cultural Skin

Claude Lévi-Strauss' anthropological/autobiographical fieldwork in Brazil, which he published in *Tristes Tropiques*, provides a significant postcolonial view of the indigenous other in Brazil.[7] His viewpoint is deeply intersubjective as he explores his own reactions to his experiences with indigenous groups in the Pantanal and Amazon regions of Brazil. His viewpoint is, I think, closely allied to contemporary analytical discourses which view self and other as linked together into a complex mosaic. Lévi-Strauss' attempt to understand the indigenous Brazilian other without judgment or preexisting categories is the hallmark of the postcolonial approach in anthropology. This postcolonial approach offers much that can be helpful in conceptualizing our current analytic practice. Postcolonial thought helps us to privilege a pluralistic view of the psyche that is not dominated by one "colonial" viewpoint. It is interesting that Freud often spoke of the analyst as a conquistador who needed to help the analysand subdue the dark forces of the unconscious. Analysis began with this particularly colonial metaphor. Jung, while less the conquistador than Freud, spoke of engaging the unconscious in a healing dialogue for the purpose of integration and individuation, but he still privileged Western culture and spoke with traces of Eurocentric colonial superiority of the less evolved, "primitive" cultures. There is much we as analysts can learn from Lévi-Strauss, who tried to let the myths, religion, and art of indigenous cultures speak for themselves without prematurely imposing theoretical categorizations onto them. In his structuralist approach, much like a contemporary Jungian psychoanalyst, he looked for the invariant elements, the archetypes embedded in myth, and he found that myths were created out of a basic (invariant/archetypal) need for order in the human psyche. He found that myths were devised to help resolve conflicts between opposites, much like Jung's use of the transcendent function.

My own research in Brazil has focused on the acquisition of cultural identity through the early transactions between self and other, especially those interchanges which involve the skin, such as holding, touch, and skin painting. I have looked at how the self and other in their diverse dialectics give shape to individual and group identity, to a kind of cultural skin in which one can experience social containment. I have been researching the function of the skin, as it is the area around which our first transactions take place. I have been developing the concept of a primary skin

Figure 5.1 Traditional face painting.

function as the foundation of our experience of a container and the concept of a cultural skin as a container of collective experience. In the anthropological work that I have done in Brazil, I have focused on the emergence of both a primary skin function and a cultural skin or social container.

Given my interest in the primary skin function and the idea of psychic skin, the indigenous Brazilians are especially interesting because they utilize skin painting as an important ritual that promotes the evolution of both individual and cultural identity. For the indigenous Brazilians, skin painting confers human dignity on the individual. It ensures the transition from nature to culture, from beast to civilized man. It is interesting how for these people skin paintings represent the origins of culture. Skin painting varies in style and pattern according to caste, and it expresses differences in status within a complex society. The paint, I am told by the anthropologists with whom I worked at the Museu do Indio in Rio de Janeiro, is made from a mixture of vegetable dies and monkey fat. Hours are spent on painting the skin, and it therefore involves much touching of the skin of the other. The paint stays on the skin for long periods of time and is not washed off for long periods of time. In the Mbaya culture, which is organized into castes, nobles displayed their rank by stenciled body painting or tattooed designs, which were the equivalent of coats of arms. All facial hair was removed, including the eyebrows and eyelashes. To be a man in this culture, it was necessary to be painted; to remain in the natural state was to be no different from the beasts. Skin painting therefore provided a means of initiation into culture.

I have been struck by the deeply aesthetic nature of Brazilian skin painting and was intrigued that the body itself became the first object of aesthetic interest for a large number of indigenous groups. Perhaps this is a piece of data that points to the importance of the body as one of the origins of an aesthetic attitude in culture. My work with infant observation is another area where the aesthetics of the maternal body and its often overwhelming beauty for the infant are linked to formative experiences of self and other and lead to the evolution of a capacity in the infant for both aesthetic and spiritual experience.

The Skin in Analytical Psychology

I believe that the precursor of the capacity for symbolization, and by this I mean the capacity to utilize thought, image, and emotion in an integrative manner for the purpose of psychological growth and development, has as its foundation the sensorial development of the infant during the first year of life. In this regard the development of sensorial differentiations, through the use of touch, smell, taste, sight, and sound, and the infant's experience of the skin as a defining boundary between what is experienced as internal, as opposed to what is experienced as external to the self, are fundamental to psychological development.

The psychological experience of the skin in infancy is fundamental as it leads to the development of a concept of an internal space where symbolization processes can take place. I think of this internal or potential space as being able to contain imaginal functions such as occur in states of dreaming, reverie, and imaginative activities (like active imagination).[8] My interest in the psychological function of the skin began several years ago when I was doing research into Jung's infancy and childhood and the impact that this had upon the evolution of his psychology.[9] In *Memories, Dreams, Reflections*, Jung's autobiography written when he was 83 years old, Jung talks about his infancy and childhood with a great deal of candor and insight.[10] When Jung was 3 years old, his mother was hospitalized in a Swiss psychiatric hospital for several months for what appears to have been a severe depression. Jung says that her hospitalization was related to difficulties that were surfacing in the parental relationship. During his mother's absence, he was taken care of by a maid. He also developed a severe skin disorder, eczema, that he connected with the separation of his parents and his mother's hospitalization.

I thought it probable that Jung's severe eczema was linked to the sense of psychic catastrophe that he experienced upon his separation from his mother. It was as if he was unable to contain torturous and painful emotions within himself, and they burst out in a somatic form as a severe skin disorder. Jung states,

> I was suffering, so my mother told me afterward, from general eczema. Dim intimations of trouble in my parents' marriage hovered around me. My illness, in 1878, must have been connected with a temporary separation of my parents. My mother spent several months in a hospital in Basel, and presumably her illness had something to do with the difficulty in the marriage.[11]

Freud was the first to allude to the importance of the psychological experience of the skin in his seminal theoretical work *The Ego and the Id*.[12] Freud states that "the ego is first and foremost a bodily ego; it is not merely a surface entity, but is itself the projection of the surface."[13] In the English translation of this work, he added a footnote to this statement and noted that "the ego is ultimately derived from bodily sensations, chiefly from those springing from the surface of the body. The ego is thus a mental projection of the surface of the body."[14] Freud's intuitive insights into the bodily origins of the ego have served as a guidepost for the analytical investigations that have taken place since the time his statements were made. Freud's metaphor focusing on the surface of the skin is an important one to reflect upon. Freud's hypothesis that the ego is a mental projection of the surface of the body implies that the ego, which provides our orientation to reality and the external world, is formed by the psychological experience of the surface of the body, the skin. In this regard the experience of the skin is the earliest foundation for the development of the ego and hence the primary mediator of psychological experience. The skin provides the first mental scheme of the "I" (the self) and the first psychological experience of boundaries. The psychological skin becomes the first delineator of internal and external experience, the mediator of the first object relationships, and the mediator of the first experience of the self.

I think that Freud's observations have been confirmed by the work of investigators both within the field of developmental psychology as well as within the field of psychoanalysis. For instance, Piaget's work on the origins of intelligence, play, and symbolization shows with ample detailed observations of infants and their development that the infant begins to organize his experience through his bodily interactions with his environment.[15] The first schemes or internal maps in the mind are, according to Piaget, sensorimotor schemes, and the first sensorimotor schemes form the foundations for all later cognitive and emotional development. For Piaget, all intellectual and emotional development begins with the sensorial aspects of the infant's experience. What this means is that the way in which the baby moves its body, the way the mouth and lips move to encounter the breast or bottle, the way the arms reach out to engage the realm of inanimate and animate objects such as mother have a lasting impact upon the developmental trajectory of the baby. The skin is the envelope in which the body is contained, and it is the skin which provides the points of contact with the external world and which acts as a delineator of boundaries between what is experienced to be outside and what is experienced to be inside the self.

In my own observations of babies, I have been struck by the infant's need to give shape to his bodily self by pushing his body up against hard and soft surfaces and by the mouthing of and grasping hold of animate and inanimate objects. The experience of the infant being securely held in the arms of the mother or other significant caregivers, and the exploration of the body of the other, especially the touching of the skin of the breast or mother's face during breastfeeding, are significant experiences that facilitate attachment and connection with mother. In addition, the way in which the baby is handled and held, which can be viewed during bathing and diapering episodes, all are important and fundamental experiences that give rise to a stable and secure sense of self as well as a stable and secure sense of attachment to a significant other.

The first in-depth study of the psychological function of the skin was made by the Kleinian analyst Esther Bick.[16] While Bick wrote only a small number of scientific articles about her work, they are of noteworthy significance. Bick introduced infant observation as part of the training for child psychotherapists at the Tavistock Institute in 1948. Bick envisioned infant observation as providing a firsthand experience into the development and evolution of psychic life in the infant during the first two years of the baby's life. This technique is now widely utilized as a foundation for the analytical training of Jungian, Kleinian, and Freudian child analysts. Infant observation as conceptualized by Bick helps analytical candidates conceive vividly the infantile preverbal experiences of their child analysands.

In Bick's article titled "The experience of the skin in early object relations," she postulates that the psychological function of the skin is akin to a holding function and that the skin is experienced by the infant as holding together the parts of the personality which are not yet differentiated from parts of the body.[17] Her thesis is that in its most primitive form, the parts of the personality are felt to have no binding or cohering force themselves and that the skin is experienced both as a container of psychological experience as well as a sheath that holds together the primitive psyche and soma.

Initially the infant, through his experience of an adequate holding relationship, introjects the containing or mothering function. Until the containing maternal functions have been introjected, according to Bick, the concept of a space within the self where thought and symbolization take place cannot exist. For Bick, the need for a containing object leads the infant to search for an object to hold the personality together. Optimally this is the breast, which together with the secure and firm holding of mother, gives the infant an experience of being a coherent whole. My own observations of babies indicate that there is a desire for a containing experience that involves the nipple securely held in the mouth, the sucking motions that lead to a good feed, the tactile feel of mother's skin, and the experience of being securely and firmly held in mother's arms. When this deeper connection is made between infant and caregiver, it can lead to a shared experience of satisfaction, mystery, and pleasure that helps to reinforce the baby's experience of security and primary (sensory and psychological) containment. I think that this type of satisfying experience for both mother and baby leads the baby to develop a primary skin function. With the development of a primary skin function, the baby feels secure within her own skin and is able to tolerate periods of separateness from mother without undue anxiety.

Didier Anzieu, in his book *The Skin Ego*, presents the helpful metaphor of the skin ego as a kind of psychic envelope.[18] According to Anzieu, the primary function of the psychic skin is as a container or sac which retains the goodness and fullness which accumulates through feeding, care, and bathing, which the mother performs for the benefit of the infant. The skin envelope as a mental representation emerges from the interplay between the mother's body and the child's body. When the containing function is adequately introjected, the baby is able to acquire the concept of a space within the self, and he can begin to conceptualize that both he and his mother are each contained within their respective skins. When the containing function fails to develop adequately, the child will need to develop secondary skin function defenses to guard against feelings of having a fragile skin, or a leaking colander skin from which psychic contents can dangerously seep out and cause distortions in reality testing and interpersonal relationships.

Over the past 15 years I have been involved in research utilizing the Esther Bick method of in-home observation of infants and their caregivers. The Bick method of observation is closely akin to anthropological fieldwork. The observer becomes a participant observer for the first two years of the infant's life and visits the family for one hour on a weekly basis. The observer not only takes note of the infant's behavior and mental states but also has as a focus of reflection the cultural context of the observation, the influence of both the conscious and unconscious mental states of the caregivers on the ongoing development of the baby, and the impact of the observer himself upon the family.

Infant Observation With a Mayan/Hispanic Family

I observed the evolution of a primary skin function in Julia at five months, one week. Julia is a Mayan/Hispanic baby whose parents had immigrated to California from Central America. When I arrive for the observation, Mother asks me to go into the bedroom where Julia is lying in a bassinet on the parental bed. Mother is giving her a bath. Julia appears calm yet alert. Mother is speaking to Julia in Spanish with an intonation that echoes the rhythms of Julia's vocalizations. Mother gently covers Julia's body with warm water and then rubs her skin and bathes her with soap. Julia has a small rubber ball in her hand that she holds with a certain determination and focus. All the while she maintains a gaze upon Mother's face and eyes and does not either look around the room or at me. As Mother shampoos her head with vigorous strokes, Julia remains relaxed and calm, allowing her head to bob up and down a bit, responding to the strokes of Mother's hands and without uttering any sounds of protest. Mother then tells me that Julia remains calm when she has something in her hand, and then she does not cry. As mother is talking to me, she gently bathes Julia's genitals in an unselfconscious manner. Mother goes through the ritual of rinsing Julia a number of times, each time passing her hands over Julia's head, chest, arms, and legs. Julia appears to calm as Mother strokes her body, and she then closes her eyes and appears to drift into a reverie state. When Mother stops touching her, Julia opens her eyes and looks towards Mother, as if to orient herself after being in reverie. Mother continues the rinsing a number of times and lifts Julia onto her legs, turning her around so that her back faces me. She then turns her around again and says to Julia in Spanish, "How delicious is the water. Thank you, God, for the water. What would happen to us if we did not have water?" I sense Julia's pleasure in the moment and her close emotional connection with Mother. Julia has a radiant smile upon her face, and she then looks away from Mother with a strong and firm gaze. She conveys a sense of presence and embodiment in her fleshy baby's body. I feel touched and privileged in being able to witness the intimacy between infant and mother. Julia's radiant smile evokes a smile in Mother, who then continues with the bath, as she and Julia are immersed in the pleasure of their interchange.

I think that Virginia Woolf's concept of "moments of being" is a helpful one in understanding the aesthetic dimension of this experience.[19] Woolf talks about the ways in which ordinary experience can become filled with importance and that these "moments of being" coalesce within us into a pattern or mosaic that forms the "invisible and silent scaffolding of our lives."[20] According to Woolf, "moments of being" provide the foundation for our experience of self. They involve the integration of past experience into the present, providing us with the experience of a narrative of our lives. As I observed Julia during the two years of observation, I kept being drawn back to the lived "moments of being" which provided the secure foundation for her later development. These experiences provided Julia with a feeling of containment within her own skin. At first the experience of skin was primarily sensuous and took place on the surface of her actual skin. As Julia's development unfolded, the sensuality of her skin experience became more internalized and later symbolized in her play. Julia's experience of these skin episodes became encoded in her psyche and provided the foundation for emerging capacity for containment and relationship. She began to feel more comfortable in her own skin, and she could begin over time to imagine what it may be like in the skin of the other. The past experience of the skin became integrated with the present experience of self and other. Woolf poetically describes this experience of integration of past into the present as follows:

> The past only comes back when the present runs so smoothly that it is like the sliding surface of a deep river. Then one sees through the surface to the depths. In those moments I find one of my greatest satisfactions, not that I am thinking of the past; but that it is then that I am living most fully in the present. For the present when backed by the past is a thousand times deeper than the present when it presses so close that you can feel nothing else.[21]

Julia's experience of being bathed in the warmth of the water and in the warmth of Mother's words is a "moment of being" that structures and nourishes the felt experience of containment and that facilitates the formation of a primary skin function that enables Julia to feel safe and secure within her feminine body image. The experience of Mother's touch in the warm bath, the sensation of the warm water and of being contained in the bath, and of feeling securely held within Mother's mind all form the background for the emergence of this primary skin function. The experience in the bath becomes an unconscious narrative of the self where past and present can become integrated; "the present is experienced as sliding over the depths of the past, creating a fullness."[22] Woolf's insight into the impact of these "moments of being" is expressed poignantly as follows:

> I reach what I might call a philosophy; that behind the cotton wool is hidden a pattern; that we – I mean all human beings – are connected with this; that the whole world is a work of art; that we are all parts of the work of art.[23]

I believe that the anthropological, cultural, and infant observation perspectives are all uniquely helpful in fostering a deeper understanding of the importance of the self/other dialogue for development and individuation. From the standpoint of analytical psychology we can now productively shift our perspective from a one-person psychology, focusing almost exclusively upon the individual, to a more contextualized psychology that focuses on the self/other dialogue within the analytical relationship, within development, and within culture. I have found the metaphor of the psychic skin useful in helping to understand the individual in the context of their culture. In conversations with Erik Erikson, which occurred while taking a yearlong seminar with him on development, culture, and psychoanalysis, he expressed the belief based on his own anthropological experience that culture is communicated to the infant primarily through the bodily/tactile experience between self and other.[24]

As a Jungian analyst I would also place as much importance on unconscious affective communication as upon physical and sensuous experience. The experience of the primary skin function as a container of psychological, symbolic, and emotional experience is communicated to the infant through her interaction with (m)other in both the conscious and unconscious realms: in the conscious realm through language, intentional touch, and sensuousness, and in the unconscious realm through the sounds of the words, the feelings beneath the touch and gaze, and the rhythms of interactions in space and time. The skin as experienced both within the context of cultural and individual development provides an important container for psychological, emotional, and symbolic experience. As the primary skin function evolves, the cultural and individual experiences are melded together into a powerful aesthetic and spiritual mosaic which takes form first on the surface of our skin and throughout our development provides the invisible scaffolding of our lives.

Notes

1 See the discussions on infant observation research in the context of analytical psychology, psychoanalysis, and attachment theory in Michael Fordham, *Explorations into the Self* (London: Academic Press, 1985); Esther Bick, "The Experience of the Skin in Early Object Relations," *The International Journal of Psychoanalysis*, no. 49 (1968): 184–186; and Mary Ainsworth, *Patterns of Attachment* (New York: John Wiley, 1978).
2 Buarque de Holanda, *Raizes do Brasil* (Sao Paulo: Companhia das Letras, 1936). Unfortunately this seminal work in the field of Brazilian anthropology has not been published in an English translation. Buarque de Holanda is considered to be one of the fathers of modern Brazilian anthropology.
3 Gilberto Freyre, *The Masters and the Slaves (Casa Grande e Senzala)* (Berkeley: University of California Press, 1986).
4 Roberto Gambini, *Indian Mirror: The Making of the Brazilian Soul* (Sao Paulo: Axis Mundi, 2000).
5 Jean de Lery, *History of a Voyage to the Land of Brazil*, trans. Janet Whatley (Berkeley: University of California Press, 1990). This important work, one of the first about on the encounter with indigenous peoples in Brazil, was originally published in 1578.
6 Gustavo Barcellos, "Chega de Saudade do Brasil: Uma Visao Arquetipico da Bossa-Nova," in *Anales del II Congresso Latino-Americano de Psicologia Jungiuiana* (Rio de Janeiro: Impresín Cuatro y Cero Ltda, 2000).
7 Claude Lévi-Strauss, *Tristes Tropiques*, trans. John and Doreen Weightman (New York: Penguin Books, 1973). Lévi-Strauss first published his memoirs of his anthropological work in 1955. His work is filled with interesting reflections on the philosophical and psychoanalytical nature of his fieldwork in Brazil.
8 Donald Winnicott, *Playing and Reality* (London: Tavistock, 1971).
9 Brian Feldman, "Jung's Infancy and Childhood and its Influence upon the Development of Analytical Psychology," *Journal of Analytical Psychology*, no. 37 (1992): 255–274.
10 C.G. Jung, *Memories, Dreams, Reflections*, ed. Aniela Jaffe, trans. Richard and Clara Winston (New York: Random House, 1961).
11 Jung, *Memories, Dreams, Reflections*, p. 8.
12 Sigmund Freud, "The Ego and the Id," in *The Standard Edition Vol. XIX*, trans. James Strachey (London: Hogarth Press, 1924).
13 Ibid., p. 26.
14 Ibid. This footnote appeared in an English edition of this work published in 1927.
15 Jean Piaget, *Play, Dreams and Imitation in Childhood*, trans. C. Gattegno and F.M. Hodgson (New York: W.W. Norton, 1962). In this work Piaget is very sympathetic to

Jung's psychology, which he studied while a student in Zürich. As an analysand of Sabina Spielrein, he was also exposed to Jung's approach to analysis.
16 Esther Bick, "The Experience of the Skin in Early Object Relations," *The International Journal of Psychoanalysis*, no. 49 (1968): 184–186.
17 Didier Anzieu, *The Skin Ego*, trans. Chris Turner (New Haven: Yale University Press, 1989).
18 Virginia Woolf, *Moments of Being*, ed. Jeanne Schulkind (London: Harcourt Brace, 1976).
19 Ibid., p. 73.
20 Ibid., p. 72.
21 Ibid., p. 98.
22 Ibid.
23 Ibid., p. 72.
24 Erik Erikson, personal communication with author in 1976. The seminar with Erikson took place in 1975–1976 during my postdoctoral fellowship at Mt. Zion Hospital in San Francisco.

Chile

Chapter 6

At the Far End of the World

Exploring the Chilean Cultural Isolation Complex

Claudia Beas and Javiera Sánchez

In 2009, the Legatum Institute issued its Prosperity Index,[1] where Chile was ranked 36th out of 104 countries and third in Latin America, after Costa Rica and Uruguay. This Prosperity Index takes into account various factors, including economic fundamentals, democratic institutions, personal freedom, and social capital. Although Chile ranks similarly to that of other developed countries on several of these factors, its ranking is alarmingly low on the social capital index. "Social capital" was described by Fukuyama as a people's ability to work together, to come together around certain shared standards and values.[2] It is the result of the capacity to relate to one another socially, to be able to trust other people, or have a common set of norms based on honesty and reciprocity. On the social capital index, Chile ranks 85th. Less than a fourth of the Chilean population believe that the people surrounding them are trustworthy, and 80 percent believe that friends are not important – a variable in which Chile ranks in last place.[3]

Likewise, according to the Social Cohesion Survey for Latin America carried out in six countries, Chileans show the least number of friends per person and the highest percentage (20 percent) of people who state they have no close friends.[4] A national survey conducted in Chile reveals that the country's youth mistrust their neighbors (76 percent), their bosses (56 percent), and their coworkers or fellow students (51 percent).[5]

Something doesn't click with Chileans when it comes to trusting or bonding with others; it appears to be very difficult for them to engage in and maintain friendships. As a rule, the group to which Chileans primarily belong is their family; they scarcely interact with their peers and infrequently come together around sports, the arts, or common hobbies. What is it about Chileans that makes it so hard for them to make friends and to trust others? Why is it so difficult for them to cut loose from their original family and relate to their peers? Why do they tend to isolate themselves? We believe that this phenomenon is associated with a "Cultural Isolation Complex."

This chapter will seek to understand how this cultural isolation complex has developed and how it plays out today in Chile. We will explore several factors that we believe have contributed to the development of this complex. Among them are Chile's geography – the fact that Chile is surrounded on all sides by imposing

DOI: 10.4324/9781003400820-10

natural boundaries; Chile's history, where the trauma of the Spanish Conquest plays a crucial role; the influence of the Spanish and their Catholic hardline conservatism; and the reactivation of the Conquest trauma as a result of the long dictatorship of Augusto Pinochet that isolated Chile for 17 years (1973–1990) and instilled in its citizens a fear and mistrust of others; and finally, the role of the mother as the axis and core of the family unit. We will also seek to understand how the cultural isolation complex operates today in daily life throughout Chile. To this end, we will examine the different polarities that are characteristic of this complex: isolated/bonded, trust/mistrust, submission/domination, and superiority/inferiority. By exploring this complex, we will attempt to address the collective experience that appears unconsciously in the social group identified as the "Chilean people."

Geography: At the Edge of the Map

Chile is located along the southwest coast of South America, at the edge of the continent, at the far end of the world. It is a long and narrow strip of land that runs 4,200 kilometers, surrounded by natural boundaries.[6] To the north, there is a vast dry and barren desert: the Atacama, the driest in the world. To the south, the glaciers; to the west, the vast Pacific Ocean, which separates Chile from Australia and Asia; to the east and running from north to south, the Andes mountain range, which amounts to an actual wall that inevitably separates Chile from Argentina and Bolivia.

These uniquely isolating geographical characteristics, and the fact that Chile is the longest and narrowest country in the world, make it a very difficult territory to connect with in terms of communication and transportation, both domestically and with the rest of the world. Additionally, these geographical features and Chile's vast length are factors that determine the varying climates: some regions are arid, dry, and hot; others feature a Mediterranean climate; still others are covered with rainforests and glaciers.

In referring to archetypes, Jung states that "the only way to explain how they generate is to assume that they are the decantation of human experiences that are repeated over and over."[7] In this context, we may ask ourselves about the effect that living surrounded by these natural boundaries for centuries has had upon the Chilean identity. How has waking up and going to sleep every day hemmed in by the ocean, the mountains, the desert, and the glaciers affected the peoples of this land, from the pre-colonization period of the indigenous people through the period of colonization and throughout the era of the republic? What is it like to be born and to die trapped within a geography that is conducive to cloistering and insularity? Living in Chile causes a sense of isolation similar to that of living on an island, though perhaps increased by the all-pervading and permanently insurmountable Andes Mountains.

Based on these factors, we may assume that in the collective unconscious of the Chilean people the experience of insularity and geographical cloistering is strongly present as a result of the "decanting" of the repeated experience of living surrounded by these natural boundaries.

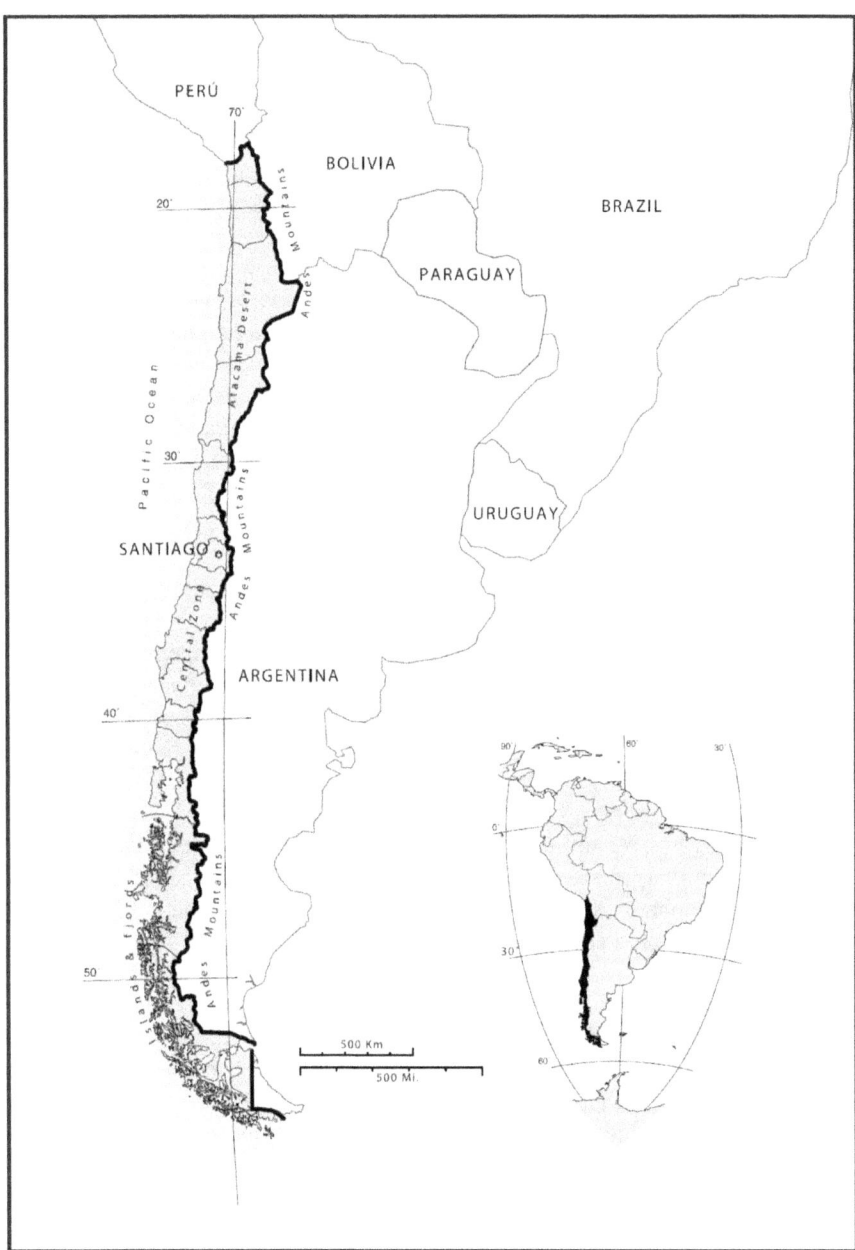

Figure 6.1 The geography of Chile.
Source: Map courtesy of El Mercurio © 2012

History: Trauma, Submission, and Mistrust

Singer and Kimbles state that cultural complexes frequently arise from collectively experienced traumas.[8] Following their lead, we will focus on the traumas resulting from the Spanish Conquest and from the recent Pinochet dictatorship, which lasted from 1973 to 1990. We believe that experiencing these traumas has been central to the development of a lifelong experience of exclusion and mistrust in our national identity.

The Chilean people – as well as other Latin Americans – are the result of the mixing of races that took place during the Conquest and colonization. This mixing of races occurred violently, with bloodshed. It entailed trauma, a disruption of continuity, and took place between the conquerors and the conquered, between the evangelizers and the converts, giving rise to a collective consciousness where "in each individual both the 'one' and the 'other' – the dominator and the dominated – coexist."[9] In this respect Montecino points out that in the native Andean worldview, the Conquest was a *Pachacuti*, a cosmic catastrophe, where the world is born anew and is now inhabited by half-breeds who carry within themselves both the Spanish subjugating conqueror and the conquered native.

The Spanish Conquest cannot be segregated from the Catholic religion and evangelization since the Spanish conquerors arrived in the New World in the name of the crown and in the name of God. Their mission was to evangelize the natives, and they conducted that mission as a military operation. Larraín states that evangelization was a war to the death between God and the enemies of Spain, which included pirates and Protestant countries as well the *Mapuches* (the natives of Southern Chile).[10]

> It was an aggressive military religiousness in which evangelization took the form of a military undertaking. . . . The war to the death against the natives and their exploitation by forced labor in the *encomiendas* (land grants) thereby acquired divine protection.[11]

The evangelization of the natives was hard and merciless. It sought to undermine their roots, their mores, and their spirituality in order to impose upon them a new belief system – a Spanish and Catholic one. To this end, the first measures implemented by the Spanish missionaries toward evangelization were to destroy the natives' sacred places, their religious icons, and anything associated with their beliefs since they were considered a menace to the Catholic creed. In the Spaniards' view, the natives were subhuman and inferior. For instance, Barros Arana referred to the natives as being incapable of creating bonds of affection. He portrayed them as drunkards, lazy, cannibals, and lacking in intellectual and moral abilities.[12] The strategies to convert the natives to Christianity were very diverse. Violence, coercion, and repressive methods were used. These actions were intended to eliminate ancient traditions, authorities, and values, labeling them as perverse and inadmissible. The Spaniards' strong belief that they were the bearer of a superior religion led to this devaluation of the natives' own religion. Evangelization was sought as a civilizing force by the Spanish.

In fact, according to Jorge Gissi, the Spaniards imposed their identity and culture on the natives by disrupting the natives' own, preexisting culture, one which in the past had supported a social cohesion in the native community that was the basis of family relationships, mutual support and protection, and the defense of the community itself. He points out that as a consequence of this disruption, the deculturization process, and the consequent collapse of community structures, the natives' self-esteem and self-image were undermined, leading to the generation of a culture of resistance and mistrust.[13] It is evident that the Spaniards did not acknowledge the natives as equals who had a right to be different but rather assumed that they should be assimilated into the "true" Catholic religion. The concept of being different is thus strongly ingrained in the collective conscience not as a positive attribute but as a disrupting factor. Anything new and different is deemed threatening and must be attacked; anything coming from abroad, from far away, anything foreign, is symbolized as something that undermines the foundations of one's own identity.

Given these premises, the foundations for the development of the cultural isolation complex were laid at the historical, religious, and sociopolitical inception of the country. The period of conquest and colonization became ingrained in the conscious/unconscious psyche of the people of Chile in a set of polar opposites around conquest and revolt. On the one hand was the figure of the conqueror as evangelist, and on the other was the figure of the native as rebellious and subversive, who must be subdued in order to achieve unity. At the limits of this polarity these same figures turn into their opposites: the conqueror is seen as the violent and destroying oppressor, and the native is deemed a brave and heroic protector of his own people. An alternating polarity of almost irreconcilable positions takes root in the community. The conquered/conqueror dichotomy generates its own splits in the cultural unconscious around the polarities of trust/mistrust and inferiority/superiority. These kinds of tensions make what is familiar and recognizable highly desirable to feel secure, while what is unknown is viewed as alien and fearful.

As the years went by, Chile began to be inhabited by Spaniards, creoles (offspring of Spaniards born in Chile), half-breeds (offspring of Spaniards and natives), and natives. Rank, advantages, and power in society took on that same order. Therefore, those excluded and oppressed were no longer only the natives. The creoles and half-breeds were also excluded by the Spaniards from all political and economic processes. The resentment about this caste society was so intense that one of the strongest, driving forces that mobilized the revolt toward independence "was the *de facto* creole's exclusion and discrimination."[14] The creoles created an enigmatic problem for the state: they were not foreigners or Spaniards or members of a still nonexistent republic. The exclusion of creoles from participation in the government was one of the primary forces that led to the creation of Chilean nationality and identity. It is easy to see how the reality and feeling of exclusion became associated with an inferiority complex and a constant looking towards Europe and the United States as being superior. Their looks, philosophy, science, economy, and progress were to be imitated. This created another awkward split in the Chilean psyche: many things foreign are idealized, but at the same time they are feared when they are near.

The Chilean feelings of exclusion and inferiority did not end with Independence and the birth of the Republic in 1818. Although the natives, half-breeds, and creoles were marginalized by the Spanish Crown early in the formation of the country, in time the excluded creoles became the oligarchic elite that dominated the country politically and economically. They, in turn, marginalized the rest of the population, which was a mixture of the beginnings of the bourgeoisie and large groups of people living in virtual serfdom or surviving on the outskirts of large cities. This was the next wave of those who felt excluded, and they in turn contributed to the profound political polarization and civil unrest of the 1970s.

The national identity of the incipient Republic did not become totally consolidated until the victory over Bolivia and Peru in the Pacific War (1879–1883).[15] This is not a minor issue as it signals the reemergence of "the other," a new opponent from whom the nation needed to defend itself. "Thus, a national identity based on war relies on the need to have an enemy to destroy."[16] This logic, based on the "other" as enemy, is also seen in internal relationships, both with the *Mapuches*, the natives of Southern Chile, and during the dictatorship (1973–1990), when the term "internal enemies" was used to refer to political adversaries. We therefore see an intensification of the trust/mistrust polarization, which leans towards the pole of mistrust. Thus, the signification of the "other" as an enemy who must not be trusted is already evident in the very roots of Chilean's identity as a nation. Furthermore, when national identity is forged as a result of victory in war, the polarities embodied in the concepts of victor/defeated, superiority/inferiority, and subjugation/submission become part of how a people views itself, and in the case of Chileans, they came to see themselves as the triumphant and superior group that subjugates others.

In the twentieth century, and specifically during the 1970s, the specter of authoritarianism reappeared in Chile, thereby opening old wounds which have not yet fully healed. Internal tensions and divisions were apparent in the country during the government of the leftwing *Unidad Popular* that brought Salvador Allende to power in 1970. Allende died during the right wing coup led by the Chilean army commander-in-chief Augusto Pinochet in 1973. The ensuing dictatorship took the tensions between right and left to a level of polarization that had horrific results and has left the Chilean psyche with deep scars.

> Although the Allende government caused political divisions in the country and raised the hostility and aggression levels between supporters and adversaries, thus hindering any sense of shared fraternity, the military government went from aggression and hostility to torture and physical elimination of the vanquished "others" who were no longer deemed to be part of the community.[17]

To eliminate the Marxist legacy and to rid society of the left wing other, a number of methods were used. The first strategy was the "cut and clean-up operation"; the main objective of which was to break down the goals of the *Unidad Popular*. In addition to this, several initiatives were implemented that were aimed at "recovering national heritage" and "vindicating the sense of nationality." According to Larraín, the marginalization of those who had supported the *Unidad Popular* took several forms during the military government.[18] "Exclusion" was carried out in many ways. Many Chilean citizens were forced into exile; others who were outside of the country were not allowed to return; many were refused passports, and still others had their citizenship revoked. Exclusion also took place on the domestic front by isolating those who remained in the country but had supported the previous government. Suspected partisans of the previous *Unidad Popular* were turned in, tracked down, fired from their jobs, or submitted to massive house searches. Insecurity and terror were once again ingrained in the collective unconscious through horrors that were reminiscent of those suffered by the natives at the hands of the Spaniards. People were filled with the dread of being killed, tortured, or losing loved ones.

In the official language used during this period, these policies were initiated to root out an infection of mind and body in the Chilean people:

> The aforementioned considerations require a cultural policy which within its scope of competence will firstly be aimed at uprooting once and for all the source of the infection that has spread and may still spread throughout the body politic of our country; and secondly, that will be effective as a means of eliminating the flaws of our mindset and behavior.[19]

Repression extended to all spheres of public and private activity. As early as 1975 the military regime controlled the media, the universities, and the political and cultural organizations. "Among other measures, personnel were fired from government institutions and universities, books were burned, walls were washed clean of political slogans, men were forced to cut their hair and shave; street, district, and school names were changed."[20] Anything that was reminiscent of the previous government had to be expunged from history, as it represented the opponent and was a sign of evil. Along with this generalized campaign of restoration, a nationalistic authoritarian organization emerged which implicitly or explicitly sought to redefine the mores and perception of social reality.[21] Once again, a large oppressed social group was forced to undergo a process of disruption and deculturization. Polarization and projection were used as ways to establish and maintain control. It was ingrained in the collective consciousness that the other is the "enemy" who must not be trusted, just as it was in the early stages of the Conquest. The oppressor/oppressed, superiority/inferiority, excluded/included polarities were thus reinstated. Once again, as in a circular, repetitive history, those in power were persuaded that they were the bearers of a divine truth that had to be safeguarded "for the good of the family and the fatherland." Meanwhile, in their shadow, everything that was "evil" was projected onto the other, the enemy, the opponent, who had to be subdued and eliminated.

In the recent period of transition to democracy which began in 1990,[22] Chileans have gone through a gradual and sustained process of civil, political, and cultural awakening. However, the symbols and scars of the Pinochet dictatorship run so deep in the national psyche that they have hindered the full rebirth of a culture of democracy. The collective memory of the trauma of the dictatorship joins forces in the cultural unconscious of the Chilean people with ancestral memories of the older repression under the Spanish conquerors. In the history and psyche of Chile, this has created the foundations for a potent cultural complex. In 1990, with the return of democracy, a new national myth has been encouraged that advocates the unity of all Chileans. However, in spite of all the talk of inclusion and reconciliation, the Chilean people are still unable to break free from their cultural isolation complex.

This new national myth conceives of Chile as the "Jaguar of Latin America." According to Larraín, Chile has been experimenting with the idea of itself as an enterprising and successful country, where the economy has become the gravitational center, consumption is the new highest value, and the successful entrepreneur is seen as the new hero.[23] This is a Chile that both conquers world markets and, at the same time, looks upon itself as separate and different from the rest of Latin America. The best example of this emerging attitude was on view at the International Fair of Seville in 1992, where Chile put an iceberg on display at its stand, seeking to convey that our country is different from the rest of Latin America. The iceberg was intended to symbolize that Chile is a cold country, reminiscent of Europe and the United States, and not in any sense like its neighbors, the tropical "banana republics." Moreover, "the perception of being different, persistently reiterated in the media and by politicians, elicits accusations of arrogance and not very friendly responses from our neighbors. Some international analysts have spoken about the "growing isolation of Chile in Latin America."[24] Tironi points out that in the 1990s the self-image of the Chilean people underwent a radical transformation, "from the self-effacing and pessimistic stance that, according to historians, has been a distinctive feature of the Chilean character, it changed into a proud and optimistic attitude – and suddenly even arrogance."[25]

If we analyze the National Bicentenary Survey, we can see that one of the manifestations of patriotic pride is the belief that our country is different from the rest of Latin America. Further research concludes that 57 percent of Chileans believe that Chile is a very different country than the rest of Latin America, and 55 percent believe that Chile would benefit more by strengthening ties with developed countries and moving away from Latin America.[26] The new Chile, seeking to break free from the feeling of inferiority, has arrived at the other nonintegrated pole of superiority. It is a Chile that attempts to hide from its cultural isolation complex but fails to do so, and though it now seeks to include its fellow countrymen, its feelings of superiority and tendency toward exclusion are brought to bear on its relationship to other countries on the continent. Therefore, in the 21st century the question is whether Chile wishes to integrate with the rest of Latin America or to once again repeat the cultural isolation complex by moving away from its neighbors and attempting to live a new myth of superiority by feeling "different and exceptional." Along with this attitude of conscious superiority comes the projection that everything that is undesirable (corruption, chaos, low economic growth, etc.) is related to the *other*, which today is no longer embodied by Chilean natives or local political adversaries but by the people and governments of other Latin American countries.

"We Have But One Mother" (Direct Translation of a Popular Spanish Saying)

Personal complexes aside, it is possible to observe the existence of cultural complexes that develop from traumatic experiences shared by a group of people and which are repeated over time. We believe this is precisely the case with Chilean society concerning its family dynamics and the central role played by the mother. The mother's role as the gravitational center of the Chilean family also significantly effects the cultural isolation complex in the following way: the mother dominates the domestic sphere, and the weakened male figures are unable to help the children step out into the world. The result is that the children remain isolated from the public sphere. The mother acquires most of the power in the family, especially over the children, and the father's access to the household's affections is gradually diminished. The dominant role of the mother figure in Chilean family dynamics contributes to the isolated/bonded duality equation, tipping heavily to the side of isolation, which in turn reinforces the cultural isolation complex. The National Bicentenary Survey shows astonishing data, revealing that

> Chileans value family life above all else. That is where they find their main source of satisfaction, to the point where they express a greater inclination toward maintaining contact with their family than establishing multiple friendship relations.[27]

However, the most revealing thing is that when the data is examined in greater depth and detail, it can be concluded that this strong family tradition is very closely associated with the filial relationship to the detriment of marriage or fraternal relationships, which are rather weak. Yet the strength of the filial bond does not involve the father to the same extent as the mother. The data compiled from the 2007 Bicentenary Survey show that the paternal role is relatively devalued, especially concerning the father's ability to establish order and authority in the home.[28]

In the average Chilean home, the mother reigns supreme, and the bond established between mother and child is stronger than the bonds established between the child and their father, siblings, mates, or friends. A powerful mother complex is coupled with the lack of a strong father figure to help loosen the bonds of the mother-child dyad. The father seems unable to help the child differentiate from the mother or to help the child step out from the domestic world into the outer world.

The characteristics described by Jung concerning the archetype of the mother – the loving mother and the terrible mother, the mother as kind, protective, supporting, and at the same time, devouring, seductive, and poisonous – appear to be hypertrophied in Chilean family dynamics.[29] The image of the mother embodies both the luminous and dark side of motherhood. She is capable of protecting, feeding, and nurturing a helpless, vulnerable, and needy child. However, her dark side is capable of preventing this same child from growing, failing to nurture it, and experiencing the child as an extension of herself or as her own property. That is the devouring mother.

Jung points out that in its positive aspect, the maternal complex "is the motherly love that is featured among the most moving and unforgettable memories . . . and is the secret root to all change . . ."[30] In its negative aspect, the maternal complex is represented by a woman whose single purpose is to give birth. Four key aspects can be seen in such a case. Firstly, the man is viewed by her as a mere accessory, an instrument of procreation, and is assigned his place among the children as just another person who needs her attention and care. Additionally, the woman's own individual personality is secondary since she lives her life through her children, who are simply an extension of her procreative, maternal role. Furthermore, this woman's eros is only developed in the context of her role as mother. Any eroticism, in terms of a relationship with a man, is absent. Finally, in spite of all the display of maternal sacrifice, such a woman's need to be a mother and reaffirm her maternal identity prevails over the child's need to grow, even to the point of destroying her child's own personal life and personality.[31]

Among Chilean woman, the exaggerated mother complex naturally extends itself to the worship of the Virgin Mary. Thus, the National Bicentenary Survey reveals that

> the Marian fervor remains very much alive and appears as supporting many Catholics' adherence to their faith: The Virgin is the main rallying issue in prayer and personal requests, and participation in celebrations, processions, and pilgrimages in her honor continues to be immensely popular in Chile. The power of Marian cultism goes far beyond the boundaries of Catholicism; it finds adepts among Evangelicals and even nonbelievers as well.[32]

This kind of maternal complex that we see both in the mother-child relationship and in the Marian fervor may be explained historically. Montecino proposes that a central narrative for the foundation of Latin America is the Marian allegory since this myth resolves our problem of origin: that of being children of a native mother and an absent Spanish father. This myth assigns "the female and male categories specific qualities: mother and son, respectively."[33] This rigid conception of the female as mother and the male as son leaves out and obliterates the male father figure, as well as all features of sexuality, both male and female.

Montecino maintains that the conquest of America began as a venture comprised entirely of males who "violently or tenderly ravished the native women, engendering half-bred descendants who were initially despised."[34] This loathing of the half-breeds came from both the natives and the Spanish. They were neither Spanish nor natives, but alien to both, including their mothers. Usually the abandoned mother kept the child, who became a *huacho* (a term that refers to both illegitimate children and orphans), and the Spanish father became an absent parent.

The mother-*huacho* family model was extended to the colonization period, during which the men continued to have native or half-bred concubines despite the arrival of Spanish women. However, this family model in which the mother was the central gravitational force was not limited to Spaniards but included all social classes because the prolonged Arauco War and the mining and farming-based economy fostered constant male migration.[35] "The women ran estates and families alone for months or even years at a time, their children socializing with female servants and relatives . . . the female image becoming very powerful."[36]

Montecino maintains that when the republic came into being in 1818, there was an attempt to change the family model – at least theoretically. Single mothers and concubines were frowned upon by a society seeking upward mobility. The author believes that during the nineteenth century the upper classes of Chile established a monogamous family model based upon the notion of a strong father figure, while the middle and lower classes favored one centered on the mother – with an absent father.

The best example of this is Bernardo O'Higgins (1778–1842), whom Chileans consider to be the founding father of the nation. He was an illegitimate child, or *huacho*. He was the son of a creole mother, Isabel Riquelme. His father was Ambrosio O'Higgins, an Irishman who worked for the Spanish crown and became both governor of Chile and viceroy of Peru. Ambrosio O'Higgins was an older bachelor who impregnated a teenager, Isabel Riquelme, and then abandoned her.[37] Isabel gave birth to Bernardo, who grew up to become a military figure and national hero who was central to Chilean and Latin American independence. His upbringing embodies the family model centered on the all-providing mother and absent father.

Chilean women faced an exasperating paradox. They were expected to be virgins and mothers at the same time. However, they made this paradox their own in living a myth that demanded that the son always remain a child – an asexual, eternally loyal, and attached child, a "clinging mommy's boy." The women gain a sense of accomplishment through the dyadic relationship they establish with their sons, abandoning as "useless" the other man, the partner, the non-child, the child of another, who may become a sexed man and a mate. The woman's drama/dilemma in this model is that she only fits in as a mother. The man-child's drama/dilemma is that he only fits in this model as a son. In Jung's words, this kind of mother is the woman "to whom we were entrusted as children and at the same time were left at her mercy."[38]

Consequently, the hypertrophied mother complex, with its luminous and darker aspect, is at the core of Chilean society: the "holy mother" who provides care and protects, allows anything, and is unconditional in her love, but who also does not let go of the child. Thus, the bonds to home are powerful and the possibility of stepping out into the world is limited. For the child, the motherly bond is placed above friendships; the child stays at home rather than going out into the world; only the family is considered to be reliable, while the role of the community or public space is experienced as something to be mistrusted. Thus, the heroic task of individuation is thwarted. Chile's geographical isolation is brought home to the family level, where the mother's body represents the land with mountains, deserts, ocean, and glaciers that trap the child and prevents it from escaping.

Final Analyses: The Remnants Under the Shadow of Our White, Glistening Mountain Range

It is easy to see how the cultural isolation complex became ingrained in Chilean society. Living in cloistered, insulated geographic conditions resulted in a psychologically isolating experience. In addition to the geography of isolation, Chileans suffered a series of historical traumas, most notably the Conquest and colonization, and much more recently military dictatorship. During the Conquest and colonization, natives and half-breeds suffered exclusion, suspicion, submission, and inferiority. The horrors of the dictatorship brought this back to life generations later, recreating the trauma of the Conquest for a portion of fellow citizens who suffered what their ancestors had endured. This included hiding and suppressing their beliefs and thoughts for fear of being killed, tortured, or losing their loved ones. In addition to the isolation of geography and the traumas of history, a family model centered on a hypertrophied mother complex creates sons that find it extremely difficult to differentiate themselves from their mothers. These same sons tend to give highest priority to the families in which they were raised and especially the bonds they have with their mothers, thus inhibiting their stepping out into the world and relating with their peers.

Geography, history, and a particular style of family life have all contributed to the difficulty we Chileans have relating socially, associating with our peers, and most importantly and above all, being capable of trusting others. We live trapped in this cultural isolation complex with a failure to develop the more positive sides of the polarities of isolated/bonded, mistrust/trust, submission/domination, and inferiority/superiority. Our tendency to identify with the isolated, mistrust, submission, and inferiority sides of these polarities is silently expressed through many of our behaviors, feelings, and beliefs.

It is hard to know the exact role that this cultural complex plays in Chile's development as a country, but as analytical psychologists, we are curious about the question of its unconscious influence on our behavior as Chileans and how we might go about addressing it more consciously. Undoubtedly, the cultural isolation complex affects how we appear both from the outside in, and from the inside out, of the country. For example, from the inside out we perceive ourselves as being hospitable and welcoming to foreigners, which – paradoxically – is the main thing for which we are criticized from the outside in. We are seen by foreigners as a closed, mistrusting society in which it is very difficult to become integrated. A clear manifestation of the difference between how we view ourselves and how others view us can be found in the traditional waltz, "Si vas para Chile," written by Chito Faró, a song that moves all Chileans, particularly when we are traveling abroad. Following are the lyrics to one of its verses and its chorus:

> Should you go to Chile,
> please pass by where my loved one lives.
> It is a tiny and lovely house
> sheltered by the slope of a hill.
> The hamlet is known as Las Condes,
> between the hills and the heavens.
> And if you look down the valley,
> you will see a brook whispering by.
> *The peasants and hamlet dwellers will meet*
>   *you, dear traveler,*
> *and you will see Chileans' love for a friend who is*
>   *a stranger from abroad.*[39]
>   [Author's translation]

This verse is one of the best-remembered in Chilean popular music and is often cited to stress the courteousness Chileans show to foreigners. However, we believe that this verse, rather than expressing reality, expresses instead a profound national desire. We all sing it from the bottom of our hearts because it expresses something we aspire to but cannot achieve, because collectively we have experienced too much abandonment, exclusion, rejection, and abuse. The gap between the security we seek and the insecurity we experience continues to be a wide one. It is far easier for us to identify with the feelings of exclusion in the isolated/bonded polarity, along with an exaggerated desire to be accepted and to establish warm relationships. The dream of every Chilean after years of exclusion and subjugation is to be able to trust others who are different and alien.

Our cultural complex is manifested in a national characteristic that our Latin American neighbors frequently observe. Chileans often use diminutives in their speech, placing emphasis on how people are doing us a favor, even in situations when we are only asking for something to which we are entitled. For example, it is very common while at a restaurant to hear, "Excuse me for bothering you, could I have a small glass of water?" or "Could you bring a little more sugar?" These are ways of making our requests seem smaller and reflect our national wish not to cause a disturbance. We tend to tell ourselves that being gracious about our "small" requests is done out of courtesy when in reality, under the surface, we suffer a huge unconscious inferiority complex, insecurity, and a great longing to be accepted.

The same behavior can be observed along the trust/mistrust spectrum, in which there is a huge need to trust and feel secure. We go to great lengths to show kindness and helpfulness when we trust somebody, and we have many national events in which there are large demonstrations of solidarity, such as the rescue of the 33 miners who were trapped for two months 700 meters underground. Chileans experienced this traumatic event as a heroic act of belief in our nation. Another example is the Teleton, a televised charitable event, the object of which is to collect money for the disabled. The event is one which brings all of Chile together and where we can demonstrate our generosity through the large sums of money we donate. We publicly express our great desire to progress together, but in fact our behavior is more generally governed by a deep suspicion of our neighbors and coworkers.

Perhaps it is time for us Chileans to ask ourselves who we want to be to ourselves, to our fellow citizens, and to the world. Having recently celebrated the Bicentennial of our Independence (1810), we would do well to learn how to begin trusting our neighbors, coworkers, and peers.[40] We would also do well to learn how to include others who are different from us. It is time to begin trusting our neighboring countries without feeling we are superior to them and inferior to Europeans.

Given our geography, our history, and our model of family dynamics, we have learned to suppress and repress anything different or unfamiliar. As Chileans, it is imperative that we become more conscious of our fears of the unknown and the unfamiliar, with the hope that such consciousness might allow us to face these fears and accept diversity and differences as qualities that could foster growth and bring us closer to real integration as a people.

This task of becoming aware of the fact that we are simply one more Latin American country that is neither greater nor lesser than the others would open us up to others. It would make it easier for us to establish positive working relationships with our neighbors at home and abroad. Who we are today has its roots in the past. This is why it would be wise for us to look back at our origins, to look for keys that will help us understand the present, and to develop a vision for the future of Chile as a nation. By considering our identity – our strengths and our complexes – we also address the future.

Notes

1 The Legatum Prosperity Index (2009). Available at www.prosperity.com.
2 Francis Fukuyama, "Social Capital and the Global Economy," *Foreign Affairs*, vol. 74, no. 5 (1995): 89–103.
3 The Legatum Prosperity Index.
4 Encuesta de Cohesión Social en América Latina (2007). Available at www.ecosocialsurvey.org.
5 Universidad Diego Portales (2009). *Participación de Jóvenes*. Available at www.comunicacionyletras.udp.cl/files/Resultados_Encuesta_jovenes_UDP_FEEDBACK.pdf.
6 Ana María Errazuriz, Pilar Cerezeda, José Ignacio Gonzalez, Mireya Gonzalez, María Herniquez, and Reinaldo Rioseco, *Manual de Geografía de Chile* (Santiago: Editorial Andrés Bello, 1998).
7 C.G. Jung, "Sobre la Psicología de lo Inconsciente," in *The Collected Works of C.G. Jung, Vol. 7, Dos Escritos Sobre Psicología Analítica*, trans. R. Fernandez (1943; repr., Madrid: Editorial Trotta, 2007), § 109.
8 Thomas Singer and Samuel L. Kimbles, "Introduction," to *The Cultural Complex: Contemporary Jungian Perspectives on Psyche and Society*, eds. Thomas Singer and Samuel L. Kimbles (New York: Routledge, 2004).

9 Sonia Montecinos, *Madres y Huachos. Alegorías del Mestizaje Chileno* (Santiago: Catalonia, 1991), p. 45.
10 Jorge Larrain, *Identidad Chilena* (Santiago: LOM Ediciones, 2001).
11 Ibid., p. 237.
12 Ibid.
13 Jorge Gissi, "Identidad, Carácter Social y Cultura Latinoamericana," *Estudios Sociales*, no. 33 (1982).
14 Larrain, *Identidad Chilena*, p. 85. The beginning of the Chilean War of Independence from Spain was on September 18, 1810. This is when the First Government Assembly (Primera Junta de Gobierno) took place, and it is the date that is traditionally celebrated as the Chilean independence day. The War of Independence lasted until 1826, when the last Spanish troops surrendered. The Declaration of Independence was on February 12, 1818.
15 War between Chile and the Peru – Bolivian Confederation.
16 Larrain, *Identidad Chilena*, p. 157.
17 Jorge Larrain, "Identidad Chilena y El Bicentenario," *Estudios Públicos*, no. 120 (Spring 2010): 5–30.
18 Ibid.
19 L.H. Errazuriz, *Dictadura Militar en Chile. Antecedentes del Golpe Estético-Cultural*, 2008, p. 146. Available at http://cursos.puc.cl/ieu20051/almacen/1305772712_mmonteal_sec1_pos0.pdf.
20 Errazuriz, *Dictadura Militar en Chile*, p. 139.
21 See José Juaquin Brunner, *La Cultura Autoritaria en Chile* (Santiago: FLACSO, 1981).
22 The transition to democracy began on March 11, 1990, when Pinochet handed over power to the democratically elected president Patricio Aylwin. This ended the dictatorship that began in 1973 with a coup d'état. Nevertheless, there is an ongoing debate between scholars as to whether or not the transition to democracy has actually been completed.
23 Larrain, *Identidad Chilena y El Bicentenario*.
24 Ibid., p. 25.
25 Tironi, in Larrain, *Identidad Chilena y El Bicentenario*, p. 172.
26 Encuesta Nacional Bicentenario Universidad Católica-Adimark, *Los Chilenos del Bicentenario* (Santiago: Ediciones Universidad Católica de Chile, 2010).
27 Ibid., p. 38.
28 Ibid.
29 C.G. Jung, "Los Aspectos Psicológicos del Arquetipo de la Madre," in *The Collected Works of C.G. Jung, Vol. 9i, Los Arquetipos y Lo Inconsciente Colectivo*, trans. C. Gauger (1954; repr., Madrid: Editorial Trotta, 2002).
30 Ibid., p. 172.
31 Ibid., p. 167.
32 Encuesta Nacional Bicentenario Universidad Católica-Adimark, *Los Chilenos del Bicentenario*, p. 60.
33 Montecinos, *Madres y Huachos*, p. 39.
34 Ibid., p. 48.
35 The Arauco War was a long-running conflict between la Capitanía Genral de Chile, which belonged to the Spanish Empire, and the Mapuche people. The conflict began in 1536 and lasted until 1818, when Chile declared its independence. The conflict did not cease after the independence of Chile. This new phase of the war which now involved the Republic of Chile and the Mapuche people came to be known as the "Araucanía Pacification." The result was the occupation of the Araucania territory by military invasion, a process that took place between 1861 and 1883.
36 Ibid., p. 54.

37 Gonzalo Vial, *Chile Cinco Siglos de Historia* (Santiago: Editorial Zigzag, 2009), p. 517.
38 Jung, "Los Aspectos Psicológicos del Arquetipo de la Madre," p. 172.
39 Chito Faró, "Si Vas Para Chile," 1942. Available at www.musicapopular.cl/3.0/index2.php?op=Artista&id=1079.
40 The process of independence began with the establishment of the first national government ("Junta de Gobierno") on September 18, 1810, and finally culminated with the signing of a Declaration of Independence in 1818.

Colombia

Chapter 7

In the Shadow of the Virgin Mary

María Claudia Munévar

One day in 1999, the clock was about to strike six o'clock in the afternoon. I was standing at my window, holding my baby in my arms, looking down at the school in front of the apartment building in Bogotá, Colombia, where we had recently moved. It was a seven-square-meter window on the fourth floor which did not yet have curtains and which placed me about ten meters from the gate of the school. This school was for the children of wealthy parents who had academic issues and had been expelled from different institutions around the city. It gave them the opportunity of completing two grades in one year.

I was just admiring how beautiful the mountains looked in the distance, when I saw two young boys around 16 years old walking on the sidewalk towards the school. Simultaneously, a motorcycle stopped at the school gate, and a teenager around 16 or 17 years old jumped off. He calmly walked up behind one of the two boys I had been watching, shot him, and then sauntered back to his motorcycle, got on, and drove off as if nothing had happened. Everyone at the school started screaming and ran inside for cover, except for the victim of the shooting. He took some steps forward, looking for the door of the school, and then turned to gaze up in my direction. He soon fell and, after trying unsuccessfully to get up a couple of times, died.

I remained at the window, petrified. My body, my psyche, my instincts were paralyzed. Neither my survival nor my protective instincts were activated. I continued standing there, with my baby in my arms and my three-year-old daughter alone in the bedroom.

The event that I am narrating took less than a minute, but for me time stopped. I stayed frozen at my spot at the window until after the boy died and the crowd in the schoolyard began to react to the shooting. Only then was I able to acknowledge what I had seen. I hugged my baby tightly and ran to the other room to see if my daughter had seen the shooting too. Fortunately, she had not.

I froze because I had seen a picture of horror or a demon. But even more unsettling was to realize, in trying to make sense of what I had witnessed, that this demon was not only part of my history but of the history of the Colombian people.

DOI: 10.4324/9781003400820-12

Development of the Complex

During its colonization period, which took place between 1550 and 1810, Colombia suffered deep wounds generated by the trauma inflicted upon it over the course of many years. Thousands of people were deceived, abused, exiled from their territories, and uprooted from their traditions by the colonizers; thousands of women were abducted and sexually harassed by foreigners, while their own men – their spouses, fathers, brothers, and sons – could do nothing to protect them. These women gave birth to incalculable numbers of children without fathers because the men who had impregnated them did not want to parent their offspring.

This experience left in the Colombian people a trauma that not only annihilated most of the pre-colonial Colombian culture and claimed untold lives, but also broke the sense of community, creating a cultural complex based on power imposed by force from the outside and solely for the colonizers' own benefit. We were robbed, stripped, humiliated, harassed, abused, and excluded from our own land by others that came from abroad. Our ancestors learned through their repeated exposure to violence that the personal power needed to accomplish anything for themselves or their community was not based on the ability to influence others through respect and authority. Rather, influencing others and achieving personal goals can best be accomplished through manipulation, force, and violence.

When a human being's basic dignity is degraded and he or she feels used by others for their own welfare and profit, it can be difficult for this person to value himself or herself or others. Thus, the abused learns to become the abuser. The abused, when first violated, is initially taken by surprise and has a natural wish/expectation to be protected or rescued. However, when he realizes over time that he will not be protected or rescued, and that, on the contrary, he will continue to be victimized, he represses or splits off from consciousness that part of his psyche that is wounded. He makes way for a new part of himself to develop, one that learns to seize power through force, fueled with all the rage and pain that lives within himself as a victim. He learns to do anything to protect himself and to recover the control he lost when he was victimized.

Thus, a cultural complex, which has been born out of the accrual of repetitive experiences and memories throughout our history, continues to be fed with new violence, generating new traumatic events. And this, in turn, continues to fuel internal fragmentation and external projections. The purpose of this paper is to show how the phenomenon of *sicariato* is a manifestation of this complex. *Sicariato* comes from the word *sicario*, which translates into English as "hired assassin." It refers to the act of hiring and training young people who come from vulnerable communities to become killers for hire. In the act of *sicariato*, the pain, humiliation, helplessness, and abandonment that began during colonial times continues unabated, yet now it is not imposed by foreigners, but by ourselves.

At the time I witnessed the murder of the young boy from my apartment window, I was just finishing my master's degree in ethics and human rights. In an almost literary way, I had been studying for the previous year and a half national and international treaties setting forth individual and collective rights.

In observing the shooting, I found myself caught in a terrible irony that weighed on me heavily – on the one hand, I was witness to the murder of an innocent boy and, on the other hand, in a few short months I was to present my thesis on the topic of "The Right of Children to Care and Love: A Guarantee of Human Dignity and Respect for Human Rights" ("El derecho de los niños al cuidado y al amor: garante de la dignidad humana y del respeto por los derechos humanos"). My objective in the thesis was to emphasize the sense of dignity and humanity that underlies and supports children's rights to care and love. I had analyzed how the failure to guarantee these fundamental rights is one of the main causes of a cycle of violence that for many years has prevented Colombians from being able to live together peacefully.[1]

Now, 12 years later, I understand how this problem is part of a bigger one: a particular cultural complex that affects Colombian people. In this chapter, I want to show how this cultural complex has permeated the collective and individual psyche of my fellow countrymen. The complex is activated in vulnerable groups who suffer from exclusion in the Colombian society. For diverse reasons, many individuals and groups of people are marginalized and, for all practical purposes, do not have a place in mainstream society. For the most part, this marginalization is not done consciously, but happens subtly, in unnamed and unplanned ways.

There are groups of people whose rights have been taken away or who never had certain rights in the first place. They wander around full of contradictory feelings, oscillating between desires for acknowledgment, approval, and a sense of belonging to feelings of deep hatred, resentment, and a desire for revenge against those who have excluded them. As a result, these individuals end up becoming shadows of the social order. This cultural complex has at least two poles: victim and perpetrator. The very same children who have been displaced, abandoned victims become the perpetrators, the *sicarios*, of acts of violence against those who are viewed as holding/abusing power, and they in turn become victims of the *sicarios*. Both poles feed this perverse, destructive relationship which is driven by the complex, repeating itself over and over again in the same collective behaviors and emotions that arise from exclusion, abandonment, and humiliation, which turn into a thirst for vengeance and the desire to seize power and fulfill other needs.

The World of *Sicariato*

It is in the context of this cultural complex that the phenomenon of *sicariato* emerged in Colombia. The word refers to young people from marginalized areas, most without a father figure, that are hired by others to hurt or kill someone for a few Colombian pesos. Typically, these young hired killers cross themselves before the image of the Virgin Mary before they commit their crimes, and often their own mothers, for whom they have assumed the role of protective male since an early age, serve as their silent accomplices.

Our society is not able to grasp that the phenomenon of *sicariato* is a manifestation of a cultural complex. Rather, society beholds *sicariato* in a state of terror, remaining frozen as I was when I witnessed the shooting I described earlier. Or it tries to ignore or get rid of this phenomenon with ineffective controls as a way of denying it, keeping it at a distance. Then, another murder occurs. The cycle begins anew. Each time, our society seems surprised that it has happened again; we collectively cross ourselves as if the event were a foreign demon, not a cultural complex whose strength depends on society's continued unconsciousness of what is really happening psychologically.

The *sicariato* phenomenon in Colombia has taken many lives throughout the years, not only the lives of the people who are killed, but also the lives of the children and teenagers who, by entering into this life as hired assassins, condemn themselves. It is a pathological cultural complex that fosters putting a price on human lives. It is a complex that has grown in strength through years of oversight and abandonment, of disregard and exclusion. It announces itself with the horror and cruelty of each new shot fired. It remains untreated and untreatable as a silent disease. The government argues over statistics about the increase or decrease of *sicariato* murders each year. And people keep waiting for a miracle that will make it disappear someday. What is it in our society that facilitates this dissociation between fact and reality? What keeps us from inquiring and learning about the meaning of *sicariato* for our culture and how we might address it?

After a period of violence in Colombia in the 1950s caused by the expropriation of land through the violent expulsion of peasants and the fierce confrontation between the Liberal and Conservative parties, people from the countryside sought refuge in the hillsides of cities such as Medellin and Bogotá. When this happened, the government did little to protect these people and was often even an accomplice in the abuse of internal migrants from rural areas. Nevertheless, people filled with dreams of a peaceful and better life continued to migrate to the cities. What they found when they arrived were few opportunities for work or establishing a comfortable lifestyle for themselves. Soon, they lived in such poor conditions that they could not satisfy their basic needs.

From the beginning, they were seen and treated as another excluded group. The rest of society did not try to help them solve their basic educational, health, or other emotional and recreational needs, which are essential for the healthy development of any human being. Rather, they were viewed as an inexpensive labor force, willing to work in whatever kind of job was offered. Their traditions and their old lifestyle slowly disappeared, as well as their dreams of a better life for themselves and their children, away from the violence in the countryside. Later, in the early 1980s, armed groups such as the M-19 (Movement April 19th) and the EPL (People's Liberation Army) provided military training to young people in these poor neighborhoods during the peace negotiation process with then president Belisario Betancur, which later failed. These rebel groups saw a source of potential followers in the children of these rural immigrants and trained them as little soldiers. However, after the breakdown of the negotiations and the dismantlement of the settlements, the guerrillas left the children/soldiers behind, unprotected and exposed to many risks. At the same time, drug-trafficking, which started around 1975, was booming and offered the promise of an easy way to obtain a better life. Like the rebel groups before them, drug traffickers saw in these young people trained for fighting a useful resource for the drug war they were initiating, and the young people saw in the drug traffickers the promise of a life of extravagance and the opportunity to take the law into their own hands.

At that time (the early and mid-eighties), drug traffickers were viewed with fear and respect. They were recognized as both murderers and benefactors, especially among groups living in marginal neighborhoods. Among the drug traffickers, there were some who had no education or normal job opportunities but who had nevertheless reached the sky's limit: they had everything, and they could do anything. Many of them were seen as heroes in their own neighborhoods, where they inspired loyalty and devotion. They were admired by women and surrounded by a protective circle that was willing to defend them with their own lives.

Since the murder of the Colombian justice minister Rodrigo Lara Bonilla by two 17-year-old men on a motorcycle, on April 30, 1984, it became obvious that drug trafficking had infiltrated the highest political class in Colombia. Lara Bonilla had started an open fight against drug trafficking and contested Pablo Escobar's position as alternate congressman by proving his involvement with drug cartels. After ordering the assassination of Lara Bonilla, Escobar became one of the most feared drug dealers in Colombia. Even more appalling than the extent to which drug trafficking had penetrated every class in Colombia was the fact that Colombian children and teenagers from marginal parts of our society were being hired and trained as *sicarios* or hired assassins.

By 1999, when I witnessed the shooting described at the beginning of this paper, it was publicly acknowledged that there were places in Medellin, Colombia, where young people were trained to be assassins. These places were called *escuelas de sicarios* and were located in the very communities in which these children were raised and where life was going on as usual.[2]

Because this Colombian cultural complex originates in multiple traumas over a long period of time, it is now simply part of our cultural life and repeats itself in any new situation in which our people feel excluded, humiliated, or deprived. The young people in these conditions live without adult figures that are able to provide the care and protection that they need. It is easy for them to become entangled in the complex of victim/perpetrator. They start as victims, but they become perpetrators by taking the power of life and death into their own hands. They try to achieve with violence what they have not been given or been able to provide for themselves. They become the perpetrator, even if this leads to their own death. For a while, these young people who kill to survive become someone; they begin to obtain recognition and temporarily convert their hopelessness into power. We know from psychology that the more complexes are dissociated, the stronger they get. They are like magnets attracting whatever nourishes them. In this case, they are nourished by death and violence.

The actions of *sicarios* are irrational and nonsensical. They confront us with the horror of an unconscious complex. When I was brutally confronted by witnessing the murder, I experienced a surprising emotional ambiguity because I was unable to see the darkness or even the evil in the teenager who was shooting. I wondered what had happened along the way to make that kid into a cold murderer who used a gun to kill another boy his own age. Was the *sicario* cared for and protected with dignity by adults? Was he seen and treated as a valuable member of society? The answers to these questions are obviously "No." *Sicarios* come from vulnerable communities where they are used by others to carry out their misdeeds. I was awakened to the shadowy realization that something very dark is moving in our society and that it is not only linked to these young boys or to those who use them to commit crimes.

This Colombian complex has claimed many victims. I witnessed one and, in trying to understand it, came to the realization that one teenager was murdered and another one, the one hired to execute him, gave his future away. The truth is that in the moment hired assassins use their weapons to murder others, they lose their freedom. Their will is no longer their own. Their survival instinct has been perverted so it now serves death. Their instinct for creativity now serves an auto-destructive compulsion. Jung described the five instincts as "self-preservation, sexuality, activity, reflection, and creativity."[3] Jung explained that the creative instinct can also lead to destruction. It can activate archetypal defenses, which in the case of these young people can be very primitive and dangerous to them because of their relative lack of ego development. Weisstub and Galili-Weisstub note that trauma has an impact on the development of the individual's normal psychological defenses:

> Trauma to an autonomously functioning ego with more differentiated defenses has a different significance than trauma to a relatively undifferentiated and unprotected psyche. In the undifferentiated psyche, the significance of archetypal defenses is relatively greater. When the ego is not developed, the damage is more catastrophic. The psychic defenses, such as splitting and projective identification, are more primitive and archaic. The inner world is full of rage and violent aggression, which is split off or dissociated into fantasies or archetypal forms, which threaten to turn against the self and others. There is not an adequate ego to deal with the rage or with the split-off forms which are invested with aggressive, destructive energies. The self is constellated in a basically negative way and does not provide positive guidance.[4]

Identification With the Image of the Hero

Part of the problem is that *sicarios* achieve a new status in their own communities once they become hired assassins. These young boys see themselves, and are seen, as rescuers and heroes, because they can take care of themselves as well as their mothers, their girlfriends, and their loyal friends or *parceros*.[5] But while they clearly know how many thousands of pesos they will get for their crime, are they aware of the emotional price that they also will pay for it? The fact is that the momentary recognition they achieve is as insignificant as the amount they charge for a killing. For a brief time, they are seen as heroes. In their communities, they are admired by the younger children, envied by their peers, and respected by the older ones. But *sicarios* seem oblivious to the dark, destructive force that is moving through them.

Sicarios seem to identify with an aspect of the hero myth, specifically with the first stage of it where the hero is an embodiment of the child hero archetype. However, the hero myth does not develop further in the *sicario*. He does not go on to bravely confront challenges that might lead to more consciousness but rather acts unconsciously, playing out the destructive shadow of the collective with his acts only giving his life meaning for only a short time. He does not acquire new knowledge but instead experiences fragmentation and suffering. He does not connect with that aspect of the hero who, in time, has a living connection to the Self. Though the hired assassin may be trying to find within himself the power of the hero to rescue himself from poverty and helplessness, he fails and is swallowed by the collective shadow. What inner resources do the hired assassins have for facing and integrating the unconscious complex that is driving their behavior? What level of conscious development have they acquired that would allow them to distance themselves from the dark energies that come from the collective shadow?

The children and teenagers who become *sicarios* grow up in conditions of extreme deprivation. They are barely able to survive. Even as the country overall is growing economically, becoming more productive and attracting investors, there is a forgotten part of the population that is unseen, unrecognized, and unintegrated into the prospering society. And it is from this invisible population that the *sicarios* come from. As the larger cities attract tourists who can enjoy all the beautiful and interesting things that Colombia has to offer, the ugly side is forgotten as if it belongs to someone else.

In Colombia, the population is categorized socioeconomically by the National Statistics Administrative Department (DANE) into one of six categories, classifying housing according to poverty levels, public utility services, and location. Those living at level 6 enjoy a lifestyle that meets all the conditions of a decent life; those living at levels 1 or 2, which includes most of the population, can barely fulfill their basic needs. Below these levels, there are some people who live in extreme poverty and cannot even find food. This last group is categorized as living in a "vulnerable" situation.

According to the 22nd edition of the Spanish dictionary from *La Real Academia Española*, "vulnerable" is defined as "That which can be physically or morally wounded or hurt."[6] Based upon this definition, vulnerability exists in relation to others. *Sicarios* come from and belong to vulnerable communities in Colombia. Society ignores them and the violence they act out, which, in fact, is precipitated by a split-off and unconscious aspect of the collective, cultural psyche. The horror created by *sicariato* remains "outside." Society says that this horror belongs to "them." As long as society does not acknowledge that this situation emerges from its own collective, cultural unconscious, it increases the autonomy of the cultural complex. The collective maintains the feeling of being in control and protected, ignoring the fact that this huge collective shadow grows and threatens life on a daily basis. The collective plays an oppressive role towards people such as *sicarios* by abandoning them to the world of the unconscious.

Those who eventually become hired assassins often first work in groups that provide security to drug traffickers. They progress to offering similar services to more organized criminal groups and then, eventually, they begin to freelance. Even today they kill one another, not for money, but to prove their strength and power to each other and to defend conquered territories. The proliferation of gangs is out of control. The past simply seems to repeat itself endlessly. The cultural complex determines attitudes, behaviors, relationships, one's view of oneself, and one's view of life. Meanwhile, the continuous exclusion and segregation of groups of impoverished people offers fertile ground for the kind of split-off barbarism that gives birth to the *sicarios*. Why are these young people unknown until they become identified as *sicarios*? While growing up, those in risk of becoming *sicarios* develop an identity that has special characteristics related to their way of talking, dressing, mixing with people, and having fun. Their manner of perceiving the world and themselves is expressed through their behavior and attitude. They wear particular accessories such as baseball caps, jewelry, scapulars, sneakers, and ride motorcycles. They have a special language that uses code words which identify them to one another. They close neighborhood streets to host extravagant parties that offer a striking contrast with the surrounding poverty. Society does not pay attention to these special meanings and, in general, denies the whole situation until something terrible happens again. Then it feels attacked and takes a defensive position.

Something bursts inside young hired killers when they murder someone. Although they might unconsciously identify with the child hero archetype by setting out to accomplish a difficult task, they remain trapped in an unconscious state that reflects a more primitive, barbaric stage described by Jung as the trickster.[7]

The Meaning of the Virgin Mary

Sicarios take drugs frequently and spend what they have earned for killing someone at a party that goes on for days, as if this could calm their anguish and extinguish their connection to what they have done. In this way, they celebrate the tragedy of their life, of their action, and what it represents for the collective.

They try to lessen the unbearable despair and anxiety that causes them to act impulsively and compulsively by invoking the image of the Virgin Mary. The phenomenon of *sicariato*, in fact, has been linked since its beginning to the Virgin Mary, represented by the image of María Auxiliadora (Mary Help of Christians), her most popular image in Medellín. The *sicarios* go to her for protection and entrust to her the burden of their crimes, which is why María Auxiliadora also has been called "Our Lady of the Assassins."[8]

In legends and stories, the Virgin Mary is viewed as a good mother, capable of giving her children what nobody else can. She receives human beings without judging them or expecting them to be free from sin. Even though the Virgin's value has not always been so honored by the Church historically, she has gained institutional recognition in recent times. The devotion and fervor expressed in her name has given her enormous importance to those who worship her. The Virgin Mary, as one of the many embodiments of the Great Mother archetype, responds to the need of people to feel protected and accepted despite their human weaknesses.

For the young killers, the Virgin seems always willing to shelter them and to witness the repeated sacrifice of her son(s). For that reason, *sicarios* usually wear *camándulas*, a kind of rosary around their necks. They pray, go to mass, and bless their bullets. They need to believe in something; they need to feel protected. The archetype of the Great Mother, embodied in the image of the Virgin Mary in Colombian culture, is described by Erich Neumann as acting as a container: "sheltering needy mankind beneath her outstretched cloaks."[9] These young men seem to seek, in the last minute of their destructive act, something sacred or divine, which is contained in the image of Holy Mary.

The hired assassins' devotion to the Virgin Mary helps them justify their actions and presumably guarantees their eternal salvation and the privilege of the beatitudes. In that way, one can think of the *sicarios* as acting *in the shadow of the Virgin Mary*. She takes anyone in as one of her children. Somewhere in the collective unconscious, there seems to be an archetypal figure that is capable of holding all these atrocities.

There are thousands of children who live in the marginal neighborhoods of Colombia. Their dignity, which one would hope would be a birthright of all children, is not acknowledged. Instead, some of these dispossessed children find some kind of recognition in their communities by becoming hired assassins. Death turns into a profitable business, and illegality becomes a way to achieve some economic reward.

The fragmented physical environments of these impoverished communities become a reflection of the inner worlds of its inhabitants. Human degradation spreads. Hope fades away, and the cultural complex takes new lives with it. Fear, hatred, and violence result in the transgression of conventional collective values and reveal the sinister side of Colombian reality, where vulnerable children are used by criminal minds. These minds are able to take advantage of the children because the only figure available to them as an imaginary protector is the Virgin Mary.

Facing the Complex

What happens to the vulnerability and innocence of a child who has lived in adversity, when their daily experience exposes them to some of the most sordid aspects of human nature? They will try to protect themselves and gain some control, and they will try to satisfy their uncared-for needs. Donald Kalsched talks about trauma by describing it as follows:

> Trauma is about pain so "utter" that it swallows up normal developmental processes, leaving an "abyss" or "basic fault" between self and world outwardly

and ego and Self inwardly. Fortunately, the story does not end with this cleavage because the human psyche has enormous self-curative powers.[10]

Colombian history was fractured in the Conquest by trauma. These young men who have become hired assassins have entered into and remained embedded in a traumatic experience that recreates the trauma of the Conquest while fragmenting their own history. As a country, we have continued to suffer trauma that has been ignored, justified, and addressed with statistics. Our traumatic history has been marked by a violence that not only damages us psychologically but has made it difficult for us to realize the enormous potential resources we have as a people and country.

Rafael Lopez Pedraza has said that "the hero and virgin are predominant elements in our myths, cults and psychology . . . from a religious, ethnic and linguistic point of view, it can be said that this is a basic level of our identity."[11] We might hope that the unconscious identification of the *sicario* with an aspect of the hero archetype and his regression in pursuit of nurturing care from the Virgin Mary might lead in time to a progressive movement in the collective psyche. Otherwise the psychic balance of individuals and of our society is in great peril.

The language that *sicarios* use is instructive as a window into their psychology. When talking about what they do, the *sicarios* use a vocabulary that infantilizes and/or makes less cruel their own violence. It is also a way of avoiding the mention of death. They refer to the victim as "*muñeco*" (dummy); the act of killing is called "*acostar, quebrar*, or *tumbar*" (to lay down, crush, tumble); the weapon is called "*fierro*" (burner); the state of being dead is called "*frio*" (being cold); the million pesos they earn is called "*melon*" (melon); the person who hired them is "*patron*" (boss); the act of shooting is "*sonar*" (whack); if they are killed or arrested, it is called "*perder el año*" (to flunk); when they show skill and loyalty, it is referred to as "*probar finura*" (to be crisp); finally, when they die they call it "*viajar*" (to take a trip).[12] This use of language, inventive in its own way, suggests that the conscious mind of the *sicario* is working hard to protect him from the reality of his actions, just as the collective seems to protect itself from recognizing the reality of its complicity in perpetuating a cultural complex grounded in humiliation and revenge.

All of this suggests that as a society, Colombia needs to focus its attention on the children and teenagers from vulnerable populations at a much earlier age, rather than judging them or fearing them later after they have entered the life of the *sicario*. These young people are part of our society and are expressions of its ills and failures. The current response to the situation is to send the hired assassins to prison or to a detention center. Sometimes, they are sent back to their families. But what do these actions accomplish when the murders have already happened? Is it really a solution to send them to jail or to set them free? The truth is that we honestly do not know what to do. State representatives turn to laws and regulations that do not address the magnitude of the problem. So *sicariato* continues unabated, and the criminal organizations continue to use these young people with relative impunity since they cannot be prosecuted as adults under the law. To make matters worse, some judges have been linked to the very criminal organizations that hire *sicarios* and have helped criminals go unpunished.

The development of a vulnerable child who is a victim of economic and cultural poverty into a hired assassin represents a remarkable journey from victim to executioner in a short period of time. The lesson these youngsters learn is that the strongest person prevails. Many of them are seen in their communities as redeemers and, after some time, everyone fears them because they have the power to decide who lives or dies. In time, their aggressiveness and capacity for the violent harming of others is no longer relegated to their "business" deals; rather their learned aggression becomes a reflex response to any kind of situation or gesture perceived as a challenge. They begin to fight over territory, making their communities even more insecure zones for the inhabitants and for the *sicarios*. The paradox is that this insecurity grows out of their initial desire to feel secure. As time goes by, the *sicarios* forget why they kill. Death just walks beside them, sometimes with a cold-blooded cruelty that is horrifying. Finally, death ends up in front of them rather than walking by their side.

The *sicariato* phenomenon is one of the bleakest manifestations of a Colombian cultural complex. These children mature precociously, driven by the instinct to survive. The solution to this horrific problem may occur when Colombia decides to help and shelter these vulnerable communities that the *sicarios* come from and give them a real place in our society. Otherwise, the darkness that they carry for the collective persists in the form of continuing destruction and self-mutilation. These young killers were children once, and if we cannot understand why they live, maybe we can try to understand why they die. Children around these young killers see, admire, and imitate them. We need to offer those who would emulate the *sicario* the possibility of seeing their lives as having some sort of potential other than becoming hired assassins.

The Colombian population needs to be able to look inward to recognize that this cultural complex belongs to the whole country and not just to the marginalized communities that spawn the *sicario*. We have created several programs in our more marginalized communities which are aimed at children and their families to develop libraries and academic scholarships with the purpose of taking these future teenagers away from violence. But for society as a whole, it would serve us well to also focus on increasing our own awareness about our cultural complex of victim and perpetrator, which has a long and repetitive history in our traumatized country.

Notes

1 María Claudia Munévar, *El derecho de los niños al cuidado y al amor: garante de la dignidad humana y del respeto por los derechos humanos* (Unpublished M.A. thesis, Cali: Universidad del Valle, 2000), pp. 7–8.
2 Training facilities that existed during several years in the municipality of Sabaneta, near Medellín.
3 C.G. Jung, "Psychological Factors Determining Human Behavior," in *The Collected Works of C.G. Jung, Vol. 8, The Structure and Dynamics of the Psyche*, trans. R.F.C. Hull (New York: Bollingen Foundation, 1960), §§ 237–241, § 245.

4 Eli Weisstub and Esti Galili-Weisstub, "Collective Trauma and Cultural Complexes," in *The Cultural Complex*, eds. Thomas Singer and Samuel L. Kimbles (New York: Routledge, 2004), p. 158.
5 Closest friends, often considered part of the family.
6 Real Academia Española, *Diccionario de la Lengua Española, Vigésima Segunda Edición*, vol. 10 (Alcala: Real Academia Española, 2001), p. 1576.
7 C.G. Jung, "On the Psychology of the Trickster-Figure," in *The Collected Works of C.G. Jung, Vol. 9i, The Archetypes and the Collective Unconscious*, trans. R.F.C. Hull (Princeton: Princeton University Press, 1959), § 465.
8 Fernando Vallejo, *La virgen de los sicarios* (Bogota: Alfaguara, 1994).
9 Erich Neumann, *The Great Mother: An Analysis of the Archetype* (New York: Princeton University Press, 1963), p. 325.
10 Donald E. Kalsched, "Working with Trauma in Analysis," in *Jungian Psychoanalysis*, ed. Murray Stein (Chicago: Open Court, 2010), p. 281.
11 Rafael Lopez Pedraza, *Sobre Héroes y Poetas* (Caracas: Festina Lente, 2002), p. 23, p. 31.
12 Alonso Salazar Jaramillo, *No nacimos pa semilla: la cultura de las bandas juveniles de Medellín* (Bogota: Cinep, 1990), pp. 213–223.

Mexico

DOI: 10.4324/9781003400820-13

Chapter 8

The Right to Exist
Mexico's Spiritual Colonization

Jacqueline Gerson

Living in Mexico for most of my life, I have come to appreciate different things about this country to which both of my parents immigrated when they were quite young. I was born in Mexico, a land that seemed very remote and foreign to my family and its history. I was raised in Mexico in the old European Jewish tradition, while simultaneously learning to speak Spanish, eat Mexican food, deeply admire Mexican art about which my mother taught me, and most importantly, to love Mexico.

I remember my parents stressing the value of an education from earliest childhood. In addition, punctuality, commitment, giving one's word to do something, and by all means, doing it on time, were principles I was taught. But these strongly emphasized values did not seem to carry much weight for those around me. My nanny Mercedes, a round *mestizo* woman with strong indigenous traits, would promise to come back from her vacation on a certain day, but more often than not, she would arrive a few days later. Not only that, but when she took her day off to rest and visit her mother, usually on Sundays, she frequently did not return on Monday morning, as she had promised to do. Instead, she would arrive Monday night or even on Tuesday. When she finally came back, my mother would reprimand her for being late. Every time this happened, a similar exchange took place. When my mother voiced her frustration and annoyance with Mercedes, Mercedes either muttered an excuse or, more likely, kept quiet as my mother yet again asked her to return when she said she would. As a child, and not in charge of a home, I somehow knew that this was my nanny's way, and that it would happen again and again – as it predictably did. I had a deep connection to my nanny; I knew she loved me as I loved her, and I would embrace her every time I saw her returning home to us.

Growing up, I lost that wise connection children have of relating to the other, to the newness in life. I became an adult, living in Mexico and finding myself in deep distress over what I learned to be a common trait in Mexican people: the uncertainty that what is said, or promised, will ever match what actually takes place, with the inevitable reaction to this lack of follow-through being one that is soaked in emotion, of frustration and disruption.

This pattern can be seen in different ways. For example, when trying to understand the word *mañana*, which literally means "tomorrow," one must adopt its

DOI: 10.4324/9781003400820-14

native, rather than literal, meaning. In Mexico, it is a commonly given answer when things aren't ready when they are supposed to be or commitments are not fulfilled as was agreed upon. *Mañana* must be understood to mean nothing more specific than "sometime in the future, hopefully." To not understand this basic reality of Mexican life can feel, at best, naïve.

Another clear example of the discrepancy between what is said and what is done can be particularly apparent on Monday mornings, as it happened with my nanny. It is a day that is difficult for workers to arrive on time. This phenomenon has become so common here in Mexico that Mondays have been baptized teasingly as "Saint Monday," meaning that not showing up to work on Monday has become a sacred practice, enacted on an individual basis, as needed, but so frequently repeated that it almost feels like our way of life.

On one of these Monday mornings I got ready for the plumber to arrive at my home to fix a pipe that had broken and was about to flood my kitchen. I had called him and described the situation, and he had kindly and empathically promised me that he would arrive early Monday morning. I myself had a full day of patients at my office, plus an early emergency, and was counting on this worker to appear so that I could leave my house on time and do my own work. As I was waiting, I felt not only the craziness of frantic modern life but my old European upbringing demanding punctuality and follow-through on commitments made, in the plumber's work and certainly in my own. He never arrived.

That particular Monday morning, in the midst of my experience of frustration, impotence, and anger, I also had a glimpse of my childhood wisdom: that this is the way it is in Mexico, and it has been so for years and years. I remembered this same situation recurring in all kinds of different instances since I was a child! I also remembered being able to embrace my nanny, even when she came home late on Mondays, even though anxiously expecting her and wishing for her timely return myself. Immersed in this experience, I began to think of these kinds of events as part of Mexican reality, as part of the Mexican psyche. It was on that morning that this paper was born.

I began thinking that this common Mexican trait is curiously connected to how courteous, pleasant, and warm Mexicans are towards people. When addressing a Mexican, a *mestizo* (Mexicans are the result of the mixture of Spanish and indigenous blood), to ask for some type of service, information, or even for an invitation, one will most likely get a helpful, kind, and accepting response. One will very seldom hear "no" for an answer; rather, Mexican people agree, accept, and verbally assent to whatever the other is asking for, wanting, or needing.

One can never tell what will really take place afterwards, or if the agreed-upon request will be fulfilled at all. In relating to the other, no matter what the socio-economical level or cultural class, one seldom hears sentences that are direct and clear. On the contrary, answers and opinions, when given, are ambiguous or contradictory, but nonetheless nice, kind, and good-spirited. Many times, responses are affirmative to what the other is stating in an interrogative mode. Silence is another common answer – one that doesn't mean "yes," doesn't mean "no," but includes both, and at times could mean neither.

This kind of behavior that characterizes the *mestizo* people not only makes communication difficult but, at times, incomprehensible. One doesn't know what to expect. Because of this common response, Mexicans have been judged in a simplistic and superficial way as not being smart enough, as being irresponsible, not committed, lazy, even liars – not to mention other derogatory adjectives.

I believe that this particular trait in the *mestizo* people has two polarities: one making promises that are not kept, and the other demanding something that is wanted, needed, presumably agreed upon, and expected to take place. These polarities "foster the creation of 'primitive self care systems,'" an idea developed by Donald Kalsched, that paradoxically work against the self.[1] I feel that a similar mechanism creates, in an entire society, a cultural complex in which the *mestizo* people identify with being the victims, even though they also unconsciously act out the aggressor role. This complex "perpetuates an archetypal field in which the culture's wholeness is repeatedly conquered."[2] This is a phenomenon to be understood

> in the light of the psychology advanced by Tom Singer and Sam Kimbles ... [as] a cultural complex, that is, a complex in the Mexican psyche that operates not only on a personal level, but at a collective level too. It has the power to possess any Mexican since it operates throughout our population, arising as it does out of the very essence of the Mexican culture.[3]

It is an impressive equation when two people facing each other act out the cultural complex. One person is wholeheartedly manifesting his or her need for work that represents the other's field of expertise and on which the expert depends for his living. I heard the plumber respond to my request to fix a broken pipe of water – "I will be in your house Monday morning, for sure, don't worry" – while sensing a different agenda that I know operates in every Mexican mind. This agenda, while vastly differing in specifics from person to person, shares one common theme: the full meaning of an exchange does not accurately correspond to the actual words that are spoken. There is another, hidden agenda. "I will come to your home Monday" means "If I need to say this now, I will say it, since clearly, this is what is expected, but who knows if it will happen."

I wondered, what is the "other agenda" that is being honored? There must be another agenda that is operating, that corresponds to a different way of measuring time, of understanding commitment and relationship – established values – above all, an agenda that serves other gods and that, unknowingly, *mestizo* people are venerating. This unspoken, unacknowledged agenda imposes itself and is enacted with no compassion for the other, or for the *mestizos* themselves, who are severely judged, at times even mistreated, for this behavior. Trust is lost in such a relational field, and instead, there is shame, resentment, and anger on both sides: one for the lack of response, the other for a demand that lacks empathic relatedness.

Pondering these questions in what turned out to be a chaotic Monday morning, and with many more Monday mornings resonating in my memory, I felt a deep need to understand what is being manifested in this dynamic. It was then, while waiting and wondering in my kitchen about this most interesting aspect of our Mexican culture, that a powerful image appeared in my mind, as if sent by the mercy of the gods to help me continue my workday in spite of my threatening broken pipe and feeling flooded with frustration: in the midst of my kitchen, I saw, in my mind's eye, the image of "El Templo Mayor," the main temple of the Aztecs, the center of Mexican civilization where power resided. Just recently, El Templo Mayor began to resurface right next to the Metropolitan Cathedral in Mexico City's "Centro Histórico."

As the reader most likely knows, Mexico was conquered by Spain in the sixteenth century, as were most Latin American countries, except Brazil. At that time, what is now known as Mexico City used to be a magnificent Aztec city called *Tenochtitlan*. According to Mathew Restall:

> When Bernal Diaz first saw the Aztec capital he was lost for words. Years later, the words would come, many of them when he wrote a lengthy account of his experiences as a member of the Spanish expedition led by Hernán Cortes against the Aztec empire. But on that November afternoon in 1519, as Diaz and his fellow conquistadors came over the mountain pass and looked down upon the Valley of Mexico for the first time, "gazing on such wonderful sights, we did not know what to say, or whether what appeared before us was real" ... Diaz struggled to describe what he saw – the metropolis of Tenochtitlan, studded with pyramids, crisscrossed with canals, seeming to hover on a lake that was "crowded with canoes" and edged with other "great cities" – derived from his shock at realizing that the world was not what he had perceived it to be.[4]

Confronted and threatened by this other new world, with such unknown beauty and magnificent development, the Spaniards embarked upon the Mexican conquest, which was consummated in a most devastating way when the Spanish conquistador Hernán Cortes finally took the city of Tenochtitlan in 1521. The story of the Mexican conquest is most interesting and meaningful for anyone wanting to learn about this tragic historic episode. However, in this chapter I want to focus on the colonization process that took place right after the traumatic conquest and lasted for the next three hundred years. For that purpose, there is a deeply symbolic and relevant image that illustrates how this process took place, and it is precisely the image that appeared to me that Monday morning while waiting for the plumber to arrive.

Let me describe what used to be the actual layout of Tenochtitlan, the capital of the Aztec empire, which had as its geographical center what was believed to constitute the center of the universe for the Mexican people (or Aztecs): El Templo Mayor (the main temple). It was precisely in the main temple where both the real and the symbolic power of the Aztec empire was located, the sacred place where myths were reenacted. El Templo Mayor was the first construction to be built when the Aztecs arrived in this land, and it represented the navel of the world, the sacred space from which religion, culture, power, and well-being would develop and emanate.

There were other transcendent buildings in this sacred area of the city of Tenochtitlan, such as the Temple of Huitzilopochtli, god of war; the Temple of Tlaloc, god of the rain; a temple for Quetzalcoatl, god of light, order, movement, urban structure, and civilization; a temple for Tezcatlipoca, god of the night and temptation, antagonistic to Quetzalcoatl; there was a temple for the sun; for the goddess Cihuacoatl, protector of the race and of fertility; for the goddess Chicomecoatl, goddess of the corn; as well as for Xochiquetzal, goddess of beauty; and many more meaningful buildings that together constituted the sacred space wherein ritual ceremonies, intended to facilitate communion with the gods, took place.

When the Conquest occurred and the Spanish colony began to settle in the new territories, the colonizers strategically built what remains until this day: the Mexican Metropolitan Cathedral, right on top of the major temple of the Aztecs. Not only that, the cathedral was actually built with the same stones that once formed El Templo Mayor. This relevant fact constituted not only a statement of Spanish power and domination but was also a significant step in the attempted evangelization of the Indians, in the religious syncretism that took place in the new conquered territories – which were baptized as "the New Spain" at the beginning of the sixteenth century.

For almost five centuries it was believed that whatever was left of El Templo Mayor, if anything, remained buried under the imposing colonial building of the Mexican Cathedral. But on February 21, 1978, in a construction area under the supervision of Compañía de Luz y Fuerza del Centro (the Mexican electricity

Figure 8.1 Mexican Cathedral standing alone as the major symbol of existing culture for 500 years.

company), workers in charge of changing some electrical wires "suddenly hit upon a stone that forbid them to go on further in their task, [so] they stopped the work until the next day when they called the INAH [National Anthropology and History Institute] since the surface of the found stone had some engravings."[5]

This finding aroused restlessness in the twentieth-century Mexican people and gave rise to different opinions about digging at this site and perhaps uncovering the main temple of the Aztecs. This is how the project to rescue El Templo Mayor got started. In fact, the work covered a surface of 12,900 square meters, and it took almost five years to get to the point where it now stands. Thirteen buildings of modern Mexico City had to be demolished to fulfill the scope of this project.

Nowadays the archeological site of the Templo Mayor stands in the Historic Center of Mexico City, right by the Mexican Cathedral and by the Palacio Nacional (House of Government), the place that represents the ruling power not only of the city but of all the country. Amazingly, in the twenty-first century, the Templo Mayor, together with the remains of the other divine temples, is standing with its royal and sacred ambiance, framed and contained by the main colonial buildings that paradoxically enhance the magnificence of the Mexican culture. When one is standing right there at the center of what was the "Aztec navel of the world," one can feel the magic that rediscovering and remembering brings. Watching the long line of hundreds of people waiting to enter the site – a phenomenon that takes place every single day of the week – one experiences a feeling of reverence for the long-buried Templo Mayor.

Figure 8.2 The reemergence of El Templo Mayor in the heart of Mexico City, near the Mexican Cathedral.

There is a magnificent museum as well that contains astonishing treasures that were simultaneously uncovered when digging at the archeological site. By 1980 there was an art exhibition organized around the many significant pieces that were discovered, which was held at the Palacio de Bellas Artes (Palace of Fine Arts). Among the pieces that were displayed, the sculpture of Xiuhtecuhtli, Old Lord of Fire, was widely admired. For some unknown reason, there was no specific security system in place to keep the artifacts safe. Eduardo Matos Moctezuma, who was in charge of the excavations as well as this art exhibit, asked one of his helpers to take special care of this piece. The next morning this helper called Matos and said,

> Remember asking me to specially look over the sculpture of Xiuhtecuhtli? Well, the guard in charge just came to let me know that while carefully watching over Xiuhtecuhtli, he was able to witness how a woman with a *"rebozo"* [Mexican shawl] arrived to honor the piece. While admiring the newly recovered Xiuhtecuhtli, she said, as in prayer facing the sculpture: "You have suffered so much, but you are finally here."[6]

The Templo Mayor, as well as the culture, beliefs, and traditions that emanated from it, were buried, totally unacknowledged, silenced for centuries. Since the colonization of Mexico, there has been only one officially recognized language as taught by the conquistadors, which is Spanish; one official religion, the Catholic faith, brought by the Spanish missionaries; one official government; and one official way of measuring time. Nevertheless there is, and there has been for centuries, another side to the officially and brutally imposed new culture. The other side, like the Templo Mayor, has remained buried, neither seen nor acknowledged. It is the silenced one; the one that is not spoken about; the one lacking reverence for the gods of the Spaniards, for their beliefs; the one lacking consideration for this different way of understanding the world, and life, and the measure of time.

It is, I believe, that abandoned and resentful side of the Mexican psyche, the unacknowledged, which is acted out via missing appointments, chronic tardiness, saying one thing and meaning or doing another. When feeling threatened by the imposition of the new culture and the destruction of all that was cherished of their own, the *mestizo* people developed "primitive self care systems" as a means of survival in the face of abusive treatment by the conquistadores and colonizers.[7] Indigenous people didn't say *no* to what was asked of them because their lives depended upon giving a compliant answer. But the *no* response was, and still is, acted out in their behavior.

Even now, centuries later, there is no pride in other ways of living than the one taught by the colonizers, in speaking a language other than Spanish, or in believing in a different religion than the one imposed by the colonizers. Not only is there no pride in any other way, there has been hardly any space for other ways to appear in the everyday life of the *mestizo* across the centuries. The brutal imposition of the culture brought by the Spanish from Europe has inspired many to give voice to the struggle endured by the Mexican people. A well-known historian,

Miguel Leon Portilla, wrote a book that he evocatively titled *La Vision de los Vencidos* (*The Vision of the Defeated*). In that book he quotes an important document considered to be the oldest manuscript written by indigenous people. Interestingly, it is housed in

> the National Library of Paris, under the title of *Unos Anales Históricos de la Nación Mexicana* (Historic Annals of the Mexican Nation), written in Náhuatl (the Aztec language) by anonymous authors from Tlaltelolco around 1528. . . . For the first time, it is expressed, not with little detail, the destruction of the culture, as seen by some of the survivors.[8]

This genocide of a culture was, and still is, most important. Restall notes,

> In colonial times, Spaniards sought to confine history by harnessing it to what may be the simplest trope ever invented to explain human behavior, differences between people, and the outcome of historical events – the trope of superiority. . . . In its most extreme form, indigenous inferiority was expressed in terms that denied Native Americans their humanity. Juan Gines de Sepulveda . . . openly stated that natives "hardly deserve the name of human beings." Even full conversion and subjection to the Spanish empire could only partially turn these "barbarians" into civilized men.[9]

When even humanity is denied, the only possible voice left is the one that can ensure survival. That is the voice that will speak – the one the colonizers demand to hear – when the right to exist as human beings is threatened. But words that are spoken under these conditions are not owned, so they have no roots to sustain or support established commitments. Under such circumstances a Mexican cultural complex was born, a complex that arises in the gap that exists between the assumed logic of spoken promises made and acts that are expected to follow, but that, in fact, do not. Feelings of anger, resentment, and frustration arise in both parties: on one side, because what is said does not match what is done; on the other side, because one's authentic voice has no freedom and hardly any space within which to be heard in the world.

There have been several attempts to explain what takes place in the Mexican culture, in the Mexican collective psyche. Mathew Restall, in his book *Seven Myths of the Spanish Conquest*, writes about the myth of the cultural and spiritual Conquest, when he notes that both native tongues and native clothing have survived into the present.

> The aspect of native culture of greatest concern to Spaniards was religion, as Christianization provided the empire with the rationale and justification that transcended and was supposed to disguise the mundanely self-serving realities of colonial expansion. . . . Franciscans and other Spanish friars and clergy hoped to utterly destroy all traces of native religions, to wipe the slate clean

and establish a new church free of pagan accretion on both sides of the Atlantic. They certainly succeeded in bringing Catholicism to native America, but if the purpose of the spiritual conquest was to install a Christianity free of local cultural variation, that conquest was not completed in the sixteenth century.[10]

From a historical point of view, the dynamic that took place between conqueror and conquest is seen as a problem of miscommunication. Restall notes that

> historian James Lockhart has called the process of cultural interaction in colonial Mexico one of Double Mistaken Identity. According to his interpretation of this process, "each side of the cultural exchange presumes that a given form or concept is functioning in the way familiar within its own tradition and is unaware of or unimpressed by the other side's interpretation."[11]

From a psychological point of view, there are different ways to look at this cultural complex that pervades the Mexican psyche. One interesting perspective is D.W. Winnicott's contribution when he talks about the

> false self [that] functions to protect the true self; it runs the gamut from normal social politeness in order to defend against exploitation and annihilation. Unlike the true self, which shows flexibility, bounce and imaginative reach, the false self displays rigidity, over-determination and a seeming deadness.[12]

In Mexico, at times, one may feel as though one were in a culture where things are said or done without conviction or authenticity, where one hears merely what is expected to be said.

> The individual then exists by not being found. All that shows . . . is our false self successfully functioning to keep our true self hidden. We feel futile and in social terms contribute instability to the group, for what others believe our self to be we know is bogus – that is the false self defense. The inner tension we feel between hiding safely and feeling futile, because not truly alive, we replicate in the group by daring others to find us and then defeating them or by condemning them for never bothering to look for who we really are.[13]

Another interesting idea is C.G. Jung's understanding of psychic material that is excluded from the dominating consciousness as if it has no right to exist; material that is not understood or rejected completely contains its own moral implications. This notion refers to a concept which Jung called the *shadow*. "The shadow," Jung says,

> is a moral problem that challenges the whole ego-personality. . . . The inferiorities constituting the shadow reveal that they have an emotional nature, a kind of autonomy, and accordingly an obsessive or, better, possessive quality. . . .

On this lower level with its uncontrolled or scarcely controlled emotions one behaves more or less like a primitive, who is not only the passive victim of his affects but also singularly incapable of moral judgment.[14]

In light of this Jungian concept, we can see that every human being, no matter his or her race, nationality, or gender, has a "lower level" of personality. When this lower level is confronted by the opposite, as seen in the other, profound emotion will awaken and possibly give rise to moral problems. The Spaniards, when confronted with the inconceivably different ways of the indigenous people, acted out in quite a primitive manner by viewing these people – and their advanced civilization – as less than human and certainly inferior to them. The Spaniards' identification with medieval values, and highly prized beliefs in their inherent superiority, made it impossible for them to relate to the newness that they discovered in this faraway land. On the other side, the indigenous people initially believed that the Spaniards were the saviors of the ruling empire of the Aztecs, and they even projected onto the Spanish conqueror Hernán Cortes the awaited god, Quetzalcóaltl.[15] In that instance, they surrendered their own authority, yielding their right to the other, to the conquistador.

As noted previously, the *mestizo* people carry both Spanish and indigenous legacies not only in their blood but in their psychology as well. The conqueror-conquered poles are present in the Mexican psyche, and it is the identification with one of these polarities that creates the Mexican cultural complex that gives the other no right to exist. One side of the equation loudly demands work and the completion of the work within a specified time period; and the other, silently, seeks consideration of its mythological, ritualistic, and contemplative way of living life's cycles.

One can act out this cultural complex when presenting a demand to another with feelings of righteousness of what is wanted and understood, or the other may feel ashamed and unable to set limits, falling into victimhood. On both poles feelings of resentment arise: on one hand because of the lack of punctuality, commitment, and the fulfillment of promises made; on the other, because of the lack of understanding, consideration, time. I believe it is very dangerous to fall into identifying with one pole or the other. But this is the tendency in Mexico, which fosters the enactment of the cultural complex by one projecting onto the other the side of the equation he does not recognize, acting it out, even nowadays, as was done 500 years ago.

As I sit here writing this paper, I sense the interplay of both sides of the equation in me now. On one hand, I know I have a commitment to fulfill and a specific date to deliver this paper; I know that other people, co-editors, editor, publisher, and other authors depend on my work being done on time. This is not an open-ended task. I have a due date to deliver my paper, just like the plumber, whom I was expecting to arrive at my home that Monday morning. But even further, I do not have only the external commitment to the others to fulfill, I have in myself an internal demand to do my work. My inner voice requires that I work thoroughly and faithfully so that my inner demand for punctuality, quality, and responsiveness does not activate an inner cruel conqueror – with an endless ambition of demanding more, better, faster work – to take over my peace of mind and my good spirit. If I allow this to happen, that is, if I can't limit my own inner demands upon myself, if I yield authority to that endless demanding inner voice, being unaware of this psychic dynamic, I could end up projecting it onto the external world – onto people and coworkers – giving them the power of "The Conqueror," since I myself would be unable to redeem the cruelty of my own potential mistreatment and abuse.

I believe that we must be very careful in delimiting the power of imposing and demanding from ourselves and from the other. Not being aware, not taking responsibility, we may fall into the dynamic of this cultural complex and react against the imposition as though it were "The Conquest," leaving us unable to write, or work, or respond – or to arrive on time on a Monday morning. In my case, I would not deliver my paper on time because there would be no paper to be delivered. Under an imposed regime of demand and expected work on time, I would most likely become paralyzed, unable to flow with ideas. I would then be acting exactly like the plumber who did *not* arrive on Monday morning as he had promised he would do. I would have to excuse myself from writing for this volume, like my nanny used to do on Mondays, and most likely I would have no words to do so because I would feel terribly ashamed. That would certainly be a complete enactment of this cultural complex.

Fortunately, my own "buried gods" have surfaced while "digging" in my personal analysis for years. I have felt enlightened by rediscovering and remembering silenced "gods," and I have learned to venerate them. My gods have to do with pleasure, dance, playfulness, joy of living. These inner gods exist in that place in my mind where my nanny Mercedes lives. They now feel the right to exist in the external world, and they fight for their time and space. Allow me to share this intimate memory: when I was a girl, I used to go to the park with Mercedes. I remember her spotless white apron, which she used to put over the grass for me to sit on, so as not to soil my clothes. I soon discovered that sitting in her lap was even cozier, warmer, more loving. So I would run to play with other children for a while and then return to Mercedes' lap, and she would embrace me warmly while saying that I was the best girl in the world. I loved it. I still do. While at the park with Mercedes there was no judgment, no measure of time (Mercedes literally never wore a watch), no demands, no expectations. I was "only" hugged. I discovered playfulness, joy, and pleasure in life.

So during the many hours that writing a paper takes, I often "go" to the "Mercedes space" in my mind. There I flow with ideas. I dance with other authors. I play with interpretations and different meanings, which my mind so eagerly embraces. And I also trust that there will be a paper to deliver and that it will be ready on time, as I have promised it will be.

"At the park, with Mercedes": it is only there, in that embracing, playful space where there are no demands, where time is measured by processes and relates to the inner, where one can listen to what one feels and needs, where being in intimate contact with the other and with the other in me – that bodily, sensorial, and verbal communication are cherished. However, I can't indulge for too long in this psychic space that I so much enjoy because then this paper, or any paper, could go on and on as I, in this playful mood, add something more beautiful, more meaningful, *ad infinitum*. But if so, I could also get lost in pleasure.

With this example that is so familiar to me, I hope I have been able to convey the interplay of the roles of European conquistador and indigenous conquest – both polarities in this Mexican cultural complex. These two polarities can actually represent, when contained, our two legs allowing us to walk in life. In order for this mutuality to take place, both sides need to be recognized in their luminous as well as their shadow aspects, in the risk of identifying with only one or the other, in our own participation in relating with the other, and in the constant risk of projecting onto the other what hurts us to see in ourselves. This, I believe, is what our "new-old" historic center is telling us, now holding at its core the old Catholic Cathedral standing together with the newly resurfaced – but even older – Templo Mayor.

One can turn one's sight to the new image that we now have at the center of Mexico City: the Templo Mayor, framed and surrounded by colonial buildings, cohabiting after a very dramatic shared history, desperately needing to relate to each other – Spanish and indigenous, new and old, built with the same stones, faithfully reflecting the architecture constituting the Mexican *mestizo* psyche.

Figure 8.3 The two major structures in Mexican culture, the cathedral in the background and the foundations of the Templo Mayor in the foreground, appearing side by side as symbol of hope that the Mexican psyche may come together.

But there is much work to be done. Mexicans have to go on "digging," not only literally, but even more importantly, psychically, in order to become conscious of a magnificent heritage to be cherished, making the space and having the right to exist together, proudly, in our city, in our country, and in our psyches.

Notes

1 Donald Kalsched, *The Inner World of Trauma: Archetypal Defenses of the Personal Spirit* (London: Routledge, 1996).
2 Jacqueline Gerson, "Kidnapping: Latin American Terror," in *Terror, Violence and the Impulse to Destroy*, ed. John Beebe (Einsiedeln, Switzerland: Daimon Verlag, 2003), pp. 91–92.
3 Jacqueline Gerson, "*Malinchismo:* Betraying One's Own," in *The Cultural Complex: Contemporary Jungian Perspectives on Psyche and Society*, eds. Thomas Singer and Samuel L. Kimbles (New York: Brunner-Routledge, 2004), pp. 35–36.
4 Mathew Restall, *Seven Myths of the Spanish Conquest* (New York: Oxford University Press, 2003), p. xiii.
5 Eduardo Matos Moctezuma, *Proyecto Templo Mayor* (México City: DGE Ediciones/Turner Libros, 1998), p. 13.
6 Ibid., p. 16.
7 Kalsched, *Inner World of Trauma*.
8 León Miguel Portilla, *Visión de los Vencidos* (México City: Universidad Nacional Autónoma de México, 2000), p. xvii.
9 Restall, *Seven Myths*, p. 132.
10 Ibid., p. 74.
11 Ibid., p. 76.
12 Ann Belford Ulanov, *Finding Space: Winnicott, God, and Psychic Reality* (Louisville, KY: Westminster John Knox Press, 2001), p. 48.
13 Ibid., p. 61.
14 C.G. Jung, *Aion: Researches into the Phenomenology of the Self, The Collected Works of C.G. Jung*, Vol. 9ii (Princeton: Princeton University Press, 1959), § 14–15.
15 Jacqueline Gerson, "Longing for Quetzalcoatl," in *Psyche and the City*, ed. Thomas Singer (New Orleans, LA: Spring Journal Books, 2010).

Chapter 9

The Broken Bridge

Exploring the Mythic Core of Mexican Cultural Complexes

Claude Juvin and Rocío Ruiz

When we began our research for this chapter, we found ourselves immersed in many complex questions arising in ourselves, in our country, and in the world. This has opened us up to a deeper perspective about our contemporary Mexican culture and society.

Everyone has heard about Mexico being a "macho" country with men who wear big hats and carry guns. They are pictured as abusing their poor and submissive wives. We have also heard a great deal about the rising prevalence of violence in Mexico: kidnappings, murders, dismemberments, beheadings, assaults, and aggressive behavior, even madness, at many levels of the government. In the Northern town of Ciudad Juarez, rampant drug dealing and the murders of numerous women have received huge notoriety.[1] During the past several years, more than three thousand young working women have been killed and their abandoned bodies found in the desert. Local and federal authorities have not been able to stop this horrific trend, which continues without interruption.

As Jungian analysts we wonder if it is possible to make any sense out of the dynamics underlying the unprecedented surge in violence that has impinged upon every segment of the Mexican population. Is anything waiting to be born out of this anarchy and chaos? We know that chaos can potentially be the prelude to transformation, that out of conflict huge energies are unleashed which can eventually support a new order. But at this point, we are totally in the grips of a process that is not only frightening and destructive but shows no signs of giving birth to anything new or positive. Nevertheless, we have to hold onto the hope that the chaos and violence of contemporary Mexico has the potential to bring an authentic transformation in our society rather than a further sinking into oblivion.

Again, as Jungians, we know that symbols are expressions of archetypal patterns that organize the psyche and the world. We know that symbols communicate in depth about human health and sickness, interpersonally and intrapsychically. At times, symbols can open the way to healing and balancing the psyche. If we pay attention to the symbols that emerge in our own psyches and in the collective psyche, we may find orientation and insight into the chaos enveloping our society and discover hints as to how we might find a direction out of our despair. We know that "in countries that lack a psychological culture, concrete experience is overvalued, and little time is granted for reflection in the inner life of psyche."[2]

In this chapter, we want to take the time to reflect on our creation myths and their symbols as a way to understand the core of those cultural complexes that seem to be devouring our society with the emergence of large-scale brutal violence in our everyday lives.

Here is a version of the Aztec creation myth that is central to understanding Mexican culture:

> Before the various paradises existed, the primordial substance seems to have had innumerable mouths as she swam in the formless waters devouring all she saw ... the earth monster is the goddess ... who sometimes weeps at night, longing to eat human hearts. She refuses to remain silent so long as she is not fed, and she will not bear fruit unless she is sprinkled with human blood. Life must be sacrificed to the great creature which nurtures life.[3]
>
> Two are the gods who alternatively created the different humanities which have existed: Quetzalcoatl, the well-disposed god, the hero who discovered agriculture and industry, and the black Tezcatlipoca, the omnipotent god, multiform and ubiquitous, the nocturnal god, protector of the sorcerers and of the bad men. Gods fight and their struggle is the story of the universe; their alternate triumphs are as well creations. Tezcatlipoca was the first who began the initial era of the world.[4] In the Aztec world, the eras are called Suns.
>
> Tezcatlipoca ruled the world of the First Sun until he was defeated by Quetzalcoatl his brother. Later, however, the two brothers co-operated in the creation of the Fifth Sun by defeating the Great Earth Monster Tlaltecuhtli. This was a chaotic monster with both male and female qualities that let crops flourish on earth only if she was fed with human blood. Known as the "earth lord" Tlaltecuhtli assumed a double role, with one side having a generative function and the other an insatiable devouring of blood.
>
> Tlaltecuhtli was defeated and dismembered by these two brother gods, Tezcatlipoca and Quetzalcoatl. From the dismembered and dying body of the "Earth Lord," the two brothers created heaven and earth by throwing one half of the body into the sky where it became the vault of the heavens, and the remaining half, was formed into the earth. They also cooperated in the creation of order, plants, and humanity.
>
> At another point in the relationship between these brothers, Tezcatlipoca plied Quetzalcoatl with a beverage and, when Quetzalcoatl was inebriated, he slept with his own sister. His subsequent anguish and shame led him to burn his palace, his treasures and sacrifice himself on a funeral pyre, from which rare birds rose from his ashes.[5]

A perpetual tension exists between Tezcatlipoca and Quetzalcoatl and can be viewed in terms of a dualistic opposition of earth and wind or, by extension, matter and spirit. According to the Florentine Codex, Tezcatlipoca, whose name means "smoking mirror," is omnipresent and causes discord and conflict everywhere he goes.[6] He is a creator as well as destroyer, a bringer of fortune as well as disaster.

Tezcatlipoca appears to be the embodiment of change through conflict. He was conceived as the invisible, ever-present lord of shadows, wielding his magic mirror to see into, and manipulate, the lives of humans.[7]

Tezcatlipoca, with his potentially death dealing and enormous energies, is an archetypal force who brings to mind the contemporary bloody violence reigning over our country. "The destructive emotionality which is so easily connected with evil in a masculine type of civilization causes the feminine principle to be destructive."[8]

Quetzalcoatl, whose name means Plumed Serpent, symbolizes the conjunction of the opposites. Considered as masculine, Quetzalcoatl, originally was most likely a hermaphrodite as indicated by his compound name: the masculine "quetzal" (bird) and "coatl," which means both "twin" (which indicates his double nature) and "snake" (a creature that the Aztecs associated with the feminine psyche). Even though he co-created the Fifth Sun (the actual world), Quetzalcoatl was the only god who rejected the need for human sacrifice to the gods which had been mandated in the following injunction:

> Man has been created by the sacrifice of the gods and he has to respond by offering them his own blood. Human sacrifice was essential in Aztec religion for men could not exist without the creation of the gods, who in their turn needed that men feed them with their own sacrifices as nourishment.[9]

As a result of Quetzalcoatl's decision not to demand human sacrifice, there was a cosmic fight, and the other gods became angry, forcing him into exile after which Quetzalcoatl killed himself. The myth has it that the Star of Venus was thus born from his heart in the self-immolation. Quetzalcoatl's journey mirrors that of Venus, who wanders the darkness in search of the lost light. We could say, following Jung, that Quetzalcoatl was transformed into a spiritual being and remains in exile as "the archetype of the spirit symbolizing the pre-existing hidden meaning in the chaos of life."[10] Like a seed, Quetzalcoatl carries the potential for consciousness through spirituality and, like Venus, appears in the morning and disappears at sunset.

At the moment of Cortes' arrival at the beginning of the Conquest, the Aztecs were longing for the return of Quetzalcoatl, who, as it had been foretold in their tradition, would come back as a bearded white man. Consequently, when Cortes arrived in Mexico, "the Aztecs welcomed him as a savior, as Quetzalcoatl returning in triumph to deliver them from the evil that had befallen them and to restore their lost kingdom."[11] But as we know, that did not happen.

In analyzing the horrible events occurring today in our country, we can see the force of dark archetypal energies at work in the violent turmoil of everyday life in Mexico. As with the Aztec gods who demanded human sacrifice, we are suggesting that Mexico is currently caught in a regression to these mythic times when there was no order or referent to meaningful existence. There is only chaos, destruction, disaster, and conflict everywhere. Like our Aztec forbearers, we can believe that Quetzalcoatl's brother, Tezcatlipoca, is rampaging among us still, while Quetzalcoatl remains locked in the spirit world without the capacity to rein in Tezcatlipoca's destruction. We can see the tyrannical rule of Tezcatlipoca in the collective and in the individual psyche wreaking havoc in both interpersonal and intrapsychic relationships. Following this line of thought, we suggest that this "reign of terror" can be seen as the expression of the unconscious energy of Tezcatlipoca in the form of a cultural complex that functions "as energic emotional fields, but the dynamics are impersonal; they propel people toward feeling and action, through psychic induction."[12] The concretization of this psychic induction into the realm of Tezcatlipoca is expressed in the large number of deaths involving dismemberment, beheadings, and murders, which can be seen as enactments of the myth in which the ritual offering of human sacrifice is made to the gods. But why do the gods need this sacrifice? Why are they angry?

> The archetype of the Self is evoked by cultural complexes, which then have available to them all the energy of the archetypal and personal levels of the psyche. This can make cultural complexes very dangerous.[13]

We are proposing that the Aztec gods are angry because the Mexican people stopped honoring them. After the Conquest and evangelization by the Catholic Spaniards, the Mexican people were forced to cut their connection to their ancestral roots. The conquerors killed their priests and built churches over their temples, forcing them to pray in a Catholic way. The conquerors destroyed all the images of their gods and punished them if they maintained their traditions. With the loss of connection to their gods, the indigenous Mexican people lost connection with what rooted them in their true self and their authentic identity. A confused identity developed that included foreign and strange elements that were not their own: new language, new religion, new values, new costumes. At the same time their old ways and beliefs were not integrated into the new culture. Instead, not only was their old culture destroyed but as human beings they were excluded from the culture of the conquerors and treated as slaves. The conquerors raped the Mexican women and created a new race: the *mestizo*. The result of that "rape" is that most Mexicans today are *mestizos*.

By the end of the Conquest, the pre-Hispanic culture died forever. People who belonged to this culture were proclaimed inferior: they were treated as slaves, their religion devalued as sorcery, their beliefs slandered, and their deeper thought about the relationship between nature and spirit completely distorted. Their books were burned in public spaces as the devil's work, the wise old men and guardians of the tradition were eliminated, and the artistic creations of their god images were melted down or "drowned" in the lakes.[14]

In his concepts of deintegration and reintegration in the development of the self, Fordham said that

> in essence, deintegration and reintegration describe a fluctuating state of learning in which the infant opens itself to new experiences and then withdraws in

order to reintegrate and consolidate these experiences. During a deintegrative activity, the infant maintains continuity with the main body of the self (or its center), while venturing into the external world to accumulate experience in motor action and sensory stimulation.[15]

For Fordham deintegration and reintegration are shaped according to archetypal patterning. Disintegration, as distinguished from deintegration, is what happens to the ego when it breaks up and fragments.

Applying Fordham's theory of individual development to the emerging experience of the Mexican people, we are suggesting that they endured a process of disintegration rather than deintegration. Reintegration that fosters development of the self was not possible for the new race of people that emerged from the Conquest because the people's connection to their authentic roots was severed.

We believe that in the Mexico that emerged after the Conquest, Tezcatlipoca has reigned alone while Quetzalcoatl remains in exile. We believe that Quetzalcoatl is the light, the consciousness that must be present to illuminate the shadow that is Tezcatlipoca. If the light of consciousness is not present to integrate the shadow, the unconscious is destructively enacted, repetitiously and without meaning. Tezcatlipoca causes discord and conflict everywhere he goes. He is the embodiment of change through conflict. He is the shadow, and shadow is like the "nigredo" of the alchemists. "So it is time for destruction, loss of referents and values, confusion and back to the chaos that are necessary to connect with the opus."[16] Tezcatlipoca is a troublemaker. Someone who feels safe today, may tomorrow be a victim of his evil nature that is only satisfied by causing terror and tragedy.[17]

Jung says that in relation to the shadow "the development of human consciousness is a phylogenetic need and when the light of human conscious is expanded the weak part of the soul become darker. That is seen psychically as a fissure projected in the world."[18] It seems that with his magic smoking mirror, Tezcatlipoca cheats people into making them believe that they are really connected to their true identity. Mexican people have a new god, a religious syncretism of the Christian and the Aztec, but this new god is the result of mixed traditions and superstitions. Mexican people remain polytheistic, but instead of consciously engaging their own gods, they have mixed-up Catholic saints with Aztec images. But intrapsychically there is no reintegration. In both the individual and in the collective, there is disintegration.

Jung talks about the historical events in Germany in terms of mass psychology and compensation:

> As I have said, the up rush of mass instincts was symptomatic of a compensatory move of the unconscious. Such a move was possible because the conscious state of the people had become estranged from the natural laws of human existence. This new form of existence produced an individual who was unstable, insecure, and suggestible.[19]

Jung also emphasized that in such historical moments there are disturbances in the unconscious of many people:

> The individual's feeling of weakness, indeed of non-existence, was thus compensated by the eruption of hitherto unknown desires for power. It was the revolt of the powerless, the insatiable greed of the "have-nots." By such devious means the unconscious compels man to become conscious of himself.[20]

Likewise, we can say that our people are alienated from themselves and caught in the Tezcatlipoca cultural complex. Inside, they feel weak and insecure. Yet in a compensatory way, they act out their wish for power when they can. This power has different faces: drug dealers, kidnappers, murderers, politicians, faces of "mass man" in the collective, as well as in individuals. Everyday examples occur when wealthy people abuse their servants, or the *mestizo* people mistreat indigenous people, or when individuals are caught in the violent energy of their own lives. The Tezcatlipoca cultural complex on the personal level can be seen in all the destructive fantasies and violent acts that may result when a person takes our place in the parking lot, or a car stops in front of us and blocks our way. As a people, we have no hope. We live in despair and in depression. We go home in a bad mood, angry and fighting with our loved ones.

The following incident happened to one of this chapter's authors, but it is one which may take place on any day, to anybody, anywhere, and at any time in Mexico. All of us are exposed to such situations, which we view as an enactment of the Tezcatlipoca cultural complex that occurs on the personal and on the cultural level:

> *One day when I was driving on a major street in Mexico City with my daughter and my three-year-old granddaughter, a disturbing event happened to us from which my body is still shivering. We came to a red light. I stopped and suddenly a young man emerged in the middle of the cars yelling at me: "Stupid old woman, stupid nut, fucking crone." He began kicking the car and beating on the car windows with his fists, threatening our physical and psychic safety. I was paralyzed and did not understand what was happening or why it was happening, I could not believe what I was seeing. My daughter was frightened, at the same time trying to protect my body. She yelled at me: "Mom, do not open the window." My granddaughter was very frightened. She sat silently behind my seat, afraid to move, but her eyes were wide open. Even today when we drive by the same place my granddaughter says to me: "This is where we saw the crazy man." All the people in the cars around us sat in silence. Maybe they were paralyzed, too. But nobody tried to do anything to help us. The light turned green and I moved on. I made a left turn and once again the red light stopped me. Again, the same man came running after us, kicking on my car with murderous eyes. Finally, my daughter began to react, by opening the window, shouting for help and pounding on the car's horn. Before he ran off, the man tore off the side*

> *mirror of my car. There is a way in which this experience touched me profoundly and allowed me to see what is happening all the time in Mexico today.*

When thinking about the topic of power, we are reminded of Jung's quote: "Where love reigns, there is no will to power; and where the will to power is paramount, love is lacking. The one is but the shadow of the other."[21] As we live in an atmosphere of disintegration of the normal functioning of our culture, which has become a place of disconnection and chaos, there is no love, no Eros. There is little relatedness and an abundance of alienation. Without Eros as mediator of relationship, the connection between people is missing. The bridge between the opposites is broken: between Tezcatlipoca and Quetzalcoatl, between destruction and creation, between indigenous and Spanish blood, between light and shadow, between masculine and feminine, between consciousness and unconsciousness. "Eros driven underground becomes rage and great violence ensues."[22]

To further amplify the mythic core of Mexican cultural complexes, we will reflect on another Aztec myth, which can help us to understand the "machismo" complex.

> At Coatepec, the goddess Coatlicue kept and swept the temple. One day, as she swept, she tucked a tuft of feathers in her breast, but when she had completed her task, the feathers were gone and she knew she had become pregnant. Already the mother of 400 sons (known as Centzon Huitznahua) and one daughter, Coyolxauhqui, Coatlicue's pregnancy became a source of humiliation to her children, and they plotted to kill her. But from within the womb, Huitzilopochtli, her unborn infant son, comforted her. The Centzon Huitzinahua and Coyolxauhqui charged Coatepec, slicing off Coatlicue's head. Out of her truncated body leapt Huitzilopochtli, fully formed and dressed, brandishing his Xiuhcoatl weapon (fire serpent), with which he in turn, dismembered his sister Coyolxauhqui whose body parts tumbled to the foot of Coatepec. Huitzilopochtli then attacked his half-brothers, only a few of whom managed to flee.[23]

In this myth we can see how Coatlicue, the mother, who was impregnated mysteriously by a spirit, transgressed the law that said woman needs to have a husband to become pregnant. Her children became angry at her, and she was beheaded by her daughter and sons. Her unborn son, Huitzilopochtli, leaped out of her body fully formed and, in turn, dismembered his sister and brothers. So Coatlicue died and gave way to her son, the young and solar masculine. The archetypal energy constellated in this event is destructive: beheading, dismemberment, and dominance of the masculine over the feminine, which can be thought of as feeling and vulnerability. Huitzilopochtli was born armed, ready to kill and to reign over the mother and the feminine. Coatlicue, the mother, sacrificed herself to allow the masculine power to flourish.

Dismemberment in myths is a regular feature of the cults of the Great Mother, who is herself the destroyer, the terrible mother who castrates and destroys her son. Through all the differences, the same archetypal form reveals itself: the terrible mother upon whom life depends.[24]

In our culture, we can see how the mother is always sacrificing herself to give the best to her children, especially to her sons. She remains disconnected from her own needs and emotions. Her love is "unconditional." However, she is usually angry, frustrated, and powerless. What power she gains is through blackmailing her children, although she continues to experience herself as fragile, weak, and unprotected. This leads to a negative mother complex, which "in the son injures the masculine instinct."[25]

In a Mexican newspaper, we read, "On May 10th (Mother's day) Mexico City is paralyzed because everybody is going to spend the day with their mothers." Martha Lamas, a Mexican journalist, wrote that

> "the macho" has a lot of a mother and very little of a father. . . . The myth of the mother is the myth of maternal omnipotence, originating in unconditional love, absolute self denial and heroic sacrifice. If we take away the power of the image of the *"mamacita"* (the mother who is adorned with saintly qualities), we find a woman who is exhausted, fed up, ambivalent, guilty, insecure, competitive or depressed.[26]

Faced with such a mother, a young man cannot allow himself to be in touch with his vulnerabilities, especially his feelings and emotions. The son is caught in the negative mother complex, unable to separate from his mother and her "unconditional love." He will deny parts of himself because he cannot manage them, and carry on with life as if they simply do not exist. Such a man presents himself to the world and to himself as an impenetrable wall without any vulnerabilities. Such a son/man has to be a strong warrior, and a certain fate can be inherent in that role: historically man has been conditioned to procreate, protect his brood, and be defined by his productivity; in such a world, men are tragically doomed, they cannot achieve serenity, seldom operate out of inner conviction, and rarely get out of the killing game. Even when they win, they lose their soul.[27]

Another important aspect that points to the parallel between the myth of Huitzilopochti and modern Mexican culture is the absence of the father. The father is not present at Huitzilopochtli's birth or life, and in contemporary Mexican culture, the father is very frequently either absent physically or emotionally or both. The mother often fills the entire space of parenthood. Without a father to help the son find his way out of the mother complex, the son remains either a child trapped in dependency, or he emerges with compensatory macho attitudes that include subjugating the feminine. Most Mexican men usually emerge with some hybrid combination of childlike dependency and machismo overcompensation.

The result of these developmental adaptations (or maladaptations) in men and women in Mexico is unrelatedness and disintegration (in Fordham's sense) in both men and women. Women have lost touch with their inner needs, and men have lost touch with their feelings and soul. Both have little or no conscious connection with the unconscious, and both are destined to act out the unconscious, leading to a state of affairs well described by Jung: "only unconsciousness makes no difference between good and evil."[28] The bridge is broken between men and women, between man and his soul, between woman and her inner needs.

In Mexico, women often suffer because they can't grasp their own power. They can't take care of themselves or be responsible for their own lives. Mexican women instead frequently take care of their families, husbands, children, parents, and friends. They go through life taking responsibility for everyone else's problems but not for their own lives. They are unable to see how powerful and strong they are because they project all their own power and strength onto others, especially men. They live in fear and solitude, and with the strong conviction that without their family or their men, they can't survive. Women only have a voice when they are in the role of mother. Most of them live their life through their children. In turn, men have the "voice," including all of the overt authority. It is the men that make the major decisions for the family, including all of the financial decisions. The men are responsible for the women in their family and their children, but at the same time, they seem unable to take care of or be responsible for themselves. They are like children, who expect that all women will mother them. Power drives them and wounds them.

The myth of Coatlicue, the mother, and Huitzilopochtli, the son, is alive in a very archaic and dynamic way in the psyches of modern Mexican men and women who remain unconscious with powerfully wounded, negative animas and animuses.

> The two principles or masculine and feminine energies, in their positive aspects, are not opposites of each other; they are different energies, complementary energies. The oppositions are revealed when the negative aspects come into play.[29]

The positive feminine (Eros) carries the following values: *being, union, connectedness,* and *belonging*, and the negative qualities of *chaos, symbiosis, undifferentiation,* and *absence of boundaries*. The positive masculine (logos) carries the following values: *becoming, separation, independence,* and *differentiation*, and the negative qualities of *alienation, isolation, nonparticipation,* and *withdrawal*.[30]

These dynamics, outlined by Loomis, provide an accurate description of how negative masculine and feminine energies are the predominant forces in many Mexican people. From our clinical practice, here is a typical story of this negative embrace of the masculine and feminine, as related by a 45-year-old woman:

> *I met my husband as a young girl, and we married when I was 19. I had children very quickly, and it seemed that I had a good life. After my children were born, my husband became jealous and could not tolerate my attention to our children. He needed all of my attention. We are wealthy and have three maids, but I personally prepared his breakfast and ironed his shirts every morning. I was always responsive to his needs and available for whatever he desired. I never understood why he criticized and humiliated me in front of our children and others. I never felt the same aggression towards him, and I blamed myself for not being good enough. My sisters helped me see that his behavior was aggressive, and I was astonished. I have decided to get a divorce, and I want your opinion*

about my decision. I wonder what I will do if he asks me to stay with him. It is important for you to know that my mother, with whom I have been very close, has stopped talking to me. She is very angry about my decision. She still talks to my husband.

This woman is profoundly confused. She has no space, no thoughts or feelings of her own. She is disconnected from herself. Her only referent is her husband, although he mistreats her. She is like a little girl who loves her bad parents. Much more power lies with her unconscious negative animus, which has been telling her that she is wrong and not good enough. There is another little voice who tells her that she is not in the right place, but she cannot really listen to it. "In working with the negative animus, a space is needed for its usually silenced resentment to express its horrible, destructive ideas and wishes, because it is only when the destructive animus is able to talk to us, that any containment of his power can occur."[31]

In Mexico, men feel the need to control their wives, sometimes acting as a protective father, sometimes devaluing and humiliating them. At the same time, the men are like children, completely dependent on the care and mothering of their wives. Both men and women are unable to connect with their inner positive masculine and feminine energies and project them onto the other. They are left with a false connection. So a real bridge to relationship is broken. A 53-year-old woman described to me this image of her relationship with her husband:

He lives in a bubble, inside a capsule isolated from his emotions and from his pain. He cannot connect with my feelings, with my own suffering. If I try to touch him and enter his encapsulated world, he becomes like a monster, cruel and icy. I feel impotent and, at times, crazy. We can only have a "good" relationship if I do not try to enter his bubble and behave as if nothing of emotional consequence happens. The elephant in the room must never be seen.

This image describes precisely how the positive qualities of Eros, the feminine, are disconnected from the man's center, his emotions. There is no connectedness, no sense of belonging. Emotions are threatening to the unrelated, wounded masculine, which results in alienation, isolation, nonparticipation, and withdrawal. As in the myth of Coatlicue, the feminine has to be destroyed to give way and power to the masculine. They cannot exist in the same place. We desperately need a bridge to connect both energies.

This is the initial dream of a woman who sought analysis because she was very depressed and unable to be productive and creative.

I am in a temple. I can feel the presence of my children and my husband, but I cannot see them. Then I am in a bus with people. When I get off the bus, I realize that I have forgotten my purse and my cell phone. I cannot call my husband, and I am looking for my son because I do not know where he is. Nobody knows where he is, and I just want to find him. My son appears and takes me to a chapel by walking through streets that look like a labyrinth. It is a white marble chapel, with a dazzling bright light that blinds me. When I am able to see again, my son has disappeared. I go out looking for him, and I take a taxi. Suddenly I remember that I have no money because I lost my purse. I am also worried because my husband will be angry that I have lost my cell phone. I cannot call or communicate with anybody.

In this dream image we can see how this woman loses her identity (her family, her purse, her cell phone), perhaps in order to find a new one, alone, without any of the tools for communicating with the outer world. She finds herself in touch with the sacred and archetypal in the form of the chapel and the light that makes her blind. This sacred space may help her connect with her own strengths that could make a new life journey possible for her. Her connection with the masculine begins with her relationship to the dream image of her son, young and developing, appearing and disappearing. This journey will require a new relationship to both the masculine and feminine.

Let's shift to the male psychology in this metaphor of the "broken bridge." Following are two dreams of a 50-year-old man. He presented himself as weak, easily manipulated by women, and dependent on them, while being very nice to them.

1 I am in a place divided in two. On my side, I am with a police officer or an army officer. We are looking at the other side (the desert) where there are women. The sun is burning on both sides. One of the women looks skinny, with dark circles under her eyes, tired, hopeless, hungry, sad. We (the officer and I) are eating melons, and the juice is dripping out of our mouths. We are enjoying the freshness of the fruit in the middle of the desert, and we do not care about the women.
2 I see a cage in which there are several women, prisoners. A custodian with a lot of keys is watching them. I tell him to be very careful with the keys because these women have to stay where they are.

In these dreams the man who considers himself as being "nice to women" is astonished to realize that he has a cruel and sadistic masculine side, a "macho" man hidden in his shadow. He has to confront this cruel and heartless part of himself. In both dreams, the boundaries between masculine and feminine are marked. In the first dream, the women in the desert have no possibility of going forward. They are too weak and have no food or water. In the second dream, the women in the cage are like birds that cannot fly. The men in the dreams ignore or repress their eros, their anima. Their soul needs to be fed. But instead, their shadow enacts the myth of Huitzilopochtli who killed his sister.

Final Reflections

Following our path through Mexican mythical images, we propose that the myths of creation form the psychic substratum of our culture and account for some of its specific dynamics. The archetypal energies of the mythic substratum express themselves in the contemporary, chaotic cultural complexes devouring Mexico today. The people of Mexico have lost touch with the unconscious sources and potential meaning of their current condition, which we believe are crying out to be recognized and brought into consciousness. Jung wrote, "Disalliance with the unconscious is synonymous with a loss of instinct and rootlessness."[32]

It might help if the Mexican people became more aware of these irrational and chaotic energies that are expressing themselves in the cultural complexes in which they are caught. Such knowledge might offer the possibility of connecting with the Self. Consciousness implies relation and connection with the Self, and as Sam Kimbles has written: "the archetype of the Self is evoked by cultural complexes. This can make cultural complexes very dangerous even as it enables them at other times to inspire the collective spirit in more positive ways."[33] If Quetzalcoatl, the luminous aspect of Tezcatlipoca, could be constellated, it might be possible to find a way out of the current impasse. We can imagine the current destruction, chaos, and violence as Tezcatlipoca energy reigning alone without his opposite, Quetzalcoatl, in play. Quetzalcoatl has male and female qualities. He is the bringer of civilization, the god of arts and learning, agriculture, and the embodiment of all virtues. He balances the shadowy times with light. Quetzalcoatl is missing-in-action in Mexico, and we need him in order to reconnect and integrate the forces of human nature that are so out of balance. We believe that the light that Quetzalcoatl could bring offers the potential to reconnect with the Self and to reestablish the broken bridge.

At the same time, we also propose that the Huitzilopochtli myth informs us about the archetypal energies that influence the relationship between feminine and masculine, interpersonally and intrapsychically, in men and women. We need to remember Coyolxauhqui to reintegrate the feminine in the Mexican psyche as well as to reconnect with the positive qualities of the masculine. In the same myth, Huitzilopochtli is the leader who helps the people find Tenochtitlan, the land that has appeared symbolically in the Mexican psyche as "the place with the eagle perched on a cactus, holding a serpent in its beak." This image is the emblem of our country. For the Aztecs, the serpent symbolizes the feminine psyche, and the eagle represents the masculine spirit. The eagle holds the serpent in its beak and claws, bringing the two together as a unified energy.

In the language of our hypothesis, reintegrating Coyolxauhqui's feminine energy with the masculine energy of Huitzilopochtli requires a bridge between the broken parts. In following these mythic reflections to their core and goal, we can say that Quetzalcoatl can be seen as the Self. The longing and hope for his return symbolizes the belief that something of great value may emerge out of the chaos, disintegration, and destruction. His archetypal energy is the way to reconnect the broken pieces. Quetzalcoatl offers us the possibility of the appearance of a transcendent function in the form of the birth of the true Self of the Mexican people. Quetzalcoatl promises us a new order that may deliver us from the chaos of contemporary Mexican reality and restore the broken bridge.

Notes

1 The phenomenon of the female homicides in Ciudad Juárez, called in Spanish *feminicidio* ("femicide"), involves the violent deaths of women and girls that have been occurring since 1993 in the northern Mexican region of Ciudad Juárez, Chihuahua, a border city across the Rio Grande from the US city of El Paso, Texas.
2 Jacqueline Gerson, "Kidnapping: Latin America's Terror," in *Terror, Violence and the Impulse to Destroy*, ed. John Beebe (Einsiedeln, Switzerland: Daimon Verlag, 2003), p. 102.
3 Irene Nicholson, *Mexican and Central American Psychology* (England: Hamlyn, 1998).
4 Alfonso Caso, *El pueblo del Sol* (México: Fondo de Cultura Económica, 1983).
5 Leonardo López Luján, *Tlaltecuhtli* (México: Instituto Nacional de Antropología e Historia, 2010).
6 *The Codex Florentine*, a history in Nahuatl and Spanish, is the major work of Friar Bernardino de Sahagun. It contains the deep knowledge of elder natives that was transmitted to Friar Sahagun.
7 David M. Jones and Brian Molyneaux, *The Mythology of the Americas* (Dayton, OH: Lorenz Books, 2001).
8 Marie Louise von Franz, *Shadow and Evil in Fairytales* (Dallas, TX: Spring Publications, 1974).
9 Caso, *El pueblo del Sol*, p. 22.
10 C.G. Jung, "Archetypes of the Collective Unconscious," in *The Collected Works of C.G. Jung*, vol. 9i, trans. R.F.C. Hull (Bollingen Series, Princeton: Princeton University Press, 1990), § 74.
11 Jacqueline Gerson, "Mexico City: Longing for Quetzalcoatl," in *Psyche and the City: A Soul's Guide to the Modern Metropolis*, ed. Thomas Singer (New Orleans, LA: Spring Journal Books, 2010), p. 228.
12 Samuel L. Kimbles, "Cultural Complexes and Collective Shadow Processes," in *Terror, Violence and the Impulse to Destroy*, ed. John Beebe, p. 230.
13 Ibid., p. 231.
14 Laurette Sejourné, *El universo de Quetzálcoatl* (México: Fondo de Cultura Económica, 1998), p. 2.
15 Michael Fordham, *Explorations into the Self* (London: Academic Press, 1985), p. 64.
16 Aimé Agnel, Michel Cazenave, Claire Dorly, and Suzanne Krakowiak, *Dictionnaire Jung*, ed. Aimé Agnel (France: Ellipses Edition Marketing, 2008), p. 121. In this book, the editors organize the basic concepts and themes from Jung's *Collected Works*.
17 Paul Westheim, *La Calavera* (México: Fondo de Cultura Económica, Breviarios, 1983), p. 13.
18 Agnel, et al., *Dictionnaire Jung*, p. 120.
19 C.G. Jung, "The Fight with the Shadow," in the *Collected Works of C.G. Jung, Vol. 10, Civilization in Transition*, trans. R.F.C. Hull (Bollingen Series, Princeton: Princeton University Press, 1990), § 453.
20 Ibid., § 454.
21 C.G. Jung, "On the Psychology of the Unconscious," in *The Collected Works of C.G. Jung, Vol. 7, Two Essays in Analytical Psychology*, trans. R.F.C. Hull (Bollingen Series, Princeton: Princeton University Press, 1990), § 78.
22 James Hollis, *Under Saturn's Shadow* (Toronto: Inner City Books, 1994), p. 28.
23 Mary Miller and Karl Taube, *The Gods and Symbols of Ancient Mexico and Mayas* (London: Thames and Hudson, 1993), p. 94.
24 Michael Fordham, *Children as Individuals* (London: Free Association Books, 1999), p. 135.
25 C.G. Jung, "The Mother Complex. The Mother Complex of the Son," in *The Collected Works of C.G. Jung, Vol. 9i, Archetypes and the Collective Unconscious*, trans. R.F.C. Hull (Bollingen Series, Princeton: Princeton University Press, 1990), § 163.

26 Martha Lamas, *Madrecita Santa* (México: Periódico Reforma, October 22, 1995).
27 Jan Bauer, *Alcoholism and Women: The Background and the Psychology* (Toronto: Inner City Books, 1982).
28 Jung, *The Collected Works of C.G. Jung*, vol. 9i, § 97.
29 Mary E. Loomis, *Her Father's Daughter* (Wilmette, IL: Chiron Publications, 1995).
30 Ibid., p. 35.
31 Jacqueline Gerson, "Kidnapping: Latin America's Terror," in *Terror, Violence and the Impulse to Destroy*, ed. John Beebe, p. 98.
32 Jung, *The Collected Works of C.G. Jung*, vol. 7, §§ 195, 196.
33 Kimbles, "Cultural Complexes," in *Terror, Violence and the Impulse to Destroy*, ed. John Beebe, p. 231.

Uruguay

DOI: 10.4324/9781003400820-16

Chapter 10

The Official Story of Uruguay

The Cultural Complexes Underlying What Was and Was Not Included

Pilar Amezaga and Pablo Gelsi

Identity formation is an archetypal pattern that takes place in both individuals and nations. It is a process and not something that is acquired all at once and forever. It consists of a more or less conscious selection of certain features and characteristics, and the forgetting and suppression of others. As Christian Roesler states, "In Jungian psychology identity was always seen as something that comes, more or less totally from inside, whereas for social psychology theories identity comes from without, through internalization and imitation."[1] We believe that identity is based on both personal experiences and what others tell us about who we were, are, and will be. At the level of history, the narrative of identity formation may take on a mythical quality that itself will become part of the nation's identity. In the same way as myth, historical narrative is effective when it can continue to provide meaning to successive generations, even when circumstances change. The narrative is not necessarily a textual chronicle of past facts; rather, the important thing is that it is capable of giving meaning to identity.

We can establish certain links between what Richard Kradin proposes regarding family myth and what we will call "Official Story" in this chapter. Kradin maintains that the family myth represents an imaginary description that stresses the importance of certain values within the family, the family's values in relation to the collective, and the family's position with regard to strangers.[2] As with Kradin's description of family myth, we hold that the Official Story of Uruguay corresponds to a historical description of our nation that was developed by the state in order to provide a set of values, facts, and historical characters that serve as a frame of reference for the cultural identity of our nation. Research on identity as proposed by Roesler suggests that there are a number of narrative patterns that the members of a culture or society can use to account for their histories or personal lives. It has been shown that individuals choose to tell their stories following a limited number of narrative guidelines that reflect archetypal patterns. It is also suggested that the process of identity formation consists, to a certain degree, of people becoming familiar with and using culturally typified story patterns and incorporating them into the process of building their personal histories.

Julio De Zan adds a conceptual distinction between memory and history that, in our view, is very helpful to our discussion. The author highlights the role of memory in the narrative that gives rise to identity. He shows how the narrative of historiography can be transformed into an Official Story that paradoxically loses what is characteristic of narrative, such as its fluidity, its nature as a process, and its modifiable quality.[3] It is as if the Official Story attempts to crystallize a seamless, unique, and unchanging identity, following the Eriksonian model. Erik Erikson maintained that identity will remain unchanged for the rest of our life once we reach adulthood.[4]

This allows us to postulate that what this crystallization leaves out, what is forgotten, can become an unconscious fragment – at times a pathology – at the cultural level of the psyche in the same way that occurs with individuals, creating a phenomenon which is called a cultural complex. In the same way as occurs with the fragmentation of the mnemonic records of our personal history, a fragmentation of the data and facts that we receive through the taught history of our country also takes place. The contribution of Jungian psychology to the understanding of this phenomenon is that what is forgotten and fragmented comes together in the form of a complex that becomes an unconscious part of identity and expresses itself in an uncontrolled and stereotyped manner.

This complex becomes manifest within a culture and also in the relationship with other peoples and cultures. An individual's use of memory may be impaired by different psychic pathologies. Thomas Singer and Samuel Kimbles assert that

> cultural memory, as we understand it from the point of view of the cultural unconscious, is not a warehouse or a retrieval process but a living, dynamic field. . . . We believe this place or energy field of transformation is organized by cultural complexes.[5]

Or as Nora Pierre says,

> Memory is the recollection of an experienced or imagined past. . . . It is by nature affective, emotional, open to all transformations, vulnerable to all manipulation, subject to remaining latent for long periods and to abrupt awakenings. Memory is always a collective phenomenon, even though it is experienced psychologically in an individual manner. Conversely, history is an always problematic and incomplete construction of what has ceased to exist, but left traces behind.[6]

In the case of Uruguay, this identity had to be created after the birth of our nation. That is a peculiarity of our people and plays a fundamental role in our history and our identity. Thinkers, artists, politicians, historians, and educators all made their different contributions toward creating what would become the Official Story, the basis of the national Uruguayan identity.

Uruguay, like any nation, archetypically sought to forge an identity for itself and, to do so, has followed certain patterns in the construction of its history. In this paper we will analyze some of the characteristics of this Official Story, showing how it disregarded essential foundational aspects that make up identity and that today express themselves in the form of cultural complexes that interfere with the functioning of our nation and how we relate to it.

Our thesis is that towards the end of the nineteenth century and the beginning of the twentieth, a proposed Uruguayan national identity was structured, giving rise to an artificial identity based on foundational myths built through historiographical accounts of the nation's development. As we shall see, this artificiality is based on the prioritizing of certain facts and values above others that are excluded and remain in the cultural unconscious in the form of complexes. We do not mean to imply that Uruguayan identity is pure artificiality. What we mean is that Uruguayan identity is the result of a historical process, an evolution, and not a predetermined intuition of destiny.

It is mandatory to begin with Uruguay's birth trauma. No Uruguayan fails to know deep down in his/her heart that Uruguay became part of history as a "buffer state," a term that we will explore shortly. It is a persistent ghost that cannot be eliminated even by the tenacious efforts of our old historiography to censure this fact. It is the most intensely repressed knowledge in all of us, embedded in our unconscious, because it is the most disturbing.[7]

And as Dr. Tomás Sansón Corbo stated in an interview with Marcello Figueredo on the occasion of our country's bicentennial celebrations,

> Uruguay suffers the traumas of an unwanted child who senses an accidental and hazardous existence.... The Uruguayan national being was in question from the moment in which it began the official operation of establishing its foundational frames of reference.... The construction of an "us" was built on weak foundations that do not withstand the onslaughts of a globalized world and of the MERCOSUR [Common Southern Market] project, which require cultural and identity strength.[8]

This was recently reflected in the fact that on the occasion of the celebrations of the bicentennial of our independence from Spain in 1811, the meaning of this national commemoration was once again placed in question.

A Brief History of Uruguay's Origin as a Buffer State

The creation of Uruguay as a nation, its geographic location, and its population density are relevant today and always have been. These factors have had a continuing influence on the construction of our cultural complexes: Uruguay, officially the Eastern Republic of Uruguay, is the second smallest country in South America in terms of surface area (176,000 sq km) with the third lowest population in South America (3.4 million inhabitants). It is situated like a small wedge between the two countries with the largest surface area of the subcontinent, Brazil and Argentina. The capital and largest city of Uruguay is Montevideo, with 1.2 million inhabitants, and its metropolitan area accounts for 58.5 percent of the total national population.

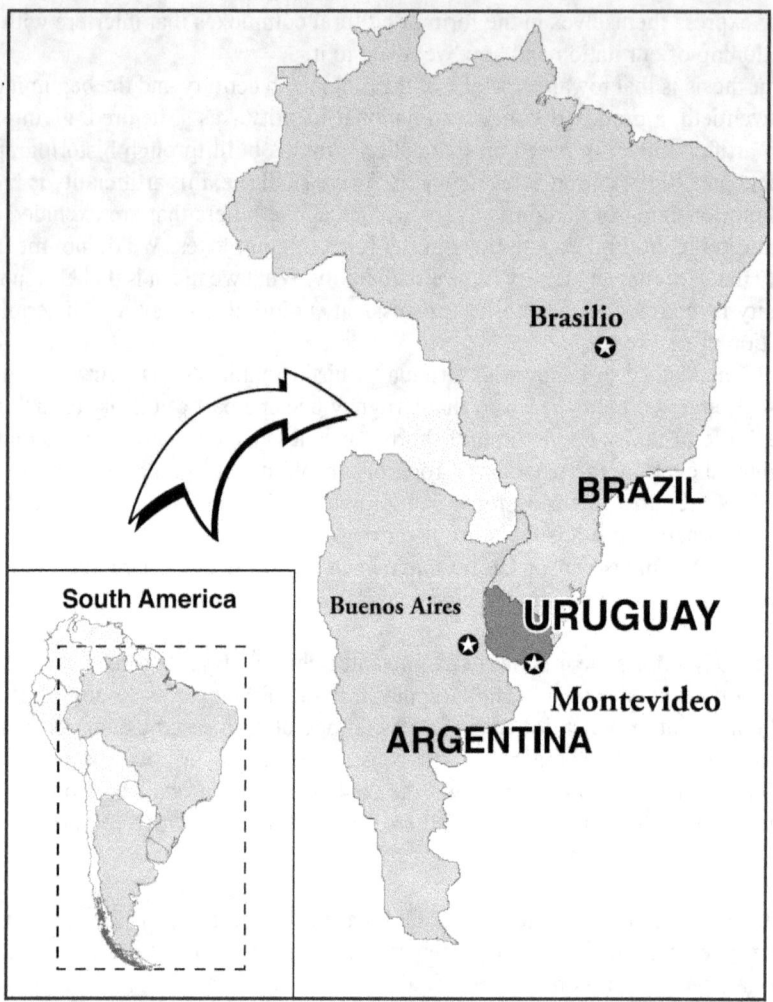

Figure 10.1 Uruguay as buffer state between Brazil and Argentina.

Uruguay is a country that geographically and politically was conceived as part of larger units. During the Spanish colonial period, it was part of the viceroyalty of the Rio de la Plata; during the efforts to achieve independence (1810 to 1820), it was part of the Federation of the United Provinces of the Rio de la Plata; and during the Brazilian dominion, it was a province of the Brazilian Empire. But as of 1830 it became an independent nation. This gradual dismemberment and achievement of independence is a process that we can find in the origins of many other countries, but unlike them, in the words of historian Gerardo Caetano, "Uruguay was born prior to the Uruguayans, the State preceded the nation."[9]

In this same vein, Professor Dr. Pablo da Silveira says,

> History knows of many cases of peoples who fought for their political independence without ever having achieved it, or only temporarily. . . . Rarer, however, is the situation of a country that had to face identity problems after having achieved its political independence and (at least according to certain interpretations) without really having sought it. That is the case of Uruguay.[10]

The current Uruguayan territory was "discovered" by the Spaniards and was part of the Spanish colony until the beginning of the nineteenth century, when it achieved its independence from Spain. It was known initially as "Banda Oriental" (which also included part of the current Brazilian state of Rio Grande do Sul). This name came from its geographic situation as the easternmost territory of the viceroyalty of the Rio de la Plata.

Anthropologist and social scientist Daniel Vidart asserts that the territory was considered to be "a useless strip of land"[11] because it had no material wealth, no organized indigenous civilization, and therefore, no culture prior to the Spanish colonization. It had practically no inhabitants and its only interest for the Portuguese and Spanish empires was for expansionist purposes.

Because of its in-between location, its borders varied according to the disputes between the neighboring powers. For example, the first city that was founded in the territory of the "Banda Oriental" was the so-called Sacramento Colony, considered today a World Heritage site. It was founded by the Portuguese in 1680 and conquered by the Spanish that same year. The following year it was recovered by the Portuguese, and it changed hands seven times during the course of the following century. The geographical boundaries of the "Banda Oriental" were never very clear. During the Spanish colonization it had no defined frontier; it was more like a frontier in itself. The name Uruguay is an indigenous name that was used to designate the name of a river, "the river of the painted birds." Uruguay is the name of a river but not of a country. In reality the country does not have a name; it is simply "the area that extends from the River Uruguay outward."[12] As the "Banda Oriental" had no precious metals or other riches that would interest the Europeans, for a long time it remained virtually uncolonized. The eastern territory only began to elicit some economic interest when livestock-rearing was introduced in 1600.

It was not until the Spanish founded Montevideo (the current capital of Uruguay) in 1726 and after they had created the viceroyalty of the Rio de la Plata in 1776 (the seat of which was Buenos Aires, the current capital of what we now know as Argentina) that Uruguay achieved territorial stability as a Spanish colony, a situation that lasted up to the beginning of the nineteenth century.

During the wars of independence from Spain at the beginning of the nineteenth century, the political proposal of José Gervasio Artigas, considered leader of the "Orientales" (the people of the Banda Oriental), was to form a federation – the Federation of the United Provinces of the Rio de la Plata – made up of the current provinces of Corrientes, Entre Ríos, Santa Fe, Misiones, Córdoba and Buenos

Aires, and the Banda Oriental. Except for the latter, nowadays the rest are all provinces of the Republic of Argentina.

In 1816 there was a new invasion by the Brazilian Empire, and the "Banda Oriental" became part of the empire under the name Cisplatina Province. Toward 1820, struggles for independence – this time from Brazil – took place. In 1825 an assembly of representatives of the eastern territory proclaimed its independence from Brazil and reiterated its wish to be a part of the Federation of United Provinces of the Rio de la Plata. Finally, due to the intervention of Great Britain, and to the fact that the confrontations between Argentina and Brazil were leading nowhere, it was agreed that the territory should become a free and independent nation in 1828. The constitution declaring it so was adopted in 1830.

From a demographic standpoint, in 1825 around 74,000 people lived in Uruguay. This population was made up in majority by Spaniards, plus some African descendants brought in mainly to perform domestic services, and a few indigenous people from the Guarani and Charrúa ethnic groups, which were assimilated into the general population.

From 1825 on, a major European immigration took place, mainly from Spain, Italy, and the Basque country, but also from France, England, Scotland, Germany, Switzerland, Austria, Poland, Lithuania, Hungary, Slovenia, Croatia, Greece, Russia, Ukraine, and Jews from different parts of the world – Romania, Syria, Lebanon, Palestine, and Armenia. "Perhaps unlike any other part of America, the Europeans in Uruguay became acculturated, mixed their genes with the indigenous and black population, and became 'mestizos' in heart and soul."[13] Toward 1843 the capital, Montevideo, was a city predominantly made up of foreigners – 20,000 vis-à-vis 11,600 local inhabitants. In 1872, Uruguay's total population was 420,000 inhabitants, of which 103,000 were foreign immigrants. In 1950 the population rose to 2,400,000 – that is, a 32-fold growth in the course of 125 years, due mainly to successive migratory waves. This occurred because the relatively unpopulated region of Rio de la Plata became highly attractive due to its potential to generate work, mainly commerce, agriculture, and cattle raising, for the many immigrant groups from which we are descended.

With this data we want to show that, in addition to not having clear boundaries, Uruguay did not have a population with its own identity. It was a tri-ethnic population, with no defining religion, language, or culture. The indigenous population, the Guaraní that survived the various invasions, was also in Paraguay, where their numbers were far greater. Spanish was spoken, but so was Portuguese because of the proximity to Brazil in the north. It is difficult to find customs in Uruguay that could not also be found in Argentina, Brazil, or Paraguay.

The maximum wave of immigration from all over Europe took place approximately between 1860 and 1920. The influx of immigrants was such that they practically overwhelmed the preexisting population. The country's physiognomy and even its memory changed.

After years of confrontation, of *caudillismo* (rule of local overlords), and after the arrival of so many people from such varied origins, a power vacuum arose in the country's leadership, and a sort of national identity crisis occurred. The idea began to take shape that it was necessary for the ruling authorities to establish a history of the country's history, an official version that would serve to consolidate the foundations of Uruguayan nationality and identity. To this end, politicians, intellectuals, and artists made efforts to establish the fundamentals on which the Uruguayan nationality would be created. An Official Story thus came into being.

The Official Story of Uruguay and Its Archetypal Patterns

We believe that, as part of the peculiarities of the formation of our identity, a unique culture was created that is a mix of citizens whose ancestors emigrated from different places in Europe and who coexist with the descendants of the indigenous and black peoples in a homogenous culture.

This is perhaps one of our greatest virtues, having managed to constitute a unit in spite of the relative differences in the origins of our inhabitants: white Europeans, blacks of African descent, and South American indigenous people. This has made us a flexible society, open to new ideas and customs. There is a hospitality in Uruguay that is highly valued by foreigners, which speaks of our openness to diversity and the possibility of pacific coexistence.

The Uruguayan society is a melting pot where the original culture was fused into something different that constitutes contemporary Uruguay. We use the term "culture" here in the sense given to it by Dr. Pablo da Silveira: "Culture in an anthropological sense is a wealth of ideas, knowledge and interpretations that allow us to assert that we live in the same world."[14] The Official Story managed to accomplish to a certain degree what it set out to achieve. Today Uruguayans have a sense of national identity that differentiates us from other nations. We feel pride in our nation and do not wish to renounce it. We do not want to be part of a greater territory that would involve sacrificing our national identity.

As in all national identity processes, ours has not been free from difficulty. This can be seen in a shadow or unconscious aspect of our identity that is revealed in the interaction of the Uruguayans among themselves and with foreigners. This is inevitable because for a successful and cohesive identity formation to take place, it must be based on certain archetypal patterns. In general, archetypal patterns appear in the form of polarities, with one of the poles tending to be favored and its opposite repressed or denied. The identity-creating process needs to suppress the tension between poles and tilt toward one of them. The rejected pole remains in the unconscious and, as we mentioned earlier on, tends to become a complex that coexists with the official identity.

The need to create a national unity leads to the construction of a specific cultural model. In this regard, Luciano Alvarez defines it as follows:

> In Uruguay there remains in force – in crisis, but still in force – a model for conceiving culture imposed by the hegemonic project of modernization of

the late nineteenth century and initial decades of the twentieth. A Jacobin, totemic, learned, patriotic, secular, national, cosmopolitan and egalitarian cultural model . . . Jacobin because it was conceived as the only possible model, a hegemonic and official cultural model that ignored or at least underrated the multiculturalism that came in together with the immigrants' poor chattels, forcing them to pay the toll of oblivion in exchange for integration. It "folklorized" the countryman, turning him into a decorative version of a gaucho; forcibly substituted unruly religion with a totemic system of national heroes and secular or secular-leaning thinkers, and built the "Uruguayan idiosyncrasy" – the national identity – in opposition to the neighboring regions. The national historic narratives were anti-Argentine and anti-Brazilian. The cultural model also opted to be cosmopolitan and our education prided itself on being "universal" and egalitarian, shaping republicans from the classroom onward.[15]

As we shall see, the proposed Official Story is sustained by three archetypal patterns that often are present in the creation of a unified sense of identity of a people. These are the following:

1) The process of creating a sense of belonging that includes members and excludes outsiders – homogeneity versus diversity.
2) The process of establishing order over chaos, which leads to the institutionalization of an all-powerful state as a symbol of national identity that is unchanging and perpetuates itself over time. The active role of individuals and private undertaking in the construction of a country is thus blurred.
3) The process by which a predominantly patriarchal founder-hero arises, an exemplary figure in a mythical time where weaknesses and failures are ignored.

The Tendency Toward Homogenization

In the Official Story there is a tendency to establish the theme of identity in a definitive manner. The Official Story has left deep marks on our Uruguayan identity because it fragmented our history, disregarding that part of our history that we will call "Oriental," by which we mean that which preceded what we call "Uruguayan" history. Here we must specify what is meant by "Uruguayan" and by "Oriental." What is meant by Uruguayan is that which is born as a result of the migratory landslide, of foreign origin and mostly urban, whereas what is meant by "Oriental" precedes the Uruguayan history and relates more to what is indigenous, telluric, and rural. "The 'Orientales' was how they referred to themselves – the *criollos* (creoles) of a country that was originally settled on a territory with a changing and relatively indeterminate surface area called the "Banda Oriental."[16] To create an identity, the concept of "Uruguayan-ness" was promoted in the Official Story, placing special emphasis on fostering mechanisms through which the inherent differences between the immigrants and the local and indigenous population could be erased.

In its beginnings, this was a poor and fairly unrewarding land with a very scant population and no culture of its own. It was a territory with undefined borders inhabited by indigenous people, *criollos* of Spanish and Portuguese descent, and some black slaves. This dimension is rarely included in the story we are told, an omission that supports the notion that we are nothing. Perhaps a complex would not have built up if it had, in fact, been accepted that we became something on the basis of this "nothingness." If we do not include "nothingness" as a frame of reference for our beginnings, it is difficult for us to value what we have created, produced, and built. The little that was here blended with what came from abroad, and that blend is our nation today. By denying what was originally here, we are led to believe that everything we are came from outside.

It is true that what came from outside is also part of us, but even here a second denial operates, which is the reality of what happened to these same immigrants. The places they came from are valued – that is, the fact that they were European – but we forget that to a certain extent these immigrants were themselves driven out of their places of origin. Thus the nostalgia for their own culture became part of our nostalgia also. When we say that we are a European country, we deny the precarious or helpless condition of the immigrant. We forget the helplessness of our ancestors who mostly came here as a rejected people, with no place in the world in which to live. They were adventurers who began to populate our lands as a last resort, many times without even knowing whether they were in Uruguay, Paraguay, Argentina, or Brazil.

Tomás Linn says very aptly:

> That is why the famous saying, "Uruguayans are descended from the ships," has a pejorative connotation denouncing their lack of roots. Other countries whose population "descended from ships" built their identity on that basis. The United States speaks of an ethnic "melting pot," perhaps idealized but based on undeniable facts. Uruguay, which up to the 1950s experienced a migratory history similar to that of the U.S., prefers to evade the issue. They descended from ships, yes, and then populated the country. By spurning at a national level what is valued deep down inside, Uruguay denies a genuine form of identity. The day that the saying "they descended from ships" is turned into an epic story, only then will the country be able to establish its roots and project them into the future.[17]

Here is what Tomas Linn has to say about the Official Story and how it dealt with incorporating the customs of European immigrants into the educational system:

> The Official Story emphasized the homogenous aspect of the culture in a deliberate policy to strengthen, in an artificial and fragile manner, a "national" style. In the face of a population of migratory origin (where the Mediterranean European current was predominant), instead of integrating the customs that each group brought with it, these were swept away and a single way of being was

established at schools and other socialization contexts, which, being rootless, was guided by those in government. To feel Uruguayan it was necessary to forget your origins. One single lexicon and its pronunciation was imposed, and expressions brought from abroad were repressed. Nothing remained of the "cocoliche," a Galician way of speaking that was neutralized in just one generation. The expressions of the Eastern European Jews that were incorporated into the native idioms of Argentina or the United States simply disappeared in Uruguay.[18]

Homogeneity takes its toll in the sense that individuals and individual cultures are not allowed to stand out because to do so would clash with the ideal of a mythical homogeneity. For a Uruguayan, it is difficult to exhibit success, prosperity, or happiness because it threatens the ideal of equality that is also at the core of the identity created by the Official Story. No one is more than anyone else, and no one should excel. Society has to advance collectively toward the achievement of its goals as if it were a platoon of cyclists where no one can ride ahead to be the first to arrive at the finishing line. Those who are very successful are considered to have achieved their success by chance, through suspicious means, and only very grudgingly through their own merit.

The dark emotion at the root of this cultural complex is mostly envy, which in its negative aspect seeks to bring people down to the same inferior level. In our clinical practice we have seen the effects that this cultural complex has on individuals, particularly in terms of the guilt that being different generates and the fear of provoking envy. Very few have the courage to state in public that they are happy, that they possess material goods, or that they have achieved things on their own merit. *Lamentablemente estamos bien* (*Unfortunately, We're OK*) is the title of a book by Lelia Marcor, a Venezuelan journalist, in which she describes this Uruguayan idiosyncrasy. She writes,

> The feeling of guilt that many Uruguayans have because they lead a comfortable life, when there is so much poverty in the world and most of all in the country, leaves any newcomer perplexed. The thing is that the "Orientales" are committed adherents to solidarity, even if many practice their liturgy in word only.[19]

Uruguayans tend to feel guilty about feeling good, happy, being prosperous, and possessing material goods. Ostentation is frowned upon; Uruguayans are modest, austere, seldom express their emotions, are mistrustful of fame, and try not to stand out from the crowd. They must show solidarity at all times. One extreme of this attempt at cultural homogenization is secularity or repression of religiosity. Uruguayans are known for their unfestive character; a certain air of sadness pervades Uruguayan celebrations, in which dancing and movement are present only in ritualized form. There is no spontaneity where laughter and good humor are the dominant note. Our favorite celebration, aside from the traditional ones, that manages to promote a strong affective charge and involves the participation of many

Uruguayans of all ages and social strata is, believe it or not, the so-called Nostalgia Night that takes place every August 24, the night before the commemoration of the Declaration of Independence (August 25, 1825). On that occasion, people dance to the music of the 1960s.

The All-Powerful State

The second archetypal pattern we highlight in the creation of the Official Story refers to the need for order to prevail over chaos. It is important to note that the historic time in which the Official Story was created was one of crisis, discouragement, disorientation, and a need for the establishment of order. For the inhabitants of Montevideo, chaos was represented by the *caudillos* in the interior of the country, local overlords ruling over the countryside much like a kind of feudal organization. The example that was taken to embody the sought-after order was the structure and functioning of the military as a symbol of regulation, obedience, and loyalty.

The key role awarded by the Official Story to the state generates a cultural complex that leads us to conceive of private life and activity as very threatening. The Official Story was formulated by intellectuals living in the capital city. They considered what was going on beyond the city gates – that is, in rural areas, the scantly populated countryside with little communication with the capital – to be barbaric and a focal point of disorder. The places outside the capital were the dominion of the local *caudillos*, who ruled politically and economically over their respective fiefdoms. The private sphere was confused with the barbarism of the *caudillo*-led countryside, and the order found in the cities was extolled as the paradigm of patriotic virtue.

The Official Story promotes the existence of an all-powerful state capable of guaranteeing the very existence of the nation. This idea has been reaffirmed many times throughout Uruguayan history and continues to this day. It is reinforced by our educational, political, and economic policies. Whatever is trustworthy and safe comes to us from the state. The state is the guarantor of our existence as a nation and as a people. The realm of private life and activity generates distrust. It is as if the state is a selfless caretaker of the interests of the nation, and the private sphere presents a threat through which individuals might seek to exploit for their own gain what is common to all, the wealth that belongs to all. A serious consequence of this is that private individuals do not assume responsibility for themselves because responsibility lies with the state. We do not believe that we are capable of generating change if we are not under state protection.

From the end of the nineteenth century onward, the national state acquired an importance that makes it almost identical to the concept of national identity. The existence of this all-powerful, omnipresent state is a source of national pride. The notion of the central role of the welfare state that distrusts the private sector is valued. The private sector is mistrusted and associated with pettiness and egotism as contrasted with the equality and solidarity which the state guarantees.

The state is present in every national activity of interest and regulates the most minute details of Uruguayan life. The state guarantees the way of life of Uruguayans and is in charge of overseeing and ensuring the care and happiness of its citizens. Examples of this are the monopoly held by public universities until 1985 and the monopoly of the state over communications, electric power, and insurance.

Artigas as a National Hero

The third archetypal pattern underlying the Official Story has to do with the creation of a national hero. To this end, the Official Story extols above and beyond the real facts the figure of our ultimate hero, José Gervasio Artigas. It is said that Artigas fought for a nation separate from the rest of the Argentinean provinces. In reality, Artigas never strove for the "Banda Oriental" to be an independent province or nation. In fact, after his integrationist project failed, Artigas left for Paraguay, where he lived for 30 years until his death in 1850, leaving unrealized the project for which he fought and became a hero. So in truth, is Artigas a hero who fought for Uruguay? Yes, he fought, but he fought for a country that is not the nation that was created when the Constitution of 1830 was adopted. He fought for something that never materialized, and that took him into exile before seeing the birth of his child, "Uruguay."

If we confine ourselves to the Official Story, it would appear to begin and end with the figure of Artigas. His ideals appear to be unsurpassable and unquestionable. But like Prometheus and some other hero figures, Artigas, with his aspiration to integrate the Federation of United Provinces of the Rio de la Plata, proposed an ideal that, although very attractive, was too ambitious. His objective exceeded the real possibilities of integration that existed at the time and that exist today. Something that is taking place today parallels Artigas' overreaching. We are thinking of the great difficulty that is being experienced with regard to the operational capability of MERCOSUR (Southern Common Market), which promotes political and economic exchange among Uruguay, Paraguay, Argentina, and Brazil. Just like what happened to Artigas and his ideal, the MERCOSUR proposal today is no more than a tempting but unviable project because it fails to take into account the individual realities of each of the member countries. Uruguay is once again left in the role of spectator and at the mercy of the economic decisions and policies of its two elder siblings, Argentina and Brazil.

Getting back to the Official Story, its main feature was to glorify the protagonist and circumstances out of which the country was born. It set aside the human dimension of the facts and the people, their frustrations and traumas, in order to create an artificial standard that would serve as a model for the construction of our national hero. Thus, the Official Story denies our plunge into helplessness. We can say that Uruguay started off its independent life in a state of helplessness. The helplessness into which we were born comes from having been abandoned by those to whom we naturally wanted to belong (Argentina), having been forced to defend ourselves against those we were never part of (Brazil), and culminates with some stranger coming along who not only did not adopt us but told us you ARE, you are on your own (Great Britain).

The Official Story states that a Uruguayan identity existed from the outset. It tells us that we were a people who strove to be independent and wanted to create a separate nation with its own autonomy and freedom. This is the reason why Artigas and his ideology were immortalized. The extolling of Artigas' exploits and holding him out as practically the only national hero in our Official Story makes it difficult for us to value what existed before and what came later on. What existed before refers to our indigenous roots, and what came later was the heroism of the immigrants. There is a marked inability to recognize new national heroes and, in a certain sense, the heroism of daily life.

What is valued and idealized is a false success, which makes it even more urgent and important to extol the lie and deny the truth. This leads to a tendency to remain fixed in the successes of the past, leaving us unable to adjust to the present because no opportunities are offered to understand and digest our origins in mourning, loss, and "nothingness." Uruguay won the world soccer cup in 1950, and the famous phrase "Uruguayans, champions of the world" has prevailed, even though the country's team never again reached the quarter finals until the last world championship in 2010. Not being able to mourn its failures cost the national team many years when it was unable to improve its game. Traditionally, Uruguay was known to have one of the best educational systems in Latin America, but with the passing of time, Uruguayans paid no attention to the innovations that were taking place in education in other parts of the world. Our educational programs and the system as a whole are thus becoming obsolete, but we are incapable of proposing substantial changes that would initiate new trends. On the economic level, the belief that we are the Switzerland of America did not allow us to prepare for the crises that invariably strike in the global economic sphere and that have inevitably affected us.

This fixation on past successes leads to a certain deification of them and a difficulty in being alert to changes that are necessary in the natural course of life. The extolling of the figure of Artigas and the idealizing of his exploits and aspirations forces us to deny the failure of the real Artigas project. Artigas failed due to the hegemonic aspirations of Buenos Aires, which prevented his vision from becoming a reality. This actual historical reality, as opposed to the Official Story, lives on in the Uruguayan psyche as a cultural complex of conflict and ambivalence towards Argentina.

In the Official Story, Buenos Aires represents the antagonist *par excellence*, not of Artigas anymore, but instead of the struggle to become an independent nation. Uruguayans have a more problematic relationship with Buenos Aires than with the other Argentinean provinces. Our cultural complex of denying a common origin with Argentina results in a conflicted love/hate attitude towards Buenos Aires. On the one hand, we imitate its tastes, ways of doing things, and dress, and on the other hand, we delight in celebrating the defeats of our sister republic, Argentina.

Uruguayans project onto the "*porteño*" (inhabitant of Buenos Aires) the desire to be big, to be dominant. A feeling of inferiority of Uruguayans in relation to Argentineans exists due to the smallness of our country in terms of size and population, but curiously that does not occur in our relations with Brazil, which is even larger and more powerful than Argentina. This may be due to the fact that, originally, each of the United Provinces of the Rio de la Plata was of a similar size to that of the "Banda Oriental." But Argentina grew, and Uruguay shrank. The knowledge of this contraction is repressed in collective memory but surfaces in a cultural complex of Uruguay in relation to Argentina.

Final Reflections

When there is a split in some aspect of the cultural identity of a society, it leaves in the shadows – that is, in the unconscious and grouped into complexes – values, experiences, occurrences, and histories that remain unelaborated and that are fated to surface at some point in the life of a nation.

Throughout this chapter we have attempted to show how the repressed poles of three archetypal patterns operate in the form of cultural complexes. These repressed poles have been left out of our national identity as it has been set forth in the Official Story of Uruguay, which is the history that the state chose to narrate about itself.

In the case of Uruguay, the Official Story emphasized cultural homogeneity, focused the indispensable need for order and safety on the state, and built a founding national myth around a unique and unblemished hero who played a fundamental role in the birth of the fatherland.

The Official Story denied the country's origins in "nothingness." It denied the country's smallness, its natives, its *gauchos*, its blacks. It denied the diversity of its European immigrants. It denied the desire to be part of what is today Argentina. It denied the heroism of the immigrant, the importance of individual effort, its colonial origins, and it denied the precariousness, frailty, and failure of its ultimate hero.

What is unique about the Uruguayan experience is that its identity is mostly based on the Official Story. It is for this reason that anything that is experienced by an individual, and which refers to the past (mostly to a traumatic past), is outweighed by the official discourse and is the reason why we Uruguayans from time to time fall prey to a feeling of devaluation that leads us to be ungrateful to our country and fail to value what we have contributed and are called upon to contribute to other nations.

We think it is essential for Uruguayans to rescue and to bring to a conscious level as part of our national identity the polarities of our founding archetypal patterns that were repressed and that are manifest today in our cultural complexes: the acceptance of diversity, the importance of private initiative, either by individuals or groups, and the fact that history is not the result of the actions of one sole hero but of the actions of each and every Uruguayan.

Notes

1. Christian Roesler, "Archetypal Patterns in Postmodern Identity Construction," in *Cultures and Identities in Transition*, eds. Murray Stein and Raya A. Jones (New York: Routledge, 2010), p. 55.
2. Richard Kradin, "The Family Myth: Its Deconstruction and Replacement with a Balanced Humanized Narrative," *Journal of Analytical Psychology*, no. 54 (April 2009): 217–232.
3. Julio De Zan, "Memoria e Identidad," *Revista de Filosofía de Santa Fe*, Rep. Argentina, no. 16 (2008): 41–67.
4. Erik Erikson, *Historia personal y Circunstancia Histórica* (Madrid: Alianza Editorial S.A., 1979).
5. Thomas Singer and Samuel Kimbles, "The Emerging Theory of Cultural Complexes in Analytical Psychology," in *Contemporary Perspectives in Jungian Analysis*, eds. Joseph Cambray and Linda Carter (New York: Brunner Routledge, 2004), pp. 184–185.
6. Nora Pierre, quoted in Julio De Zen, "Memoria e Identidad," *Revista de Filosofía de Santa Fe*, Rep. Argentina, no. 16 (2008), pp. 41–67.
7. Alberto Methol Ferré, *Uruguay como problema* (Uruguay: Diálogo, 1967), p. 10.
8. Marcello Figueredo, *Uruguay 200 años 200 preguntas* (Montevideo: Ed. Santillana S.A., 2011), p. 339.
9. Gerardo Caetano, "Identidad nacional e imaginario colectivo en Uruguay. La síntesis perdurable del Centenario," in *Identidad uruguaya: ¿mito, crisis o afirmación?*, eds. Hugo Achugar and Gerardo Caetano (Montevideo: Trilce, 1992), p. 81.
10. Pablo da Silveira, "La nacionalidad como problema: entre Habermas y San Agustín," in *Relatos de Nación. La construcción de las identidades nacionales en el mundo hispánico, Vol. II*, ed. Francisco Colom (Madrid and Frankfurt am Main: Ed. Iberoamericana/Vervuert, 2005), p. 916.
11. Daniel Vidart, *Los Fugitivos de la Historia* (Montevideo: Ed. Banda Oriental, 2009), p. 74.
12. Jaime Clara, *Cultura, Identidad y Comunicación: Uruguay, ¿quién dice creo?* (Diss., Coloquio Panamericano, Montreal, 2002).
13. Daniel Vidart, *Los Fugitivos de la Historia* (Montevideo: Banda Oriental, 2009), p. 31.
14. Pablo da Silveira, "La educación siempre llega tarde," *Review Digital de Cultura*, no. 3 (2006): 1. Available at www.dosmil30.org/dosmil30/files/articulos/20061201a.pdf.
15. Luciano Alvarez, "Podemos darnos el gusto de la postmodernidad," in *Mundo, Región y Aldea: Identidades, Políticas Culturales e Integración Regional*, eds. Hugo Achugar, Gerardo Caetano and Luciano Alvarez (Montevideo: Ed. Trilce, 1994), p. 113.
16. Vidart, *Los Fugitivos*, p. 81.
17. Tomás Linn, "Tras una esquiva identidad nacional (4) Argentina y los que descienden de los barcos," in *Búsqueda Revista Semanal* (Montevideo, Uruguay, February 7, 2008).
18. Ibid.
19. Lelia Macor, *Lamentablemente estamos bien* (Montevideo: Ed. Sudamericana Uruguaya, S.A., 2008), p. 28.

Venezuela

Chapter 11

The Gringo Complex

Áxel Capriles M.

One popular anecdote about the etymology of the word "*gringo*" is that the term first appeared in 1846 during the Mexican-American War. The North American soldiers loved to sing a folk song named "Green Grow the Rashes, Oh!", based on Robert Burns' poem by that name. The Mexicans nicknamed the invaders "*gringos*" due to the initial words of the song. Another folk etymology reports that some Yankee battalions wore green uniforms, and the Mexicans would scream at them: "Greens, go home!" There are many more popular anecdotes about the etymology of "*gringo*," and most of them refer to the Mexican-American experience in the nineteenth century. The word *gringo*, however, seems to have had an earlier origin as it was already used in eighteenth-century Spain as a name for foreigners who spoke Spanish with an accent. That is the core of today's official meaning of the slang word. In the *Dictionary of Language of the Royal Spanish Academy*, it is a noun that colloquially means foreigner, someone who speaks a language that is not Spanish. In most Latin American countries, however, it is applied mainly to North Americans. From the Río Grande to Patagonia, with small differences in meaning (in some places, it can be a synonym for blonde-haired people) and bigger differences in value connotations (from neutral to pejorative), *gringo* fundamentally indicates someone from the US. Much more than a descriptive term, however, the word *gringo* denotes a cultural complex, a wide range of collective images with strong and pervasive feeling tones.

This complex representation is particularly relevant in Venezuelan society today. Since the triumph of the Socialist Bolivarian Revolution in 1998, the political use of the term has been charged with contempt, resentment, and hate. The rhetoric of the Bolivarian Revolution has, however, a strong echo in many other Latin American countries, such as Bolivia, Ecuador, and Nicaragua. Anti-*gringo* and anti-Imperialist pronouncements have been a leitmotiv of Latin American political discourse since the nineteenth century. There is an article on "Anti-Americanism" in the well-known Internet *Free Encyclopedia Wikipedia*. It is defined as a "broad opposition or hostility to the people, policies, culture or government of the United States"[1] found in all continents. However, in the Spanish version of *Wikipedia* the article is solely about Anti-Americanism in Latin America. While these negative feelings and opinions have been very common in the discourse of revolutionary movements, guerrillas, and leftist parties, as in student riots and upheavals, they have been routinely tempered or disguised in the oratory of Chiefs of State or in diplomatic circles.

Yet in the dominant discourse of power in twenty-first-century Venezuela, this does not hold true. In this northern territory of South America adjacent to the Caribbean Sea, *gringo* is a bad word even in the Foreign Ministry. It is the final cause, the source of all evil. During the last 13 years, in the many and long speeches of President Hugo Chávez, in his recurrent and enforced radio and television broadcasts, there has been a reiterative condemnation of American Imperialism, an explicit accusation of North America as the cause of our ills. For non-Venezuelan readers and those unacquainted with the Bolivarian Revolution and the Venezuelan political process, it is possible to search in Google or any Internet browser the words *Gringo* or Yankee, together with the name of the President of Venezuela, Hugo Chávez, and find many entries where the appellations for the inhabitants of North America are followed by accusations, insults, coarseness, and vulgarities. It is not a matter that can be discarded as an individual fixation or a personal obsession of someone in power. Politics is mass psychology, and Latin American Populism, much more than a political movement, is a psychological phenomenon.

One of the emblematic presidential harangues, of which there is a video that can be seen on YouTube,[2] took place on September 12, 2008, in a crowded political meeting where President Hugo Chávez unadvisedly announced the expulsion of the American Ambassador, giving him 72 hours to leave the country, as he screamed to the crowds: "Go to hell, Yankee of shit, there are meritorious people here" (*"Váyanse p'al carajo yanquis de mierda que aquí hay un pueblo digno"*). The phrase "go to hell, *gringos* of shit" (interchanging Yankee with *gringo*) was repeated and celebrated in all government groups and media. It made the headlines of hundreds of newspapers as well as being featured on numerous radio and television news programs.

The scatological crudeness of the language used by the highest dignitary of a nation can cause surprise, but if one had been in the audience where the speeches were delivered or had seen the television reprisals of many of these discourses, rallies, and meetings, much more surprising was the cathartic reaction of the public to these diatribes. Their reaction seemed to reflect the atavistic emotional discharge of a group that, in other circumstances, normally behave as common consumers of a Contemporary Occidental Society, wearing Nike shoes and eating at McDonalds. In Venezuelan political discourse, the word *gringo* functions as what Thomas Singer calls a *trigger word*, a word that has "the power to activate deeply entrenched cultural complexes, at the core of which are archetypal contents."[3]

> Once a cultural complex has been touched, it can easily generate "us *vs* them" dynamics in different groups of people as a consequence of the potent emotions and stereotypical beliefs that are embedded in the complex through long and repetitive histories.[4]

This "us vs them" split, the polar division of society between patriots and traitors, bolivarians and pitiyankees (imitators of the *gringos*), revolutionaries and oligarchs, poor and rich, *chavistas* and opposition, good-hearted socialists and perverse capitalists, accompanied by potent emotions, resentment, hatred or fear, has been the most prominent trait of Venezuelan society for the last 12 years. Polarization, as it is commonly called in the press, is a constant theme of public debate, and how to overcome the social split is the first topic in all projects of national reconstruction.

The animadversion against North Americans is not new. If one looks at a famous and popular humorous magazine from the beginning of the twentieth century, *Fantoches*, one finds plenty of caricatures of big, fat *gringos* despoiling the thin, poor Venezuelan people. In the first and most widely read novel about the impact of oil on our society, *Mene* (which is compulsory reading for high school students), its author, Rafael Díaz Sánchez, states basic themes of our political culture: the domination and violence of the oil companies, the oppression and destruction of our national pride, the exclusion and humiliation of our people. Poverty and underdevelopment are the result of the unjust terms of interchange between the candid and open-hearted natives and the powerful foreigners, who plunder our natural resources.

In Venezuelan popular slang, the word *caribear* means to take advantage of someone weaker than you, to deceive, to cheat, and to impose upon a credulous and open-hearted person. The expression, according to a common folk etymology, seems to have had its origin in the conflicts around the oil concessions at the beginning of the twentieth century, in particular, the one-sided terms and conditions imposed by The Caribbean Oil Company. The argument of the Imperialist exploitation is the ideological thread running through the thought of Rómulo Betancourt, the leader and founder of the Venezuelan Democracy and of the most influential political party of the twentieth century, *Acción Democrática (AD)*, considered, until the arrival of the *chavismo* (the political movement under the leadership of President Hugo Chávez), to be the best and most perfect expression of our national idiosyncrasy. The popular character in the political imagination of the members of *Acción Democrática* became flesh in the person of Juan Bimba, a poor peasant, downcast, barefoot, with a loaf of bread under his arm, the archetypal victim despoiled by foreigners of the natural richness that belonged to him.

The image of the *gringo* in the political discourse of contemporary Venezuela is full of paradoxes, contradictions, and conflicts. The animosity in the public rhetoric toward the *gringo* is only one side of a double existence; it is the reverse current of a parallel reality. First, this is true because on the individual level, in personal contacts and relationships, the negative affective tones and valuations of the *gringo* we just mentioned are rarely present or are even displaced by feelings of sympathy. Creoles are particularly open and friendly to all foreigners. Second, Venezuela is one of the most Americanized of all Latin American countries. It is, besides Panama and Puerto Rico, the Hispano-American society that has adopted more

Figure 11.1 The poor Juan Bimba (Venezuelan people) and the fat gringo exploiter.
Source: *Fantoches*. Semanairo humorísticos y de intereses generales. 1938.

fully the American way of life, its habits and traditions. It is the country that best expresses and follows North American consumerism. In the same way that baseball is our national sport, or Disney World and Miami are the first tourist destinations for Venezuelan travelers, many traces of US culture are deeply ingrained in our social behavior. As the historian John Lombardi points out:

> Lacking of rooted traditions, of the long lasting institutions of other Latin American countries, Venezuela imported the entire whole. The economic orthodoxy, the political controversy and the social aspirations arrived together with the hydro electrical plants and the steel and automobile industries, the supermarkets and the highways, the housing construction projects and the suburban residential quarters.[5]

Third, because in concrete terms, in spite of all the political animosity, the United States is, by far, our first commercial partner. Just to give the reader an idea of the commercial bond between the two countries, from the total Venezuelan exports of goods and services of $59.6 billion in the year 2009, $34.795 billion went to the United States.[6] This means that almost 60 percent of our export income comes from our supposed political enemy. Our thinking reveals a political-economical schizophrenia. Our North American neighbor is politically evil and commercially good. Selling our oil to the American Empire gives us the affluence to finance and call together allies against the empire.

Historical Traumatic Events

The negative feeling tone of the *gringo* image is not the product of psychological vagary. Yankee Imperialism in Latin America is an undeniable economical, political, and military reality. It is rooted in historical facts. The famous anecdotal remark of the Mexican dictator Porfirio Díaz, "Poor Mexico, so far from God and so near the United States," depicts a feeling well grounded in a traumatic national experience. The US expansionism that led to the annexation of Texas in 1845 and to the Mexican-American War forced the Mexican cession in 1848 of what today are California, New Mexico, Arizona, Colorado, Nevada, Utah, Oklahoma, Kansas, and Wyoming. Mexico lost near 55 percent of its territory, an experience that seems to have been anticipated by the main Latin American hero and liberator Simón Bolívar, who in a letter to Colonel Patricio Campbell wrote in 1829, "The United States seems to be destined by the Providence to infest America with miseries in the name of Liberty."[7] In this line of argument, leftist intellectuals and politicians consider Simón Bolívar the forerunner of Latin American anti-imperialist thought. They argue that his proposal of a Hispano American amphictyony in the Panama Congress of 1826 was in response to his fear that a balkanized continent, the Spanish America, composed of small and weak countries, was the perfect stage for the *gringo*'s hegemonic desires and expansionism.

In 1898, with the Hispano-American War, the US took control of Puerto Rico and gained strong influence over Cuba. In 1903, it forced the independence of Panama from Colombia and took possession of the Panama Canal Zone. In 1904, Theodore Roosevelt, in his message to Congress, enunciated what became known as the Roosevelt Corollary, an extension of the Monroe Doctrine that gave the United States the right to act as an international police force and to intervene in any country that the US unilaterally considered to have behaved badly or that lacked order. Since then, Roosevelt's "big stick" policy became the symbol of the arbitrary power of the United States over Latin America. The *gringo* became the abuser, the one who imposes his will by money or force. Over the years, US marines have executed some 20 interventions in Central America and the Caribbean and felt free to depose presidents and governments and to impose dictators to their liking and interest. They occupied the Dominican Republic from 1916 to 1924 and supported the bloody dictator Rafael Leonidas Trujillo, who ruled the island for 30 years.

They occupied Nicaragua from 1912 to 1933 and left in power dictator Anastasio Somoza. The American Embassies and the Central Intelligence Agency (CIA) have had continuous involvement, intermeddling and taking various actions in many Latin American countries. The participation of the US in the overthrow of Manuel Noriega in Panama, its role in the coups against Jacobo Arbenz in Guatemala and Salvador Allende in Chile, or in the failed invasion of Bay of Pigs in Cuba in 1961, are all concrete facts that support the discourse of the heroic Latin American resistance to the arbitrary power of the North.

With such historical background and the psychological climate it produced, even US international assistance was interpreted in negative terms. President Kennedy's Alliance for Progress was a huge plan of American financial and technical help to systematically contribute to social, economic, and political progress of Latin America. Its goals were the drastic reduction of illiteracy, improvement in public education and public health, agricultural reforms that would lead to higher productivity, and the achievement of a minimum of 2.5 percent real annual growth per inhabitant with a better distribution of income. In the initial conference, in Punta del Este, Uruguay, the famous communist and revolutionary leader Che Guevara condemned American help and all governments that had accepted it. He said that the Alliance for Progress was nothing more than alms, only a small fraction of the wealth the United States had previously stolen from us. This argument spins a continuous thread that unites the thought of political leaders, like Víctor Raúl Haya de la Torre, Fidel Castro, and Salvador Allende, with that of intellectuals, such as Gabriel García Márquez and José María Vargas Vila, or important artists, including Diego de Rivera, José Clemente Orozco, and Roberto Matta.

The Venezuelan relationship with the United States is different from that of the US with other Caribbean and Hispano American countries. At least until the development of the oil industry in the second decade of the twentieth century, European countries, such as England, France, and Germany, were much more relevant and closer to Venezuelan affairs. The main creditors of Venezuela were European countries, and it was the United States that helped to put an end to the German and British blockade of the Venezuelan ports in 1902. Unlike Mexico, Panama, the Dominican Republic, or Puerto Rico, North American troops never touched Venezuelan territory and never had effective influence to impose leaders and governments. No person or government has come into power in Venezuela due to the influence of the CIA, the FBI, the American Embassy, or any other influence from the United States. President Harry Truman had a very close friendship with candidate Diógenes Escalante, but this candidate became crazy before he could be elected, and soon afterwards a military coup brought the nationalist Rómulo Betancourt into power.

Oil companies had, no doubt, a lot of power and obtained all kind of privileges and concessions, but they had to deal and negotiate with autonomous and sovereign governments. Oil concessions were given to international oil companies, from the US as well as Europe, because Venezuelans did not have the knowledge, technology, and capacity to exploit this resource ourselves. Foreign companies' rights to undertake petroleum exploration, extraction, and commercialization in exchange for the payment of rentals, royalties, and taxes were not an external imposition; they were not the result of the use of force. Venezuela, as a sovereign country, could have closed the doors to the greed of the Seven Sisters and developed its oil industry by itself. But no, it did not happen like that. Foreigners found immense wealth in our subsoil, and they were called to take it out, to exploit it. As a result and to our astonishment, Venezuela suddenly started to enjoy a richness and progress never seen or experienced before. In less than ten years after 1923, the *gringo*'s discovery of oil in our country allowed Venezuela to jump from the backward, poor, and malaria-infected country of the nineteenth century to the twentieth century. When the Venezuelan government felt prepared to take over the oil industry in 1975, the Venezuelan Congress passed a law that reserved hydrocarbons commercialization and industry to the State, and all the companies were nationalized.

The Americanization of our way of life may be a problem of imitation or cultural weakness, but it is not one imposed on us externally by the US. In this sense, anti-American and anti-Imperialist feelings in Venezuela are much more the product of contagion and *participacion mystique* with other Latin American nations than the effect of concrete, traumatic historical events. However, Venezuela shares with other countries of our hemisphere the vague feeling that Latin American poverty and underdevelopment are the result of North American Imperialism, that the US has blocked the necessary initiatives to transform our countries. The *gringos* impoverished us and sucked our natural resources to boost their own power and economy. They are the cause of our social backwardness, economic dependency, and political instability. They have what we lack because it was taken from us. North American development is inseparable from Latin American underdevelopment. The US blocked our prosperity.

We do not pretend to discuss the truth of these generalized opinions. It is extremely difficult to engage in debate about the objectivity and fundamentals of political assumptions and beliefs. But since Venezuelan history is so different from that of countries that have really been under the dominion, occupation, or tutelage of the United States, we will distance these opinions from reality and analyze them as psychological facts, as representations of the psychological complexities that our northern neighbors symbolize and pose to us. We want to understand the role that the image of the *gringo* has in the collective psychology of present Venezuelan society. Why does it generate so many contradictory feelings of admiration and scorn, of imitation and rejection? Against the dominant opinion of the Venezuelan (or Cuban) ruling class, instead of thinking about Imperialism and American exploitation in concrete and literal terms, we will reflect on them as psychological phenomena. This is a neglected approach necessary to understand the vicissitudes of modernity and progress in Latin America. Even outside the field of psychology, in contemporary studies of economic and human development, there is a growing consciousness that it is not possible to attribute the poverty of Third World nations only to external factors without also taking into consideration the internal incapacities of the involved nations, their own limitations and inabilities.

Why does a person or a collectivity become the victim in the first place? The colonial depredatory hypothesis and the dependency theory that attributed the poverty of the countries of the periphery to the exploitation of the nations of the center and to the unequal commercial interchange between countries that bought cheap and sold expensive are unsatisfactory and can easily be refuted. Hong Kong, Taiwan, and Singapore, rich countries today, were colonies in the past, and the dragons of Southeast Asia were once part of the periphery. As the historian David Landes points out, after a thorough analysis of the wealth and poverty of nations, "if we have learned something from the history of economic development, it is that culture is what determines the difference.... However, culture, meaning by it the values and attitudes that guide the population, frightens scholars."[8] The attribution of responsibility of our problems and failures to the *gringos* shows a collective value system dominated by an external locus of control, and as can be seen in many concrete facts, it serves as a mechanism for the canalization of frustration and aggression and as a target for psychological projection.

The Archetype of the Hostile Brothers

It is common in Venezuela and other Latin American countries to talk about the rest of the nations and societies on the continent as "sister" nations. "The sister Republics" or "our Colombian brothers" are frequent expressions in the political argot. In that sense, the *gringos* are our northern brothers and sisters. But how different is that northern brother/sister society? How and why did the younger brother grow so much taller?

When the Pilgrims arrived on the Mayflower at Plymouth, Massachusetts, in 1620, the city of La Hispaniola (Santo Domingo, Dominican Republic) had already been in existence for 124 years. It had the first church on the continent, founded in 1496; the first hospital, the Hospital of San Nicolas, built in 1503; the first bishopric in 1504; the first viceroyal government; and the Royal Audiencia (1511). When Boston or New York were still precarious settlements, Mexico City and Lima were rich and important cities. When the British colonies in North America united small groupings of peasants, Latin America already had the first universities on the American continent: the Real y Pontificia Universidad de Santo Tomás de Aquino, in la Hispaniola, founded in 1538; the University of San Marcos, in Lima, founded in 1551; and the University of México, created the same year. Until the seventeenth century, no one could imagine that the modest English colonies would ever compete with the wealthy and developed Spanish colonies. What happened that in a century the small northern brother suddenly became the first economic and military power in the world?

The archetype of the hostile brothers is a repetitive motif in mythology and folklore. It appears in many cultures – in art, myth, and religion – with complex psychological implications. In Egyptian mythology, the myth of Osiris is a dramatic story of jealousy and betrayal where the mighty king-god Osiris is cruelly killed by his brother Seth. In the Bible and Canaanite mythology, it appears in different forms: in the battle between Baal and Mot, in the rivalry between Cain and Abel, and in the story of Jacob and Esau. Among the Quiche, in Central America, in the Mayan Popol Vuh, it is the story of Hunbatz and Hunchouen, who envied and wanted to kill their brothers Hunahpú and Ixbalanqué. The motif of the jealous brother or sister is also the starting point of a number of fairy tales. As C.G. Jung writes,

> Yahweh had one good son and one who was a failure. Cain and Abel, Jacob and Esau, correspond to this prototype, and so, in all ages and in all parts of the world, does the motif of the hostile brothers, which in innumerable modern variants still causes dissension in families and keeps the psychotherapist busy.[9]

Traditionally, in Jungian psychology, the hostile brothers archetype has been commonly interpreted as the confrontation between the ego and the shadow, a dominant of the psyche often constellated in conflict situations. It has to do with deception and narcissistic downgrades of the ego. In the Baal cycle, Mot is invited to a meal of bread and wine, but since he always hungers for human flesh and blood, he is offended. Baal sends messengers to provide cattle and sheep for the meal and speakers to tell Mot that Baal will always be his slave. Offense is the main reason of Mot's battle against Baal, and as we will see, submission, offense, and dignity are fundamental words in Latin America's political rhetoric against American Imperialism.

Erich Neumann interprets the motif of the hostile brothers as the archetype of self-division. He sees it as a stage in the evolution of the ego, as a sign of an incipient ego that is starting to differentiate from the unconscious but does not yet have the independence to integrate the destructive and creative elements. "This separation and the consequent emergence of the twin-brother conflict mark an important stage of the way to the final dissolution of the uroboros, separation of the World Parents, and consolidation of the ego consciousness."[10] According to Neumann, in the process of attaining self-consciousness and gaining independence from the Great Mother, the ego redirects its aggression and movement to "another male hostile to him," and "a conflict situation develops in which self-defense becomes possible for the first time."[11]

Following this line of thought and extending it to collective psychology, we might imagine that the rival brother archetype as reflected in the Gringo Complex illustrates a stage in the process of the construction of a Latin American and Venezuelan sense of collective identity. As the incipient individual ego that does not have the strength and independence to face and integrate destructive elements, collectivities, in moments of crises or during phases of reorganization and development, need to redirect the aggression and tension of its members to a hostile figure as a mechanism of self-defense to preserve a certain internal cohesion. The twin-brother conflict shows the tension of opposites in the process of separation and differentiation from the collective unconscious. The "us *vs.* them" dynamics can be seen as the enactment of the archetypal motif in the cultural unconscious, as an archaic mechanism for dealing with the problem of integration of insurmountable cultural paradoxes and conflicts until the excess of polarization and different circumstances can activate the transcendent function to find a new sense of community and purpose.

The feeling tones and the emotions of envy, resentment, admiration, and emulation are always present in the relationship with parents and siblings as they are in the Gringo Complex. Sigmund Freud was one of the first to point out the importance of envy and rivalry between brothers and sisters in the construction of the ego. In his book *The Psychology of the Masses and the Analysis of the Ego*, he writes,

> For a long period, the boy does not show any sign of the gregarious instinct or of a collective feeling. Both start to build up slowly in the nursery, as effects of the relations between children and his parents and precisely as a reaction to the envy with which the older son receives at the beginning the intrusion of his new little brother.[12]

It is because of her sisters' envy that Psyche breaks her idyllic relationship with Eros and starts her trip of psychic development. "Whatever the truth may be," said the elder sister, "we must ruin her as soon as possible. But if she has never seen her husband, then he must be a god, and her baby will be a god too. If anything like that happens, which Heaven forbid," said the younger, "I'll hang myself at once – I couldn't bear Psyche to mother an immortal. I think we have a clue to the best way of tricking her."[13] Envy is based on comparison, and it is, no doubt, a very destructive emotion. Its goal is not to obtain the desired object but to destroy it. But it is also an affect that puts us in psychic movement and impels the process of *individuation*. It is a desire to develop our dull and clumsy side.

The Greeks from antiquity had different names for envy. *Phthónos* was rancorous envy. *Zēlos* was a feeling of pain for not having certain valued qualities such as honor, beauty, wealth, or intelligence. It was an emotion characteristic of the virtuous man which could be translated as emulation in a positive sense. This differentiation is important. Envy is commonly seen as a very negative and destructive passion. It is, however, a mistake to try to understand and to interpret the passions in a literal and concrete way. It is not exactly money or fame that the envious person wants. The meaning of passion is embedded in its own pattern, and its objects are part of a language that needs further translation. Affects and emotions, *passio animi, perturbatio animi*, are movements of the soul, rituals, and symbols that express the state and needs of psyche. Maybe the symbolic and prospective interpretation of the envy motif in the nucleus of the Gringo Complex is the possibility of transforming *phthónos* into *zēlos*, of converting rancor and animosity into desires of overcoming and healthy competition. The passion of envy can be understood as a symbolic act, as a call from inside to become conscious of a lack. It represents aspects of our personality that want to be made conscious. It is an enticement of soul to develop our inferior function. In his influential essay *Ariel*, the Uruguayan writer José Enrique Rodó depicted the confrontation of two *Weltanschauungs*, the opposition between the spiritual Ariel (Latin America) and the utilitarian Calibán (North America).[14] Ariel and Calibán have many things to emulate and learn from each other.

National Identity

The concept of individuality in personal psychology is mirrored in the idea of collective identity in mass psychology. It is a very difficult and controversial concept, very much connected with other theoretical constructs such as social character, modal personality, subjective culture, or collective mentality. The idea of a social and national identity has been a constant concern in Latin American history. Already in our Republican beginnings, the Liberator Simón Bolívar addressed the theme in two of his most important political writings, the *Discourse of the Congress of Angostura* and *The Letter of Jamaica*. "We are not Europeans; we are not Indians, but a new species in between the aborigines and the Spaniards."[15] "We are a small human gender; we have a separated world surrounded by vast seas."[16] Simón Bolívar, in fact, defined the process of independence as a confrontation between two clear-cut identities: Americans and Spaniards. His decree of war to the death, responsible for much of the intense and incisive pugnacity and cruelty that characterized our war of independence, established that all Spaniards, by the mere fact of being so, were *a priori* condemned to die with no need of fair trial. Since then, a countless troop of politicians and intellectuals has discussed the issue of collective and national identity, a constant concern and a basic motif of the public discourse. But in addition to geographical casualty, such as the place of birth, or some physiognomic traits that prove the mixture of races, what else defined that "small human gender," that new American Species? If new nations were going to be born, national traits were something to have in mind. Confronted with the countless obstacles and insurmountable difficulties in implanting political ideals in social reality, Simón Bolívar soon understood the complex relationship between personality and culture and the need to take into account the distinctive traits of the *mestizo* identity in order to construct the political and legal system of the new republics. Furthermore, not only were Europeans different from us, but Spanish-speaking America was totally distinct from the Anglo-Saxon one. That is why Bolívar repeatedly insisted on the inadequacy of copying the North American Constitution or institutions. Instead, we had to create anew a political system in accordance with our own idiosyncratic way of being.

The Liberator, however, like many others after him, never expanded and deepened his intuitions; he did not go further than just stating the differences between Latin Americans and other people. Lacking a positive and operational description of the identity of the new social being and missing a comprehensive concept to make explicit what it means and feels to be Colombian, or an image to reflect the basic structure of the personality of the Venezuelan, many of the traits attributed to the Latin American people were imagined and defined in contrast to those of North Americans. In a way, we elaborated rhetorically a negative collective identity. We tried to discover who we were by finding and pointing out who we were not. Octavio Paz, the Mexican Nobel Prize Winner for Literature, wrote an influential book about Mexican culture and the Latin American sense of self, *The Labyrinth of Solitude*, a sensitive and erudite expression of this polar way of thinking:

> The North Americans are credulous and we are believers; they love fairy tales and detective stories and we love myths and legends: The Mexican tells lies because he delights in fantasy, or because he is desperate, or because he wants to rise above the sordid facts of his life; the North American does not tell lies, but he substitutes social truth for the real truth, which is always disagreeable. We get drunk in order to confess; they get drunk in order to forget. They are optimists and we are nihilists – except that our nihilism is not intellectual but instinctive, and therefore irrefutable. We are suspicious and they are trusting. We are sorrowful and sarcastic and they are happy and full of jokes. North Americans want to understand and we want to contemplate. They are activists and we are quietists; we enjoy our wounds and they enjoy their inventions. They believe in hygiene, health, work and contentment, but perhaps they have never experienced true joy, which is intoxication, a whirlwind. In the hubbub of a fiesta night our voices explode, while their vitality becomes a fixed smile that denies old age and death but that changes life to motionless stone. What is the origin of such contradictory attitudes? It seems to me that North Americans consider the world to be something that can be perfected, and that we consider it to be something that can be redeemed.[17]

It is also common in Venezuela to talk about ourselves by stating how different we are from the *gringos*. However, the elaboration and crystallization of a national identity by contrast and in opposition to the United States, a nation that does not even have a name, is not without problems. In individual psychology, a person's name is a crucial component in the construction of the ego and of the individual's sense of self identity. How does this work in collective psychology? How does the image of a nation without a real name (the United States) impact societies obsessed with the idea of national identity? (Venezuela was, for a long time, also called "The United States," but followed by the identifying substantive "of Venezuela"). In the Judeo-Christian tradition, as in many others, the name is essential to the being of things. God created the world and all that is in it by naming it. The name is the first sign of identity, and in this sense, a man without name is the shadow of one who desperately needs one. Much more than in the metaphorical sense, the Gringo Complex has absorbed much of our shadow. The US government and institutions, enterprises, businessmen, and individuals, are, in many guises, recipients and personifications of the unknown and rejected aspects of the Latin American dark side. North Americans are what we are not, and as such, they are uncomfortable objects of projection.

This polar process of identification expresses itself in the workings of a geographical psychology, in the drawing of a subjective map that divides the world in two, the north and the south, in the construction of an imaginal axis: north-south. The movements and displacements along this axis have psychological consequences that explain cultural differences. They have to do with the sense of rhythm and time, with humor and ethics, with the relationship with the body or the conception of work. They correlate with notions or stereotypes of social character. "You look like a *gringo*" (*pareces gringo*) is an expression for criticizing someone for being too formal, for taking casual promises seriously, or for being bothersomely punctual.

In Caracas, if you are invited to a dinner at 8:00 p.m., you are not expected to show up before 9:00 p.m. If you happen to arrive exactly at eight o'clock, you will most probably find the host in the shower. You would be a nuisance and stress everyone in the house. In Venezuelan social life, the notion of exact time does not exist. No one invites you for nine o'clock sharp. You are invited at an imprecise "after nine" or "around nine," where "around" means anytime between 10:00 p.m. and 11:00 p.m.

Punctuality is expected and valued in many circles and circumstances, and it is, of course, required (but not common) in the modern world of organizations, business, and work. But deep down in the cultural unconscious persists a different image of time, a feeling of dissent with the concatenation and speed of linear time, an attitude of disdain and even scorn for the northern obsession with punctuality and the value of time. If you are far away and late, still undressed in your house, and someone expecting your visit phones to ask where you are, you would normally answer with no shame at all: "I am just arriving. I am around the corner." Being pushy, rushing everyone to depart, or getting angry for having to wait for someone who is delayed does not mean respect for the other or regard for civility. It denotes stiffness, bitterness, lack of flexibility, sternness of character, bad temper, emotional stress, obsessive-compulsive traits, incapacity to be in the present, inability to enjoy life as it comes.

This appraisal of the present molds the feeling of life, not as something that passes while we work and do other things, but life, paraphrasing the Puerto Rican writer Luis Rafael Sánchez, as what we do while work, projects, goals, and other things take place. In the psychological north, the experience of the present is frequently something that has to be learned and taught. There are bestsellers that proclaim "the power of now" and schools of psychology that train people to live in the "here and now." In the southern subjective geography, the present is spontaneously lived, and on the contrary, it is long-term vision that needs to be learned. The very famous Latin America expression "*mañana, mañana*," so quoted as part of our folklore in tourists' guides or business counsel books, has been misinterpreted. It has nothing to do with the future. It has to do with the present. It means, "don't interrupt me now," "don't bother me with unimportant things that break the natural flow of the moment and the feeling of now."

This representation of time is intimately connected with the hierarchy of social values and attitudes of Venezuelans towards work and wealth. In a field study which confirmed the results of many other studies about the value system of Venezuelan society, the work ethic, and the meaning that Venezuelans attribute to laboring and productive effort, 88.9 percent of the sample interviewed declared that they did not work to become rich but to live an enjoyable present.

> For the majority, present life is the only life.... In this popular conception, what sense would it make to obtain wealth through work, when it implies, according to the manifested opinions, a greater wear and tear and a loss of life? Sacrificed work and the capitalization of its results collide with "the enjoyment now," since part of the gain that comes from the effort has to be reinvested and can't be enjoyed.[18]

The delay of gratification, an ego mechanism that the protestant work ethic promoted as the highest of virtues, requires a scale of time that goes beyond the present, a psychology that projects meaning into the future.

The antipodes pay homage to contrasting gods. While we consider Apollo to be the ruler of the northern *Weltanshaung*, the archetypal foundation of its collective consciousness, we see the South as a territory kindred to Hermes. Apollo constellates a type of consciousness guided by reason, order, and planning, moved by virtue, in the search of truth and ritual purity. Seen from this point of view, the deceitful Hermes is the archetype of the unconscious, but from the southern standpoint, this dishonest and tricky deity is the archetypal mold of a different style of consciousness open to informality and wits, an indirect vision quick to find shortcuts and bypass the rigid frontiers of order, an exit out of the boring limits of reason. For Venezuelans, the Gringo Complex, as an aggregate of representations of a world under the rule of law and order, is a counter figure that gathers all types of negative feelings and emotions, but as an element of the shadow and a partial personality that confronts consciousness with the inferior function; it is also a challenge for our cultural differentiation and particularization.

The Psychology of Failure

Some years ago, a group of taxi drivers marched in protest against the increase of violence and criminality and the conditions of insecurity in which they had to perform their work. They blocked a street of a suburb of Caracas with their cars and cartels with the list of taxi drivers recently killed. In the afternoon of the same day the president of Venezuela appeared in a national broadcast accusing the president of the United States, George W. Bush, of organizing the taxi drivers' protest as part of a bigger conspiracy against the government of Venezuela.

The CIA is considered to be behind all Latin American affairs, and the North American Empire has been accused of being the cause of almost all our maladies and failures. But this level of triviality in the attribution of responsibility, to accuse the US of being involved in a simple taxi drivers' riot, shows a deeper level of unconsciousness of the Gringo Complex. The most varied studies and empirical research on cultural values and attitudes have found that the majority of the Venezuelan population (around 88 percent) is oriented by an external locus of control.[19] Most Venezuelans attribute the cause of their actions and conditions to something other than themselves – god, chance, destiny, or someone else. In this external attribution of causality, the Gringo Complex plays an important role. If around 50 percent of the population lives in slums below the line of poverty, it is because the *gringos* stole our natural resources. If administrative corruption is pervasive at all levels of bureaucracy, it is because the vices of American consumer society distorted our natural honesty. North Americans serve as scapegoats and symbols for the rationalization of feelings of failure. As Rafael López-Pedraza writes,

> The possibility of failure does not enter into what we call the collective consciousness and its demands. When there is a collapse that we could see as failure from which we could learn and reflect, we rapidly rebound from it by clutching at another vain fantasy, advancing irrevocably to meet another failure.[20]

At the center of the Gringo Complex lies the story told in Horatio Alger's *Ragged Dick*, about an orphan shoe polisher who, working against all adversity, gains social acceptance, makes a fortune, and fulfills the American Dream. It is the religion of success, of the attainment of purpose, the philosophy of the happy end, the cult of heroic triumph over adversity. This story depicts collective representations that are opposed to the figure of Juan Bimba, the victim, the weak and exploited, but they are also representations at odds with a consciousness of failure. Both Ragged Dick and Juan Bimba are prototypes of cultures in conflict with the experience of downfall, societies that have blocked the possibility of learning from failure, one, by developing a one-sided cult of success, the other, by attributing the causes of failure to others.

The invasion of the Gringo Complex into the Venezuelan collective consciousness has triggered an "us vs. them" dynamics that, dusting off old traumas and awaking latent historical complexes, threatens to split Venezuelan society and carry its polar division to extremes. What seemed just a political weapon characteristic of nationalistic and authoritarian regimes has gone beyond the political arena, constellating all kinds of destructive emotions – fear, panic, hatred, resentment, envy – that have left scars in the whole social space of our country, in organizations, families, or friends. The anti-American discourse used to trigger cultural complexes and to divide the nation into *bolivarians* and *pitiyankees* (miserable imitators of the *gringos*), patriots and traitors, cannot be analyzed, however, as a mere political artifice or as a mechanism of defense of the elites to distract and redirect the frustration of the people. There is, no doubt, much of this in the working of the Gringo Complex, but as with all psychic phenomena, it is not just a mechanism that responds to a cause but a life dynamism with a purpose. It is part of a teleological process and has a prospective function. The constellation of the Gringo Complex as a dominant of collective consciousness gives us a picture of something extraneous disturbing the homeostasis of the social system, of the amount of libido consumed and captured by the representation of the foreigner, of unconscious cultural conflicts that require response. It is a signal that forces us to pay attention, to work and to integrate contrasting ways of understanding success and failure, to unfold an archetypal narrative of home that is not at variance with diversity, to develop bonds to people and places with different images of self and identity. The conspicuous presence of the Gringo Complex in the public debate, the abuse of it in politics, will wear away its rationalizations and projective functions and force the activation of the reflective instinct. Exhausted as a multiuse argument, depleted of its political capital, extreme exposure to the *gringo* image can transform it into the antidote that reinstalls the balance between opposite visions of life.

The Gringo Complex is the bearer of many racial and sociohistorical conflicts that hinder cultural cohesion and appear in personalized form as prejudices and aversion to foreigners with contrasting values. It is a symbol of unresolved collective contradictions that demand consciousness. We condemn the *gringo*'s cold pragmatism and the inhumanity of American capitalism, but we are furious consumers of all kinds of American goods and services. The Gringo Complex contains a cluster of representations that confront us with the archetypal themes of failure and success, of alienation and identity, of informality and order, of the sense of self and the construction of the Other. It is the historical product of the fight with the shadow in psychological geography, the container of two distinct subjective cultures that first appear as irreconcilable polar opposites until the transcendent function constructs a bridge and facilitates the symbols of *coniunctio* that move collective consciousness to another stage. It is in the tension of the opposites, in the "frontier of our differences with others," that we can give new form to the primordial images that animate our specific culture.

Notes

1. Wikipedia, *The Free Encyclopedia*. Available at http://en.wikipedia.org/wiki/Anti-Americanism.
2. www.youtube.com/watch?v=I8o0DEluoyo.
3. Thomas Singer, "A Jungian Approach to Understanding 'Us *vs* Them' Dynamics," in *Psychoanalysis, Culture & Society*, 14(1) (Palgrave Macmillan, 2009), p. 7.
4. Ibid., p. 4.
5. John V. Lombardi, *Venezuela. La búsqueda del orden. El sueño de progreso* (Barcelona: Editorial Crítica, 1985), p. 260.
6. www.bancoex.gob.ve/estadis_gen.asp.
7. Simón Bolívar, "Carta al Señor Coronel Patricio Campbell, Encargado de Negocios de S.M.B. Guayaquil, 5 de agosto de 1829," *Obras Completas*, vol. III (La Habana: Editorial Lex, 1950), p. 279.
8. David S. Landes, *La riqueza y la pobreza de las naciones* (Barcelona: Javier Vergara Editor, 1999), p. 656.
9. C.G. Jung, "Answer to Job," in *The Collected Works of C.G. Jung, Vol. 11, Psychology and Religion: West and East*, trans. R.F.C. Hull (Princeton: Bollingen Foundaion, 1977), p. 400.

10 Erich Neumann, *The Great Mother: An Analysis of the Archetype*, trans. Ralph Manheim (Princeton: Princeton University Press, 1974), p. 97.
11 Ibid., p. 99.
12 Sigmund Freud, *Psicología de las masas y análisis del yo*, trans. Luis López-Ballesteros y de Torres, Obras Completas, Tomo III (Madrid: Biblioteca Nueva, 1973), p. 2594.
13 Apuleius, *The Transformations of Lucius Otherwise Known as The Golden Ass*, trans. Robert Graves (New York: Farrar, Straus & Giroux, 1979), p. 114.
14 José Enrique Rodó, *Ariel* (Madrid: Espasa-Calpe, 1975).
15 Simón Bolívar, "Discurso de Angostura," in *Escritos políticos* (Madrid: Alianza Editorial, 1981), p. 96.
16 Simón Bolívar, *Carta de Jamaica* (Caracas: Ediciones de la Presidencia de la República, 1972), p. 35.
17 Octavio Paz, *The Labyrinth of Solitude*, trans. Lysander Kemp (New York: Grove Press Inc., 1985), pp. 23–24.
18 Silverio González Tellez y Mauricio Phelan, *¿Qué quieren los venezolanos?* (Caracas: Fondo Editorial Acta Científica Venezolana y Consorcio de Ediciones Capriles, C.A., 1992), pp. 44–46.
19 Mikel de Viana, "La ficción de modernidad," in *Un mal posible de superar. Resúmenes de los documentos del proyecto pobreza* (Caracas: Universidad Católica Andrés Bello, 2001), p. 85.
20 Rafael López-Pedraza, *Cultural Anxiety* (Einsiedeln, Switzerland: Daimon Verlag, 1990), p. 82.

Chapter 12

Latin America
A Region Split by Its Cultural Complexes

Eduardo Carvallo

The contributions psychology has made over the last 100 years have helped bring to light invisible aspects of our psyche and transform such invisibility into clearly identifiable elements, thus enriching our capacity to see reality. Despite their relatively recent discovery, concepts such as the dynamic unconscious, Jungian typology, complexes, and the collective unconscious have become references that give meaning and structure to our perceptions. These concepts have become part of a cultural consciousness that extends well beyond our limited circle of professional specialists. It is common to hear in everyday exchanges that "she is introverted" or "he has an inferiority complex." These concepts have given the general population, regardless of their level of education or psychological sophistication, a broader capacity to identify underlying psychological structures.

The increased interest in thinking about cultural complexes may be seen as an expression of the need to make another layer of the invisible visible. We are all struggling to understand the contradictory, ambivalent, and at times absurd dynamics that envelop small and large groups alike, including whole civilizations. These invisible dynamics often have very negative and destructive consequences.

I

Among the many Western cultures, the Latin American community stands out as one of the most complex. In this community one encounters a conglomeration of many different cultures, which makes very difficult the emergence of a collective consciousness that might unite Latin Americans as members of a region that share a sense of identity and common purpose. The reality is that the many different cultures and cultural complexes of Latin America prevent its citizens from sharing a worldview and from developing a sense of belonging to the same homeland.

Several years ago, I heard Carlos Urrutia speak. At the time, he was the Peruvian ambassador to Venezuela as well as an outstanding internationalist. He stated that "in Latin America we find more similarities between people from different countries who belong to the same sociocultural class than among members of different social classes within a specific country."[1] From his perspective it is easier to understand the dynamics of Latin America if we see it as made up of "horizontal countries," formed by persons belonging to the same sociocultural class, rather than traditionally as "vertical countries," defined by geographical frontiers. This observation sheds light on the reality that the social classes in Latin American countries have remained unequal and segregated since colonial times.

Perhaps unlike any other region in the world, with the possible exception of India, Latin American societies are structured along a rigid class system created from the first encounters of the European conquerors with the indigenous populations who inhabited these lands. This reality, although deeply rooted in the cultural unconscious of the region, tends to be denied and ignored at the individual level of consciousness among most Latin Americans.

II

The approaches of Joseph Henderson, Thomas Singer, Samuel Kimbles, and other authors to the cultural dimension of complexes have added new perspectives to Jung's early theories.[2] Today we acknowledge that complexes – individual and cultural – are rooted in individual biographies and in collective histories. When we read Singer's description of how cultural complexes are formed, we see parallels with the construction of individual complexes:

> Cultural complexes are based on repetitive, historical group experiences, which have taken root in the collective psyche of the group and in the individual/collective psyches of individual members of the group. . . . They are at the heart of the conflicts between many groups and are expressed in group life all the time. . . . When these complexes are triggered, all the emotion of the personal and archetypal realms gets channeled through group life and its experience. Cultural complexes are lived out in group life and they are internalized in the psyche of individuals.[3]

It is not always possible to go back in time into the history of a community to trace the origins of its cultural complexes. Nonetheless, Latin America's short-lived history makes it possible to find relatively recent evidence about changes in typical cultural patterns such as symbolic structures, rituals, traditions, social composition, and power dynamics. From this evidence, one can make inferences on how these changes have generated particular cultural complexes.

III

The history of America begins with a cataclysmic cultural clash when, in 1492, Christopher Columbus arrived in a territory that did not even appear on the maps of the empires sailing on the seas at that time: Spain, Portugal, Britain, and France. News about Columbus' adventure and the foundation of La Española spread rapidly, and many wanted to be part of it. Very quickly, fleets from various European kingdoms reached the shores of the new lands, dividing the territory among themselves from the very beginning of their explorations.

Despite the apparent cultural similarity that may exist between the European conquerors (mainly Spanish, Portuguese, and British), significant differences can be identified in the way they conquered and colonized the various regions. Such differences and their consequences were determinant in the first two major divisions of this vast territory: the Anglo-speaking North American region, and the Southern Latin American region.

Although Latin America shares a huge cultural and historical heritage, for the purposes of this paper, the following reflections are made specifically from the perspective of Spanish-speaking America, the territory conquered by Spain, that is to say, Hispano America. This huge expanse of territory – that extends today from the Rio Grande (the northern border between Mexico and the United States of America) to Cabo de Hornos and includes most of the countries in the area, plus the islands of Cuba and the Dominican Republic in the Caribbean Sea (with the exceptions of Brazil, Belize, and Guyana) – has not experienced such major transformations since the arrival of the first Spanish conquerors.

It is well-known today that by the time the Spanish arrived in this region, the native population ranged from 13 to 50 million inhabitants and was organized into more than 100 different ethnic groups.[4] Some of the most important were the Aztecs in the north, the Mayas in the middle, and the Incas in the south. These three great civilizations – the Aztec, Mayan, and Incan – became the central targets of the Conquest because of their immense natural resources, technological developments, social organization, and military capabilities.

An important aspect shared by these original communities was a polytheistic religion with a remarkable animistic influence. Their gods shared very similar creation myths with male and female deities embodying generative principles – the origin of human life, motherhood, fertility. They also had common organizational principles both for the environment and for their society. Their gods were worshipped along with others forces such as the stars, meteorological phenomena, the sun, the moon, the wind, and volcanoes, as well as sacred animals like the snake, the jaguar, and the eagle. They had creation myths as well as agricultural and funeral rituals in which their gods participated.

A contra sexual aspect balanced almost all deities; their cosmology developed following an evolutionary pattern, beginning with a chaotic state, and from which, through certain structuring principles, the organization of the world started taking the form known to us at present. This is of great importance when searching for the archetypal roots of these cultures. They share a psycho-spiritual balancing of male and female forces that are connected with the instinctual aspects of being human, such as aggressiveness, breeding, and feeding. In turn, these human instincts are linked and balanced with the laws that govern all of nature.

These deities and archetypal principles were part of the creative projects of these communities, such as pottery and jewelry in which a large number of symbols can be found, representing primordial gods, protective principles, fertility rituals, and scenes of hunting and playing. These artifacts exhibit a deep cultural connection to the spiritual and natural forces in the pre-Columbian environment.

For these cultures the arrival of Europeans meant a cataclysm: not only did they face incalculable losses at a very concrete and material level, but the psychological, cultural, and religious foundations of their culture were severely affected as well. The profound changes these peoples were forced to make can be categorized as "traumatic events," meaning:

> Any experience that causes unbearable psychic pain or anxiety ... and overwhelms the usual defensive measures.... When trauma strikes the developing psyche, a fragmentation of consciousness occurs in which the different "pieces" organize themselves.... One part *regresses* to the infantile period, and another part *progresses*.[5]

This deep trauma forms a regressive core in the structure of the Latin American psyche that must be considered in any attempts to understand the symptoms and manifestations of the cultural complexes of the region.

What were the consequences of the Europeans coming into these new territories? The impact of the arrival and later colonization of the Americas varied significantly depending on the colonizing country, be it Spain, Portugal, or Britain.

The first trips of Columbus, as well as the expeditions that followed, were made solely for commercial purposes to benefit the country funding the expedition. It was not until a decade later – after the journeys of Americo Vespucio – that Europeans became aware that they had reached a new continent. After the discovery of the immense treasures in the new lands, Spain established a commercial bridge between these territories and Europe and began the extraction of the rich resources from the territories to Europe.

This commercial interest in extracting wealth from the new lands created a particularly negative attitude of the newcomers towards the preexisting civilizations. The new lands also had an influence on the profile of those who decided to expose themselves to the risks – real or imaginary – that were an essential part of the long travels to America.

It is well-known that the first Spaniards coming to these lands had low social status, and their main motivation was to obtain enormous wealth as quickly as possible. This motivation meant that the first adventurers had no plans whatsoever for eventually settling down with their wives and families in this new land. Rather, they came convinced that, after a short adventure, they would return to their homelands and their families with large fortunes that would raise their standard of living back home.

The legend of El Dorado is a manifestation of the Spaniards' attitude of envisioning America as a fantastic place where gold and silver were available in fabulous quantities. Such an image nurtured the desire for and fantasy of obtaining easy and quick riches and became the engine that fueled countless expeditions.

The Spanish Crown turned the economic implications of the Conquest into a matter of state policy. Gaining control over large areas potentially rich in valuable minerals represented a way to sustain the immense costs of the wars that were concurrently being waged on the European continent. These goals of the Crown were shared with the Catholic Church, which became a significant protagonist in the history of the Hispano American conquest.

The aforementioned factors account for two notable characteristics of the Spanish exploration of the New Continent:

1 Spain needed to fund the European wars in which it was engaged. The spirit of conquest abroad was fed by fantasies of the easy funding of its military adventures at home. Looting and exploitation of Latin America was necessary for conducting warfare at home.
2 The Spanish understanding of the world was based on a highly structured, monotheistic religion whose main representatives were

   a the king, on whose behalf conquerors founded cities and confiscated lands, and
   b the priests, who were responsible for ensuring the salvation of the souls of the conquerors as well as the souls of the natives on the New Continent who were converted to Catholicism.

These main features define the archetypal structure of the Spanish colonization of the New World. This was a rigid and authoritarian warrior pattern within a strict monotheism that contrasted sharply with the archetypal framework among the indigenous peoples, which included polytheism, a balance between male and female forces, and a close relationship of mutuality between the indigenous communities and the natural environment.

This contrast reveals the magnitude of the cultural clash that marked the encounter between these two civilizations: on one side, the polytheistic and animistic worldview of the natives, and on the other side, the profound and rigid monotheistic religiosity of the conquerors with an exploitative attitude to the natural world. As Rafael López-Pedraza has pointed out, this clash between Spain and its new conquests mirrors a cultural anxiety within the Western tradition itself in which the polytheism of its Greco-Latin roots conflict with the later monotheism of the Western Christian tradition.[6] These two trends, the polytheistic and the monotheistic, are polar opposites and tend to mutually exclude one another. What often happens when this dynamic is activated is that one pole becomes the shadow of the other. In this case, the indigenous culture of the pre-Columbians became a shadow to the conquering Spanish culture. The natural psychic reaction to the uprising of a repressed shadow aspect is an attempt by the dominant culture to destroy it or simply make its perceived inferior adversary disappear.

IV

Two interconnected trends are reflected in the attitudes that emerged from colonial times: the *other-cide* and the "invisibilization." The *other-cide*, a term coined by Eduardo Galeano in one of his reflections on the indigenous situation in America, refers to the attempt of the "winners" of a cultural conflict to eliminate the "others."[7] Stripped of their symbols and rituals and forced to accept foreign myths that replace their most fundamental beliefs about creation and the forces that govern their lives, the conquered people seem doomed to death in both a literal and symbolic way. It is easy to see how conquered peoples succumb to *thanatos*, a death instinct.

Among other things, this state of affairs was fertile soil for the development of different diseases that came with the Spaniards. Some have asserted that there were more deaths among the American indigenous people caused by diseases transmitted to them by the Spaniards than from actual fighting during the Conquest.[8]

Invisibilization was a second consequence of the Conquest: the victors did everything possible to make the culture of the conquered "invisible." This process of "invisibilization" was partly accomplished by the ruling government's official policies that were of benefit to only one sector of the population – the conquerors. This method of ruling was notorious during the Hispano-American colonization. Official government systematically excluded and treated the indigenous people as second-class citizens. What I call "invisibilization" may well be the collective equivalent of the defense mechanism of denial, which is well-known in the psychology of the individual. Developmentally, it is an early and primitive defense mechanism that erases painful and/or intolerable psychic contents that cannot be consciously acknowledged. Making the Other invisible strips them of being able to survive, adapt, or assimilate in the dominant culture.

Throughout Hispano-American history governments have strived to treat indigenous populations as invisible, granting all privileges to the Conquerors and their descendants. However, despite these policies and attitudes, the consolidation of a hegemonic Spanish culture was not achieved. Time and again, the exclusion of native cultures was compensated for through the hidden incorporation of their symbols into colonial art. For example, many images in the so-called "Quito School" depict the Virgin Mary, but she is adorned with attributes of Pachamama, the Incan goddess of fertility symbolizing the creative principle. It is not unusual to find pictures and wood carvings of women, with the colors that usually accompany Virgin Mary's iconography, but surrounded by fruits and cobs, snakes and other animals. Images of angels with overtly feminine gestures and clothing also demonstrate how the indigenous cultures found artistic expression in the otherwise predominantly male character of Catholic religious iconography. Intermarriage of Spanish descendants with indigenous people and black slaves further contributed to a process of cultural syncretism in spite of Spanish efforts to "invisibilize" the culture of the non-Spanish population.

Despite the efforts of the Spanish to consolidate their unrivaled power, the absence of Spanish women forced the conquerors to beget their descendants in the wombs of natives and to feed them with milk from Indian and Black breasts. Through this mingling of blood and genes, the mores, customs, rituals, and images of the conquered "other" slipped through the best efforts of the Spanish to eliminate them. This "slipping through" into the cultural unconscious of these fundamental elements of pre-Spanish native culture contributed to the formation of the cultural complexes that reflect the dramatic contradictions of so many aspects of the contemporary Latin region.

V

It is not a coincidence that today a number of political movements display the flag of indigenousness and equality. Once these movements gain political power, their speech turns divisive and is filled with resentment. In terms of the opening comment of this chapter about psychology contributing to making the invisible visible, these movements are demanding that the invisible become visible. They are inevitable compensatory movements of the Latin American collective psyche that have been activated in the psychological and social dynamics of the region. It is as if a collective post-traumatic stress disorder originating in the Spanish colonization of Latin America has bubbled to the surface, revealing an encapsulated regressive core in the cultural unconscious of the population. This makes the possibility of moving toward integration and mutual cultural, psychological, and material enrichment all the more difficult to achieve. Just as individual complexes act as giant "psychic holes" whose autonomy and contradictions threaten to swallow the ego and prevent the integrative potential of the psyche, cultural complexes also act as large, magnetic black holes in the psychic structure of entire populations, hindering integration among both individuals and groups.

There remains in Latin America a tremendous difficulty identifying a unifying collective consciousness or common identity that can include everyone under the same Hispano-American banner. Today we are still cleaved by the scars and the trauma left by the encounter between Europeans and the native communities during and after the Conquest. The dynamic generated by this psychosocial reality can explain the remarks of Ambassador Urrutia, referenced earlier, where he noted that individuals from a particular social strata had more in common with each other from country to country than did people from a different social strata in a single country. Despite the five hundred years that have elapsed since the arrival of Columbus, we can still identify at least three different socioeconomic cultural layers:

1 The indigenous groups who remain identified with their native cultures. They have retained their myths and religions, while simultaneously defending themselves from the imposition of European culture.
2 The groups who remain identified with the Europeans and have maintained their direct link to social and economic power throughout the different historical periods.
3 The intermediate groups who are truly "in-between" in their genes and their cultures.

To increase the complexity of the region, these three cultural layers that coexist in parallel from one country to another and are distributed across the entire continent are intersected by the territorial divisions in which they are located geographically.

These psychosocial complexities are multiplied by the history of power related to the unequal distribution of wealth between the various Spanish viceroyalties that eventually developed into independent republics. Intense rivalries between these viceroyalties and the countries that developed out of them still scar the region and have left many wounds among neighboring countries.

As a result of these dynamics, we can identify racism, classism, and sexism as cultural complexes among others, like superiority or inferiority complexes; these last two originated in relationships based on power that were established early in the region.

As a way to imagine the magnitude of the effects of the Spaniards' power on the psyche of the pre-Columbian inhabitants, consider Luigi Zoja's interpretation of how Montezuma, the Aztec emperor, "resolved" the inner conflict that the Spaniards' arrival represented for him:

> For Montezuma, the arrival of the Spaniards is the rupture of that continuity that ruled the world. For him, the strangeness of the newcomers is not inconceivable, even if horseman and horse were taken as a single being, what would be so inconceivable about that? Just call them gods and everything becomes reasonable.[9]

This vision helps explain why still today Latin Americans tend to idealize what comes from overseas but show less confidence in local products (intellectual or material), thus expressing a cultural inferiority complex that began in colonial times.

VI

As an example of how cultural complexes manifest today in the region, I would like to make a brief statement about Venezuela's history. Venezuela is a Latin American country in a privileged situation, not only geographically (it is located at the north of the continent which facilitates commerce with many other countries around the world and guarantees wonderful weather all year) but also as a country rich in natural beauty, as seen in its wonderful landscapes, and in natural resources, with one of the greatest oil reserves in the world.

As with many other countries of the region, the people of the second socioeconomic cultural layer that we mentioned previously (those who maintained their identity with European origins) have been privileged among others since the War of Independence (1810–1820). In some way the members of this group behave as the direct descendants and heirs of the Spaniards. This class, which ruled the country for many years, did not invest in policies that could ensure the common welfare but copied foreign economic and social models, many of which were inadequate to fulfill the needs of the underprivileged. This sowed resentment in a large number of people who felt that the ruling class stole their share of the wealth of El Dorado. This is an expression of the "invisibilization" that I discussed earlier. This attitude contributed to the development of classism and racism within the Venezuelan collective. Those who were rendered invisible sought to avenge these injustices which grew over time, but they were paralyzed from taking effective action by a potent inferiority complex. They felt excluded from the major political and social scenarios.

As a result of years of corruption and bad political decisions, the economy of the country was riddled with high inflation, food shortages, and very poor public services, which triggered civic unrest and a chaotic political situation culminating in an attempted *coup d'état* in 1992 that was foiled. The increasing turmoil and chaos frightened the dominant class, who decided to open more opportunities to the voices of a new leadership. One of the leaders of this new group was Hugo Chávez, a man that was born among the "invisibilized" people. He was a potent spokesperson for those people who felt much closer to him and where he came from than to the inheritors of the Spanish legacy. He spoke for a people with deeply embedded resentments and an ingrained cultural complex of inferiority. Chávez first won the presidency of Venezuela in 1999, and his speeches have been full of anger, hatred, and resentment. He constantly reminds his constituents of the role that all previous politicians have had in contributing to the suffering of a large portion of the Venezuelan population. Chávez' repetitive rants remind me of how Luigi Zoja describes the way in which cultural complexes express themselves:

> Tales of oral tradition tend to be repetitive, as a means to help fix them in memory, but . . . that repetition becomes obsessive precisely when the trauma is described. Such obsessive repetition is not only characteristic of oral tradition, particularly when a tale of trauma is recalled, but also characteristic of how a complex behaves in the psyche – whether it is a cultural or individual complex. Every time the cultural complex is activated, there is a repetitive memory and emotion that evokes the primal trauma. Trauma, memory and emotion recur repetitively and are linked through the cultural complex to archetypal, cultural and personal levels of the psyche.[10]

And as often happens with demagogues such as Hugo Chávez, he has paradoxically installed the most virulent social and political *apartheid* that Venezuela has known in all its Republican history. He and his followers have segregated all the people that have opposed him. Chávez's *apartheid* – a contemporary form of "invisibilization" – has forced the migration of more than 500,000 Venezuelan citizens to other countries in search of work and safety that are no longer available to them in Venezuela. The State no longer guarantees the minimum police protection to many of its citizens. The reemergence of the "invisibilization" process – with the tables now turned on the previous ruling class – is directly responsible for a considerably heightened level of anxiety in the country as a whole that has increased psychosomatic manifestations in a large part of the population.[11] Most disturbing in these current trends is that Venezuela is now among the countries with the highest indices of violence and insecurity in the world, and its economy is one of the most corrupt in Latin America.[12]

VII

To conclude, we are reminded that the history of humankind is marked by innumerable wars arising out of our incapacity to make conscious the darker sides of our human nature and by the failure to integrate these more shadowy realms. This great failure of humanity has not allowed the emergence of the tolerance, mutual understanding, and peaceful coexistence that remains little more than a dream shared by many.

I remember once hearing Rafael López-Pedraza paraphrase Jung: "If we fail to see our images of horror, life itself shall bring us horror as a destiny."[13] It remains a deep human hope that isolated efforts of making more visible some of our invisible complexities as human beings might one day make our images of horror more conscious as a way of halting our more self-destructive instincts.

Notes

1. He was also a frequent visitor and expositor at our training program for Jungian analysts in Caracas between 2002 and 2005.
2. Joseph Henderson, "The Cultural Unconscious," in *Shadow and Self: Selected Papers in Analytical Psychology* (Wilmette, IL: Chiron Publications, 1990); *The Cultural Complex: Contemporary Jungian Perspectives in Psyche and Society*, eds. Thomas Singer and Samuel Kimbles (New York: Brunner-Routledge, 2004).
3. Thomas Singer, "The Cultural Complex and Archetypal Defenses of the Group Spirit: Baby Zeus, Elian González, Constantine's Sword, and Other Holy Wars," in *Cultural Complex*, eds. Singer and Kimbles, p. 22.
4. Angel Rosenblat, *La población indígena y el mestizaje en América* (Buenos Aires: Nova, 1954), p. 24.
5. Donald Kalsched, *The Inner World of Trauma: Archetypal Defenses of the Personal Spirit* (London: Routledge, 1996), pp. 1–2.
6. Rafael López-Pedraza, *Ansiedad Cultural* (Caracas: Festina Lente, 2000), pp. 31–65.
7. Eduardo Galeano, "Cinco siglos de prohibición del arco iris en el cielo americano," in *Ser como ellos y otros artículos*, ed. Eduardo Galeano (México: Siglo Veintiuno Editores, 1992), p. 3.
8. For further information, see Alfred Crosby, *Ecological Imperialism: The Biological Expansion of Europe* (Cambridge: Cambridge University Press, 1993), where the author investigates the influence of diseases in social transformations between 900 and 1900 AD.
9. Luigi Zoja, "Trauma and Abuse: The Development of a Cultural Complex in the History of Latin America," in *Cultural Complex*, eds. Singer and Kimbles, p. 78.
10. Ibid., p. 87.
11. For more information about the effects and other considerations of this situation, see Eduardo Carvallo "Psicoterapia en tiempos de ansiedad," *Revista Venezolana de Psicología de los Arquetipos y Estudios Junguianos*, no. 1 (Agosto 2005): 28–33.
12. For a further revision of Venezuela's sociopolitical situation, see Rafael Uzcátegui, *Venezuela, La Revolucion Como Espectaculo: Una Critica Anarquista Al Gobierno Bolivariano* (Buenos Aires: Libertario, 2010), p. 275.
13. Maybe one of the most of popular Jung's quotes is, "The psychological rule says that when an inner situation is not made conscious, it happens outside as fate." See C.G. Jung, "Christ, a Symbol of the Self," in *The Collected Works of C.G. Jung, Vol. 9ii, Aion*, trans. R.F.C. Hull (1959; repr., London: Routledge and Kegan Paul, 1966), § 126.

Chapter 13

Venezuela
Cultural Complexes in Contemporary Context

Margarita Méndez

Increasingly, I have seen patients in my psychotherapy practice who talk about their feelings of social, economic, and political exclusion, and this appears to express a more profound cultural complex. Such is the case, for example, of a 34-year-old woman lawyer who feels alienated and rejected by her coworkers in a military department. In turn, she despises her boss, whom she considers to be an ignorant, intellectually inferior person. She treats him with disdain, to which he responds with threats of firing her, creating much tension between them. These two individuals, my patient and her boss, come from very different strata in society. She comes from a middle-class family and has had an academic education, while he comes from a low-income background, has been trained in the military, and has made great efforts to establish a military career. As a result, they engage in constant, mutual belittling. As a therapist facing situations like this one, I ask myself, is it possible that ancestral struggles, seemingly buried and forgotten, are appearing at a new collective level today? This is the topic I explore in this paper, trying to shed light on the *psychological* consequences of historic, social conflicts in Venezuela.

I

Venezuelan cultural complexes often center around feelings of exclusion and resentment that are based on historical events and social patterns that were established during the colonial period. These complexes remain active and form the roots of our current problems. I will cite the work of several authors who have contributed to an understanding of Venezuelan social dynamics to help elucidate how these complexes appear in the Venezuelan psyche today.

The Spanish colonization of Central and South America was different from the English or the French colonization of North America. While in the North indigenous people were exterminated or expelled from their territories, in Venezuela the Spaniards mixed with the indigenous people and later with the slaves who were brought to Venezuela when the large cacao plantations were initially established. In Venezuela, the Conquest lasted a long time. For instance, in the Nueva Andalucía Province (in the Western part of Venezuela) due to the difficult terrain, the Conquest wasn't complete until the second half of the eighteenth century. At the same time, the racial mixing that started at the beginning of the Conquest resulted in a fusion of three ethnicities – the Spaniards, the indigenous people, and the African slaves – giving birth to a social richness that is reflected in Venezuelan traditions, behavior, beliefs, gastronomy, and many other features. This mixture, however, did not occur without conflict.[1] Venezuelan society was also built on violence. In addition, a caste system, based upon family of origin and color, has had long-lasting consequences on the inequities that arise from exclusion.

Naturally, this has resulted in too much conflict. We can see how the notion of "otherness" was consolidated in the *Criollos'* (the Venezuelan descendants of the Spaniards that mixed with the African and the indigenous people) society in the following ways: Indigenous people were perceived as "irrational" beings, or not of age; Black African descendants were physically stronger than indigenous people, which is why they were preferred as a slave force and did not attain the status of crown subjects; and, finally, the Spaniards were perceived as the "enemies" par excellence by the other groups.[2] As a result, we can see a syncretism, or fusion of manners and beliefs, as well as a clear opposition of interests and values.

An example of cultural syncretism is the fusion of African Yoruba beliefs with Christian Catholicism that produced the Santeria religion. Santeria religion emerged in Cuba in the seventeenth century in the melding together of cults brought by the slaves from Africa with Spanish Catholic Christianity. For example, the integration between Obatala (Yoruba god, creator – *oteosus* of the world) and the Virgin of la Merced (Catholic) and between Saint Barbara (Catholic) and Chango (Yoruba god, *orisha* of thunder). Introduced in Venezuela in the twentieth century, Santeria has become a religion that is still evolving. It is an African/American form of worship of increasing popularity. In our culture we can also see religious elements of an indigenous cult that resulted in an extended religious syncretism, like the Maria Lionza cult; this is a spiritist religion which mixes devotion to the Virgin Mary and an indigenous Artemis with African beliefs.

Although these societies were originally established through violent means during colonization, the hatred that built up as a result was seemingly forgotten. However, after more than two centuries, this hatred reappeared at the end of twentieth century with a vengeance. As the Venezuelan psychiatrist and author Herrera Luque describes, "The souls of the Venezuelan people were forged from the painful wound of offense, hatred and harm."[3]

The genetic and cultural mixes that came about in Venezuela produced particular psychological consequences that are the foundation of our collective unconscious and our cultural complexes, many of which relate to the emotions of shame and hatred. Yet it is difficult to address these complexes and the emotions they generate, because consciously we advocate and value *Egalité*, the idea that everyone is equal. The differences and disparities that exist among groups are pushed into the unconscious, and saying that everyone is equal creates certain aspirations in less fortunate social groups that cannot be satisfied. As a result, underlying the alleged spirit of *Egalité*, we find cultural complexes grounded in repressed envy and bitterness simmering in the background and which later emerge as resentment.

We understand resentment as a recurring emotion because it is repeatedly repressed. Resentment is caused by an initial trauma which, if not addressed and dealt with, continues long after the trauma that originally caused it. At the same time, the emotion of resentment becomes more diffuse and generalized. In extreme cases, the resentful person's need for vengeance based upon a real or imaginary primary offense becomes "an insatiable desire," which can never be adequately quenched.[4] Not surprisingly, many things that have happened during the course of Venezuelan history, some of which continue to take place today, are significant generators of traumas and resentment. These include slavery, disparities in income and social status, racism, sexism, and classism, in its many different forms.

During the historic period of Venezuela's War of Independence (1810–1823), which includes the First Republic, our national hero Simón Bolívar signed the so-called Decree of War to the Death (*Decreto de Guerra a Muerte'*) which transformed the Admirable Campaign (*Campaña Admirable*) into a merciless fight, under the well-known motto:

Spaniards and Canaries, expect your death, even if you're indifferent.

Since the very beginning, our society has felt the threat of division, with each sector of society fighting to overpower the other. Some believe that this Decree of War to the Death "introduced a wound in the collective memory."[5] Notwithstanding the fact that the decree was a war tactic created to define the factions – Criollos against Spaniards – it inflicted a profound wound in our collective psyche. It was later forgotten and mitigated by the racial mixing that continued to take place between the three ethnic groups.

Nevertheless, then, as well as now, strong emotions arise from our cultural unconscious to the surface, and resentment awakens as economic and social disparity prevails. This is expressed in the existence of hidden feelings of exclusion in what is intended to be an inclusive society where the various groups live a harmonic coexistence. By "exclusion," I mean the following: the lack of participation of some members of the population in the social, economic, political, and cultural life of the country. This lack of participation is reinforced and perpetuated by the absence of civil rights afforded to these groups: they are denied access to resources and basic services (including legal services, the job market, education, information technology, health systems, and social and police protection).

These disparities among the various groups that make up Venezuelan society cause increased resentment that manifests in issues of race and class. In turn, this increases intolerance of the "other" and leads to even fewer human rights and privileges being accessible to members of certain groups. The social and cultural lag in most of the population includes an important racial factor. For example, "direct or indirect descendants of old slaves and freed Afro-Americans, belong to the popular sectors with greater disqualification for jobs and less income."[6]

Thus, while the Venezuelan persona declares *Fraternité*, in the shadow of the republic lies its unconscious opposite, which expresses its autonomy in the denial of rights to less empowered groups, leaving little space for real *Liberté*. Because ethnic and cultural crossbreeding began in Venezuela when the Spanish colony was first created, the fact that inequities exist among groups and that certain groups were and still are excluded from enjoying basic rights and privileges available to other groups has not been at the forefront of our consciousness. Nevertheless, there is no denying that racial and social integration in Venezuela went only so far, and exclusion and resentment persist to this day in different ways in the lower and middle strata.[7] Different from the clear message of separatism given by societies that developed apartheid, in our integrated society "exclusion" is repressed, becoming unconscious and developing the autonomy of a cultural complex which has continued to generate conflict.

II

To explore further related aspects of the Venezuelan collective psyche, it is important to consider the founding myth of Venezuela as a republic and the main character or hero in our country's journey toward independence and his exploits: the heroic myth and the cult of Simon Bolívar (1783–1830). In our study of Bolívar, he emerges as a solar hero. The psychic unidirectionality created by focusing predominantly on Bolívar as solar hero has, in turn, constellated the solar hero's nonreflexive opposite, its shadow, its gloomy or lunar side in the collective unconscious. This lunar side of the solar hero appears in the culture as acts of destruction and barbarism.[8]

In the case of Venezuela, it is important to take into account the fact that the Wars of Independence (1810–1823), and later on, the Federal War (1859–1863), resulted in a radical break with the two previous centuries of history and ravaged the cultural, institutional, and economic reserves. The previous status quo was transformed with the promise of *Liberté-Egalité-Fraternité*.

After the War of Independence, two forms of social organization emerged: one predominantly militarist, and the other called *caudillismo*, whose domain is not exactly illegitimate, since it is based on a local type of servitude, called *peonazgo*, or forced labor. Under this system the *Criollos* hired Afro-descendants and indigenous people in a complex work relationship resembling feudalism. After a short period of peace between 1823 and 1859 that followed the independence, *caudillismo* flourished in Venezuela, when several bands, led by different chieftains, alternatively and forcibly took control, seizing the political, economic, and social benefits of which they had been previously denied.

The Republic of Venezuela had a succession of authoritarian governments and leaderships, from the end of the Federal War in 1863 until the dawning of democracy in 1958. The economy based on oil (beginning in the second decade of the twentieth century) has done little to get rid of the feelings of "exclusion" that exist among certain groups in Venezuela which are rooted in the past. And the fascination with the power of the *caudillo* can generate a psychic state and drive towards power that emerges from the cultural shadow as an activated complex. On the other hand, the *caudillo* at the same time encourages servile feelings of defenselessness in the people, provoking submission.

At the death of General Juan Vicente Gómez in 1935, the last traces of *caudillismo* began to disappear, and a slow transition towards democracy commenced. Since then, the intention to develop an authentic democracy has existed among political elites; efforts toward this end were consolidated with the overthrow, in 1958, of the dictator Marcos Pérez Jiménez and the summons to general elections in which the entire population participated. With a constitutional democracy established that same year, populist proposals promised wealth and well-being for the majority. After the loss of important socioeconomic gains achieved in the wealthy years of the late 1950s to the late 1970s, the population became disillusioned, and the old, repressed resentments emerged once more in widespread social sectors of the lower income population who were gradually becoming poorer instead of enjoying the promised prosperity of the oil economy.

However, Venezuelan democracy has undergone many different phases since that time: establishment, consolidation, weakening, and loss. A weakened, scarcely organized society has contributed to this process. Other factors, including the dependency of the productive sectors on the government and a dependence on oil income, has led to the woeful, current scenario, described by the Venezuelan writer Arraíz Lucca in the following terms: "a rich, but quadriplegic State, and an impoverished Nation that cannot find a place for development."[9]

III

What is the current political situation in Venezuela? The crisis of democracy I referred to previously had a fatal outcome at the end of the nineties, with the ascension to power – via constitutional elections – of Hugo Chavez as president and various army men, backed by leftist political leaders, who were resentful because of their exclusion during the golden hour of democratic government. These candidates were amply backed by the masses, whose benefits from oil revenue were diminished, and who were also resentful because they were denied most civil rights and did not have easy access to resources and basic services. Then, by the end of the twentieth century both situations propitiated the destitution of one *élite* by another. The post 1958 democratic *élite* was overpowered by the new socialist leaders.

In 1998, when Hugo Chavez was elected president of Venezuela, he appeared to be a sort of *caudillo*, as well as the personification of the hero, a restorer of the rights of the destitute. Since then, we, as Venezuelan citizens, have been caught up in political turmoil, and as psychoanalysts, we face the challenge of understanding how the collective psyche generates intense emotions to which the psychotherapist is exposed, as much as his/her patients.

The social friction that was generated during the Colonial period is triggered again today. Great energy is constellated in our present social conflicts and political polarization. Venezuelan cultural unconsciousness has promoted states of possession related to heroic and messianic myths, such as the hope for a savior like

Bolívar or the advent of a strong leader. These do not necessarily provide the forms to build an open society based on consensus and public discussion.

Rather, the *caudillo* encourages servile feelings of defenselessness in the people who are submissively grateful for populist promises. This distances the individual from his role as an empowered citizen and restrains him from obtaining some sort of redemption of the bitterness and hate that resentment generates. The significant degree of economic and cultural poverty present today in Venezuela promotes a parasitic, dependent relationship between those who give and those who receive, with both sides feeling benefitted, literally or symbolically. Thus, this link is perpetuated by both sides.

Sectors of the population are prey to an "inversion" of social values such as respect for private property. For example, some groups today consider it commendable to usurp and invade the property of another, openly doing so with the approval of the authorities. For these people, the archetype of the "abandoned child" seems to have been activated in its darker aspects, as they take by force what has been denied to them by life, by former rulers of the country, by the "others." As a consequence of real, and sometimes fictional, wrongdoings, revenge is facilitated by the official discourse. The abandoned child is an aspect of the archetype of the "divine child" in which the "God child" and the "hero child" share a miraculous birth as well as adversities in early childhood, such as abandonment and the danger of maltreatment. Raised on the frontier of the supernatural, the divine child represents the anticipated potential of the process of individuation.[10] Examples are Moses, saved by the waters; Thumbling, a character from the Grimm brothers' fairy tales, whose small size allowed him to help his brothers; and Dionysius, destroyed by the Titans and put back together again by his father.

When the self-healing and restorative powers of the psyche are not activated in the "abandoned child," he/she may feel entitled to find for himself, through whatever means possible, what has been denied to him/her by his parents or by life itself. The abandoned child is deprived, just like Hansel and Gretel were, when they ravenously ate the witch's little chocolate-cake house once they were abandoned by their father in the woods. They will later have to pay the price for having done so and comply with the onerous tasks imposed by the witch until Gretel acquires the strength to save herself and her brother and free them of the enchantment. However, when healing powers are not constellated in the abandoned child, psychopathic traits may arise in those incapable of facing the complex. In Venezuela the boundaries between what the abandoned child deserves and the limits that they must not violate is a very complex one. Furthermore, other factors related to our temperament, mentioned by the writer and psychoanalyst Ana Teresa Torres in the following quote, emphasize this complexity: "The confusion between equality and egalitarianism, that is, between legal, civilian equity and the self-granted right to measure up, regardless of competence, is probably a very Venezuelan feeling."[11]

To summarize: in Venezuelan history the experience of exclusion results in the expression of resentment, both individually and collectively. This combination of exclusion and resentment erupts from the unconscious seeking vengeance and retaliation. Hence, resentment becomes an insatiable passion for the justice denied to the abandoned child, who seeks legitimization in social action for the motives behind his resentment. This can be a dangerous way to mobilize social change. A person filled with resentment (in contrast to a person who is traumatized) cannot define the real cause of his rage; the rage becomes generalized and can attach itself to any number of causes. Resentment is expressed not only privately in family dynamics but socially as it emerges in the political discourse.

For Venezuela to create a fairer society, we must reinforce creative values and promote empowering programs for our citizens, based on an ethical, social referential framework. An important healing experience would be for our citizens to agree on essential ethical values at a collective level. This could lead to the transcendent function, a product of the tension between opposites, at a social level. To create "a dignified habitat, effective public health, and social security systems, as well as an educational system which leads to dignified employment, which enhances self-esteem and promotes pacific coexistence and tolerance, by providing all citizens food and sanitary resources"[12] would be equivalent to reaching a resolution through the redemption of resentment.

We can learn much from the extraordinary case of South Africa with its Truth and Reconciliation Commission, where the concept of "restorative justice" was employed, a practice that resulted in healing for many South Africans, both the victims and the perpetrators of violence during apartheid. The way restorative justice works is that the victim and offender acknowledge the grievance suffered and instead of a pardon being granted (in the Christian sense of offering the other cheek), what happens is that the aggrieved person is restored to his humanity, which has been lost due to the injustice inflicted on him by the offender. Both the victim and the offender should acknowledge what was wrong and agree that it should not happen again. In restorative justice – opposite to the "justice" of vengeance – there is no reversal of values; there is no misunderstanding between what is correct in a social and moral context and what is not.

In Venezuela, we should go back and start by respecting human rights and property and maintaining a legal system separate from political interests. But collective projections of the shadow in the form of stereotypes have increased so much that they impair our understanding of our fellow countrymen and contribute to polarizing the population into antagonistic and excluding groups. Projections turn dangerous because they promote unjustified accusations, based solely on physical appearance. Ancestral frictions and feelings of exclusion come to the surface again and again reflecting a cultural complex constantly present through the emotion of resentment. In this case, we see the previous and dangerous projection of the collective shadow (the dark, chthonic side) over the opposite one. History is filled with many ominous examples of this. In Venezuela we have seen sad situations like the attack on religious Jewish temples and the destruction of sacred images of Roman Catholics. The legal system is corrupted and responds to political interests, and human rights are in constant jeopardy.

The shadow is an archetype that cannot be made conscious in its totality, nor can it be eradicated. It most likely makes itself known through a powerful projection which can be positive or negative and most probably will be projected onto the neighbor.[13] Jung emphasizes that we all have a shadow, which is an essential part of our being human, and in Venezuela, the shadow of resentment is expressed through complexes filled with destructivity since the negative emotions have been repressed.

Resentment is a constant reliving of a pernicious emotion to which we are all prone; however, some people are more likely to overcome it than others. The gods of ancient Greece, like humans, experienced resentment, as in the cases of the following:

- Hera, who was *resentful* because of Zeus' infidelities and was motivated by a strong desire for vengeance against her unfaithful husband's lovers.
- Hephaestus, who was *resentful* because of his mother's (Hera's) rejection due to his deformity and who constantly ruminated about how he could seek vengeance for her maternal destructivity.
- Poseidon, who lived at the bottom of the ocean and was *resentful* of his brother Zeus, who had relegated him to the aquatic world, and not to the richer land world, inhabited by men.
- Apollo, who was *resentful* of his father Zeus for having forced him to serve as a slave to humans as a punishment for having betrayed him.

Resentment is a universal emotion which has been described as follows:

> This emotion appears frequently in psychotherapy; it is produced by a past event, sometimes simple and normal, which has become an autonomous complex in which the psyche has become fixed, pointing to it as the cause of all the tribulations of a lifetime. One then feels a psychic paralysis, often strongly psychotic. . . . Resentment also appears in social, ethnic and economic areas.[14]

Exclusion can generate resentment with components of rage or envy at an individual level, and rage may lead to direct aggression, which, in turn, can lead to homicide or suicide. Envy, since it's a hidden feeling, leads to the symbolic or literal destruction of what is envied or, in its stead, to some form of self-aggression of the envious individual. These emotions contaminate the mechanisms of power implicit in all social and political structures, especially when unconscious emotions take over, not only of the psychological state of individuals, but also of large sectors of a society.

IV

Tension is reflected in the way people of different strata move about Caracas, a previously integrated city. People from the west side of the city have given up going to the movies on the east side because they don't feel "included." And the people from the east part of town are not familiar with the west, the downtown commercial center, and call it "the far West." This split reflects the psychological division in our society.

The issue of exclusion also often emerges in psychotherapy. Violence and permanent anxiety, characteristics of the crisis, have produced important psychosomatic consequences in the population. A Venezuelan Jungian analyst, Eduardo Carvallo, with experience of these issues in his practice, says,

> We may see that some people suffer inside, at a level that we could say is strictly psychic: anxiety, depression, sensation of loss, with exclusively emotional expressions; while others' suffering derives from the somatic field.[15]

Since we're dealing with the complex of resentment, acting out of destructive emotions is rapidly triggered, without any reflection. We have learned how the irrational can burst forth at any moment during social chaos.

A personal anecdote serves as an example: during the difficult months following the general strike to protest against the government (Dec. 2002–Jan. 2003), I tried to reach my home in Caracas. I had to negotiate past barricades and bonfires, which the residents of our middle-class neighborhood had lit in front of their houses to block access. The middle classes were protesting against the Chavez regime for implementing policies from which they felt excluded. A new era of resentment was beginning; the population that helped raise the country through commerce, industries, and qualified jobs was now feeling excluded and pursued. As I fearfully dodged the obstacles on my way home, all of a sudden I saw an astonishing image: a 30-year-old man proudly standing next to a fire. He was attired as a medieval crusader; his outfit had a red cross over a white robe with a belt and an iron mesh over his head; he propped his sword on the ground while calmly observing the chaos which reigned all around him. This man seemed to be isolated in his inner world, perhaps in a delusional fantasy.

The elements of the irrational seem to take over consciousness in psyches exhausted by tension. This scene has remained embedded in my memory as an image of the madness that can be set off in times of social chaos and how the absurd can seem almost normal and acceptable. No one acted surprised that a man dressed as a crusader was standing there while the neighbors moved about, hurriedly burning tires and piling up all sorts of things to build the barricade. Under these circumstances, "collective processes forced us to leave our consulting rooms, to go out into the streets and to the groups in the community that wished to work from a psychological stance within our communities, as a necessary answer to the challenges we face."[16]

Since civilized discussions do not always work as a way of reaching a shared understanding among different groups, in my community I worked with colleagues in cooperation with community leaders to lead several body movement workshops to further understand areas of conflict. Through conflict-resolution workshops aimed at high-risk populations, we made a small contribution *vis-à-vis* bringing awareness to the excluding policies that every sector of Venezuelan society has endured in its own way.

Although we felt that our workshops were of some modest benefit, efforts of this type always fall short when confronted with the powerful dynamics of exclusion, which in recent Venezuelan society has involved the drawing up of a black list by the government which was publicly displayed on the Internet. This was known as the "Tascon List." Such discrimination creates a political apartheid where the more qualified people are excluded from consideration for jobs or contracts in the government.[17]

In order to help the common citizen and leaders of small communities from upper, middle, and low-income segments of the population, we developed body-movement workshops on the themes of "Tolerance and Conflict Management" from a Jungian perspective. In spite of the existing historical complexes and the opposition among factions, the participants were able to experience the possibility of softening their extreme positions and conscientiously became aware of the conflict in their own inner world.

They also were given an opportunity to experience the presence of "the other" when we proposed a dance and an enactment of a mytho-dance, inspired by the myth of Perseus and the Gorgon. Two groups were formed, each interpreting the roles of Perseus and the Gorgon, alternatively. This allowed each group to physically experience the role of the hero and the role of the Gorgon. The Gorgon inspires fear, terror, and destruction; hence this figure is a personification of "the other." The experience raised some questions for the individuals who participated: How did I feel in each of these roles? What does this say about me? How did I feel in relation to the group that was with me?

While going through the myth, we came in contact with strong emotions: some participants felt powerful and invulnerable when playing the Gorgon. They didn't experience fear and felt the "power" that emerged from belonging and being part of a group. Some people felt "wicked" when experiencing power and in trying to induce fear among the "Perseus" group. When the participants became conscious of these emotions, the complexes associated with them were neutralized, and this helped to depolarize the group.

On the other hand, those who interpreted Perseus experienced a greater range of emotions, from panic – with the desire to escape – to courage, identifying with the hero who wishes to save his group and free his people from evil (as represented by the Gorgon).

We witnessed how some participants felt threatened, and we could recognize paranoid contents based on their projections. These projections were later recalled when feelings were shared in the "experimental" part of the workshop. The objective was to work with the projection of the shadow onto the "opposite" group that was waiting in the darkness of a large studio.

We were able to sense how the shadow was present in everyone and how it was projected onto "the other." We could also observe the emergence of a very important emotion: fear. This instinct, essential for survival, often appears today in the form of panic attacks, triggering a desire to escape and avoid reflection rooted in the body.

In my experience, I have found that social conflict can produce alienation of the psychic body, hence opening the door for personal complexes, together with cultural ones, to be activated in their autonomy. The goal of the workshops we conducted was to provide a bodily and emotional experience that would allow the participants to take the insights they gained outside the boundaries of the workshop into the streets and communities where they live.

We wanted to offer our participants an experience that touched a living body: the psychic body. By psychic body we are referring to our physical body and the emotional memory that inhabits it. In our work, we prefer to work through myth and metaphor rather than definitions and concepts. We also try to reflect on the tension of the opposites and hope for the appearance of the transcendent function to resolve the conflict through an embodied experience.

Until now in Venezuela, we can see that exclusionary policies have prevailed despite initiatives to include all citizens in social benefits. Past history, collective memory, and political discourse are represented in the cultural complex of resentment, making it difficult to develop peaceful, social coexistence with equality and tolerance. We intend to keep developing body movement workshops despite government policies that have eliminated all funding for projects like this – once again reflecting an exclusionary attitude. Although this work has a limited scope, we have found that shedding light on our destructive shadow of exclusion and resentment offers a psychotherapeutic contribution to the individual in search of inclusion in the Venezuelan collective.

Acknowledgments

Special thanks to Sandra Caula, Ruth Capriles, and Valerie Heron.

Notes

1 Human genetic studies among the Venezuelan population show that most of the European gene markers come from the masculine line, which means that miscegenation most frequently passes through men. The DNA on the side of indigenous and African heritage comes mainly from the maternal line. See the research in Alvaro Rodríguez Larralde et al., "Frecuencia génica y porcentaje de mezcla en diferentes áreas geográficas de Venezuela de acuerdo a los grupos RH y ABO," *Revista Asociación Interciencia*, no. 1 (January 2001): 10.
2 However, the indigenous people were acknowledged as rational people by some exceptional people such as Bartolome de las Casas; he was a Dominican father that denounced the cruelties of the conquerors and the need to protect them.
3 Francisco Herrera Luque (1992), quoted in Áxel Capriles, *La envidia y el resentimiento como complejo histórico* (Caracas: Editorial Grijalbo, 2000), p. 2.
4 Ruth Capriles, *El libro rojo del resentimiento* (Caracas: Edit. Debate, 2006), p. 23.
5 Ana Teresa Torres, *La herencia de la tribu* (Venezuela: Edit. Alba, 2009), p. 29.
6 Ligia Montañéz, "Pointing to the Existence of Racism in a Non Racist Society," quoted in Jesus Herrera Salas, "Racismo y discurso político en Venezuela," *Revista Venezolana de Economía y Ciencias Sociales*, no. 10 (August 1993): 111–128.

7 Today, *Criollos* constitute a macro ethnos of more than one third of our population, and these are the descendants of crossbreeding between indigenous people, Spaniards, and Afro descendants, including Black Afro-Americans and Canary Islands Afro-Americans. The rest of the Venezuelan population includes important sectors of immigrants from Spain, Portugal, Italy, and Colombia.
8 Rafael López-Pedraza, *Sobre Héroes y Poetas* (Caracas: Festina Lente, 2002), p. 21.
9 Rafael Arráiz, *La democracia venezolana: un joropo que no cesa*, 2007. www.apps.ucab.edu.ve/clubderomaVenezuela.
10 See C.G. Jung and C. Kerenyi, *Essays on a Science of Mythology: The Myth of the Divine Child and the Mysteries of Eleusis* (Princeton: Princeton University Press, Bollingen Series, 1973).
11 Ana Teresa Torres, "Raíces del resentimiento," *Revista Venezolana de Psicología de los Arquetipos*, no. 1 (2005): 22–27.
12 María Ramírez Ribes, (*Compiladora*), *Cabemos todos? Los desafíos de la inclusión* (Caracas: Informe del Capitulo Venezolano del Club de Roma, 2004), p. 9.
13 "Everyone carries a shadow, and the less it is embodied in the individual's conscious life, the blacker and denser it is. If an inferiority is conscious, one always has a chance to correct it. Furthermore, it is constantly in contact with other interests, so that it is continually subjected to modifications. But if it is repressed and isolated from consciousness, it never gets corrected, and is liable to burst forth suddenly in a moment of unawareness. At all counts, it forms an unconscious snag, thwarting our most well-meant intentions." C.G. Jung, "Psychology and Religion," in *The Collected Works of C.G. Jung, Vol. 11, Acerca de la Psicología de la Religión Occidental y de la Religión Oriental*, trans. Rafael Fernández de Maruri (1995; repr., Madrid: Editorial Trotta, 2008), § 131.
14 Rafael López-Pedraza, *Emociones, una lista* (Caracas: Festina Lente, 2008), p. 76.
15 Eduardo Carvallo, "Sobre el cuerpo psíquico y el cuerpo somático, aproximación a la patología psicosomática," *Revista Venezolana de Psicología de los Arquetipos*, no. 1 (2005): 28–32.
16 Margarita Méndez, "A Country in Conflict: Emerging Historical Complexes in Venezuela and the Living Body," in *Proceedings of the 17th International, IAAP Congress for Analytical Psychology 2007, Cape Town* (Einsiedeln: Daimon Verlag, 2009), pp. 1029–1055.
17 Ana Julia Jatar, *Apartheid del Siglo XXI, La informática al servicio de la discriminación política en Venezuela* (Caracas: Publicaciones Monfort C.A, 2006), p. 55.

Index

Note: Page numbers in *italic* indicate a figure on the corresponding page.

affects *see* dissociative affects
aggressiveness 62–65
all-powerful state 170, 173–174
analytical psychology 90–93
anecdotes, ethnic 52
animal symbol 43
archetype: archetypal patterns 169–176; hostile brothers 188–191
Artigas, José Gervasio 174–176

bandeirantes 43–50, 54
Brazil: and cultural skin 85–96; and graffiti 58–83; and power 39–55; and race 26–36; and the soul 15–24
brothers, hostile 188–191
buffer state, Uruguay as 165–169, *166*

child 74–76, *74*
Chile: cultural isolation complex 101–114
city, the 58–59, 82–83, *82–83*; the child 74–76, *74–75*; cultural complex and dissociative defenses 59–60; defensive persona and aggressiveness 62–65, *63–64*; life in the city 70–74, *71–73*; negative emotions, freezing, and numbing 65–68, *65–68*; relationship and the family 68–70, *69*; repair through imagination 77–81, *78–81*; street art 60–61; symptoms of dissociative affects 61–62, *62*; traumatic unconscious and restoration 76–77, *77*
class *see* social class
clinical case: racial prejudice 33–34
coat-of-arms 42–43, *42*

Colombia 119; development of the complex 120–121; facing the complex 127–129; identification with the image of the hero 124–126; meaning of the Virgin Mary 126–127; *sicariato* 121–124
colonization, spiritual 133–145
coniunctio 76–77, *77*
cordial racism 26–28; clinical case 33–34; crossbreeding and Brazilian identity 28–30, 36; and the ethnic persona 31–33; and social class 30–31, 34–35; "Whitening of the race" 35–36
crossbreeding 28–30, 36
cultural complex 4–7, 26–28, 58–59, 82–83; the child 74–76, *74–75*; clinical case 33–34; Colombia 120–121, 127–129; crossbreeding and Brazilian identity 28–30, 36; cultural complex and dissociative defenses 59–60; cultural isolation complex 101–114; defensive persona and aggressiveness 62–65, *63–64*; and the ethnic persona 31–33; the Gringo Complex 181–196; Latin American 8–9, 198–207; life in the city 70–74, *71–73*; mythic core of Mexican cultural complexes 146–157; negative emotions, freezing, and numbing 65–68, *65–68*; relationship and the family 68–70, *69*; repair through imagination 77–81, *78–81*; and social class 30–31, 34–35; street art

60–61; symptoms of dissociative affects 61–62, *62*; theory of 7–8; traumatic unconscious and restoration 76–77, *77*; Uruguay 163–176; Venezuela 208–218; "Whitening of the race" 35–36
cultural skin 85–88; and analytical psychology 90–93; infant observation with a Mayan/Hispanic family 93–96; and Lévi-Strauss 88–90, *89*

defenses/defensiveness: defensive persona 62–65; dissociative 59–60
democracy, racial 36
dissociative affects 61–62
dissociative defenses 59–60

emotions, negative 65–68
epithets 51
ethnic anecdotes 52
ethnic persona 31–33
explorers 44–45

failure, psychology of 194–196
family: Chile 109–112; graffiti 68–70; infant observation 93–96
flag 43
"four-hundred," the 45–46
freezing 65–68

geography: Chile 102–103, *103*
graffiti 58–59, 82–83, *82–83*; the child 74–76, *74–75*; cultural complex and dissociative defenses 59–60; defensive persona and aggressiveness 62–65, *63–64*; life in the city 70–74, *71–73*; negative emotions, freezing, and numbing 65–68, *65–68*; relationship and the family 68–70, *69*; repair through imagination 77–81, *78–81*; street art 60–61; symptoms of dissociative affects 61–62, *62*; traumatic unconscious and restoration 76–77, *77*
Gringo Complex 181–185, *184*; archetype of the hostile brothers 188–191; historical traumatic events 185–188; national identity 191–194; psychology of failure 194–196

hero: Artigas as 174–176; identification with 124–126
history: Chile 104–109; traumatic events 185–188; Uruguay as buffer state 165–169, *166*
homogenization 170–173
hostile brothers 188–191

identification with the hero 124–126
identity: Brazil 28–30, 44–47; Venezuela 191–194
ideology 46–47
imagination 77–83
infant observation 93–96
isolation 101–102, 109–114; geography 102–103, *103*; history 104–109

Lévi-Strauss, Claude 88–90
life in the city 70–74

Mayan/Hispanic family 93–96
Mexico: mythic core of cultural complexes 146–157; spiritual colonization 133–145
mistrust 104–109
Monument to the Explorers (São Paulo City) 43–44, *44*
mythic core of cultural complexes 146–157

national identity 191–194; *see also* identity
negative emotions 65–68
numbing 65–68

Official Story 163–165; archetypal patterns 169–176; buffer state 165–169, *166*

parental complexes 68–70
perception of color 34–35
persona: ethnic 31–33; racial 34–35
power 39–42, *40*, 53–55; all-powerful state 173–174; forming identity 44–46; ideological bases of identity 46–47; Revolution of 1932 47–51, *49*; stereotypes 51–53; symbols and representations of 42–44, *42*, *44*
prejudice, racial 33–34
psychology: analytical 90–93; of failure 194–196

race 26–28; clinical case 33–34; crossbreeding and Brazilian identity

28–30, 36; and the ethnic persona 31–33; and social class 30–31, 34–35; "Whitening of the race" 35–36
racial democracy 36
racial persona 34–35
racism 26–28; clinical case 33–34; crossbreeding and Brazilian identity 28–30, 36; and the ethnic persona 31–33; and social class 30–31, 34–35; "Whitening of the race" 35–36
relationship 68–70
repair 77–83
representations of power 42–44, *42, 44*
restoration 76–77
Revolution of 1932 47–51
rivalry, sociocultural and typological 52–53

São Paulo 39–42, *40*, 53–55, 58–59, 82–83, *82–83*; the child 74–76, *74–75*; cultural complex and dissociative defenses 59–60; defensive persona and aggressiveness 62–65, *63–64*; forming identity 44–46; ideological bases of identity 46–47; life in the city 70–74, *71–73*; negative emotions, freezing, and numbing 65–68, *65–68*; relationship and the family 68–70, *69*; repair through imagination 77–81, *78–81*; Revolution of 1932 47–51, *49*; stereotypes 51–53; street art 60–61; symbols and representations of 42–44, *42, 44*; symptoms of dissociative affects 61–62, *62*; traumatic unconscious and restoration 76–77, *77*
sicariato 120–129
skin in analytical psychology 90–93; *see also* cultural skin
skin color: perception of 34–35; social 30–31
social class 30–31, 34–35
sociocultural rivalry 52–53
soul, the 15–24
"south" 15–24, *20*
spiritual colonization 133–145
stereotypes 51–53
story *see* Official Story
street art 60–61; *see also* graffiti
submission 104–109
symbols of power 42–44, *42, 44*

trauma 104–109; historical traumatic events 185–188; traumatic unconscious 76–77
typological rivalry 52–53

unconscious, traumatic 76–77
Uruguay 163–176

Venezuela: contemporary context 208–218; Gringo Complex 181–196; split by cultural complexes 198–207
Virgin Mary 119; development of the complex 120–121; facing the complex 127–129; identification with the image of the hero 124–126; meaning of 126–127; *sicariato* 121–124

"Whitening of the race" 35–36